Competition Law in Malaysia

Competition Law in Malaysia

Nasarudin Abdul Rahman
Haniff Ahamat

This book was originally published as a monograph in the International Encyclopaedia of Laws/Competition Law.

Founding Editor: Roger Blanpain
General Editor: Frank Hendrickx
Volume Editors: Francesco Denozza & Alberto Toffoletto

Wolters Kluwer

Published by:
Kluwer Law International B.V.
PO Box 316
2400 AH Alphen aan den Rijn
The Netherlands
E-mail: international-sales@wolterskluwer.com
Website: lrus.wolterskluwer.com

Sold and distributed in North, Central and South America by:
Wolters Kluwer Legal & Regulatory U.S.
7201 McKinney Circle
Frederick, MD 21704
United States of America
Email: customer.service@wolterskluwer.com

Sold and distributed in all other countries by:
Air Business Subscriptions
Rockwood House
Haywards Heath
West Sussex
RH16 3DH
United Kingdom
Email: international-customerservice@wolterskluwer.com

ISBN 978-94-035-2683-6

e-Book: ISBN 978-94-035-2684-3
web-PDF: ISBN 978-94-035-2685-0

The Authors

Dr Nasarudin Abdul Rahman is an assistant professor at the Ahmad Ibrahim Kulliyyah of Laws, International Islamic University Malaysia (IIUM). He obtained his LLB (Hons) from IIUM in 2002 and his Master in Comparative Laws (MCL) also from IIUM in 2008. He received his PhD from Macquarie University of Sydney, Australia in the area of competition policy and law in Malaysia. Prior to joining IIUM, he was an advocate and solicitor of the High Court of Malaya. In 2002 he joined Bank Islam Malaysia Berhad where he served as an assistant manager in the industrial relations department, and later, an assistant manager in the risk management division overseeing Sharia'h risk compliance in Islamic banking. Nasarudin teaches company law and competition law at the undergraduate level. His areas of interest are also competition policy and law, industrial relations, Islamic banking. 'He is the author of a book entitled Competition Law in Malaysia' published by Thomson Reuters and had published many articles relating to competition law and policy in Malaysia. Dr Nasarudin was appointed as a new member of the Malaysia Competition Commission effective from 1 October 2017.

Dr Haniff Ahamat is an associate professor at the Faculty of Law, the National University of Malaysia (UKM). He has been with UKM since June 2016. Prior to that, he had been an academic staff member at the Faculty of Law, the International Islamic University Malaysia (IIUM) for fifteen years. He holds an LLB (Hons) from IIUM, an LLM from UKM and a PhD from University of Essex, United Kingdom. He wrote his PhD thesis on the consumer perspectives of Malaysian and European Commission (EC) anti-dumping regimes. He is a non-practising member of the Malaysian Bar. Haniff has taught public international law and jurisprudence at the undergraduate level. He also teaches Competition Law and International Economic Law at the master's level. Haniff has researched and published on public international law, law of the World Trade Organization, competition law and law of economic regulation. His key publications include journal articles on the interface between competition law and affirmative action in Malaysia, the position of Islamic international law on free trade, and the interface between EC competition and anti-dumping laws.

Table of Contents

Table of Contents

List of Abbreviations

AAC	Average Avoidable Cost
AAX	AirAsia and AirAsia X
AEC	ASEAN Economic Community
AEGC	ASEAN Expert Group on Competition
AGM	Annual General Meeting
AMS	ASEAN Member States
ASEAN	Association of Southeast Asian Nations
BEO	Block Exemption Order
CA	Competition Act
CAA	Carrier Access Agreement
CAT	Competition Appeal Tribunal
CCA	Competition Commission Act
CDO	Container Depot Operator
CMA	Communication and Multimedia Act
CPTPP	Comprehensive and Progressive Agreement for the Trans-Pacific Partnership
CRC	Cold Rolled Coil
DGC	Depot Gate Charge
EC	European Commission
ECA	Energy Commission Act
EU	European Union
FSA	Financial Services Act
FTA	Free Trade Agreement
FTPO	Fair Trade Practice Office
FTPP	Fair Trade Practices Policy
GATS	General Agreement on Trade in Services
GLC	Government-linked Company
GSA	Gas Supply (Amendment) Act

List of Abbreviations

HMT	Hypothetical Monopolist Test
HRC	Hot Rolled Coil
IP	Intellectual Property
IPR	Intellectual Property Right
ISLAs	Implementation, Support and License Agreements
JV	Joint Venture
LRIC	Long-Run Incremental Cost
MACA	Malaysian Aviation Commission Act
MAS	Malaysia Airlines System
MAVCOM	Malaysian Aviation Commission
MCMC	Malaysian Communications and Multimedia Commission
MCN	Malaysia Competition Network
MDF	Medium Density Fireboard
MDTCA	Ministry of Domestic Trade and Consumer Affairs
MHCEOA	Malaysia Heavy Construction Equipment Owners' Association
MIHSOA	Malaysian Indian Hairdressing Saloon Owners Association
MoU	Memorandum of Understanding
MyCC	Malaysia Competition Commission
NEM	New Economic Model
NEP	National Economic Policy
PDA	Petroleum Development Act
PLKS	Pas Lawatan (Kerja Semenentara)
R&D	Research and Development
RCP	Recommended Consumer Price
RPM	Resale Price Maintenance
RRP	Recommended Retail Price
SCBA	Sibu Confectionary and Bakery Association
SEP	Standard-Essential Patent
SGEI	Service of General Economic Interest
SLC	Substantial Lessening of Competition
SME	Small and Medium Enterprises
SOI	Statement of Issue
SRA	Specific Relief Act
SSNIP	Small but Significant Increase in Price
TNG	Touch 'n Go
TPPA	Trans-Pacific Partnership Agreement
TRIPS	Agreement on Trade-Related Aspects of Intellectual Property Rights
UK	United Kingdom
US	United States

VDA	Voluntary Discussion Agreement
VSA	Vessel Sharing Agreement
WTO	World Trade Organization

List of Abbreviations

General Introduction

§1. General Background of the Country

1. Malaysia is a country located in Southeast Asia. Malaysia has a total area of 330,803 km^2. As of 2017, the total population of Malaysia was slightly over 32 million.[1] Malaysia adopts a federal system of government of constitutional monarchy. Being a federation, Malaysia consists of thirteen federal states[2] and three federal territories.[3] Malaysia has two geographic regions: West and East Malaysia, separated by the South China Sea. Two of the federal states, which are Sarawak and Sabah, and one federal territory, namely Labuan, are in East Malaysia. West Malaysia, on the other hand, comprises the remaining eleven states (most of which were formerly Malay Sultanates) and two federal territories. These states form Malaya, which was Malaysia's predecessor.

2. Malaya gained independence from Great Britain on 31 August 1957. On 16 September 1963, Malaya, Singapore, Sabah and Sarawak formed the Federation of Malaysia. Almost two years later, Singapore seceded to become an independent country.

3. Malaysia is a multi-racial country. As of 2017, the indigenous Bumiputeras (including the Malays) make up 68%, Chinese 23%, Indians 7% and others 1% of Malaysia's citizen population.[4] It is worth noting that out of the 32 million population of Malaysia, 3.3 million are non-citizens.[5]

1. Department of Statistics, Malaysia, 2017, Current Population Estimates, Malaysia 2016–2017, https://www.dosm.gov.my/v1/index.php?r=column/cthemeByCat&cat=155&bul_id=a1d1UTFZazd5ajJiRWFHNDduOXFFQT09&menu_id=L0pheU43NWJwRWVSZklWdzQ4TlhUUT09 (accessed 19 Feb. 2019).
2. The states are Perlis, Kedah, Penang (Pulau Pinang), Perak, Selangor, Negri Sembilan, Malacca, Johor, Pahang, Terengganu, Kelantan, Sarawak and Sabah.
3. The federal territories are Kuala Lumpur, Putrajaya and Labuan.
4. Department of Statistics, Malaysia, 2017, Current Population Estimates, Malaysia 2016–2017, https://www.dosm.gov.my/v1/index.php?r=column/cthemeByCat&cat=155&bul_id=a1d1UTFZazd5ajJiRWFHNDduOXFFQT09&menu_id=L0pheU43NWJwRWVSZklWdzQ4TlhUUT09 (accessed 19 Feb. 2019).
5. Department of Statistics, Malaysia, 2017, Current Population Estimates, Malaysia 2016–2017, https://www.dosm.gov.my/v1/index.php?r=column/cthemeByCat&cat=155&bul_id=a1d1UTFZazd5ajJiRWFHNDduOXFFQT09&menu_id=L0pheU43NWJwRWVSZklWdzQ4TlhUUT09 (accessed 19 Feb. 2019).

4. Being a federation, the powers of government are shared between the Federal Government and the government of each federal state. This is reflected in the Federal Constitution 1957, which is the supreme law of Malaysia. The Federal Government has control over the defence, taxation, police, foreign affairs, etc. The state governments, on the other hand, have power over land, water, agriculture, Islamic affairs, Malay and indigenous custom.

5. Malaysia is a member of various international and regional organizations, and the history of its involvement can be traced to the time it gained independence. Malaysia (through Malaya) became a full member of the United Nations immediately upon gaining independence in 1957. Malaysia's participation in international economic law treaties has also been early. Malaya incorporated the Bretton Woods Agreements 1945 into its legal system via the Bretton Woods Agreement Act 1957.[6] Malaya also became a party to the General Agreement on Tariffs and Trade on 24 October 1957.[7] This indicates the country's swift acceptance of the Washington consensus institutions. At the regional level, Malaysia became a member of the Association of Southeast Asian Nations (ASEAN) in January 1967.

§2. Economic System

6. Malaysia can be considered to adopt a free market economy. There is no clear ideological stipulation in the Federal Constitution with regards to the economic system. However, the economy in Malaysia is a mixture of private and Government-linked entities, indicating a mixed approach to the economy so as to include both open competition and State intervention. It must also be noted that despite the lack of any ideological reference in the Malaysian Federal Constitution, there are specific constitutional provisions on the special position of the Malays and natives of Sabah and Sarawak. These provisions permit reservation of a certain proportion of trade or business licences or permits as they are required by law, for the Malays and the natives of Sabah and Sarawak. And these provisions become the basis for race-based affirmative action policies in Malaysia.

7. There are three phases in which the Malaysian economic system has evolved since its independence from Great Britain.[8] This is shown in the figure below.

---

6. Haniff Ahamat, *The Legal Framework for the Inclusion of Consumer Interests Within Anti-dumping Regimes with Special Reference to the EC and Malaysian Anti-dumping Regimes* 235 (unpublished PhD Thesis, University of Essex, 2008).
7. Haniff Ahamat, *The Legal Framework for the Inclusion of Consumer Interests Within Anti-dumping Regimes with Special Reference to the EC and Malaysian Anti-dumping Regimes* 235 (unpublished PhD Thesis, University of Essex, 2008).
8. Nasarudin Abdul Rahman & Haniff Ahamat, *Competition Law in Malaysia* (Sweet and Maxwell, 2016).

Figure 1 Development of Malaysian Economic Policies

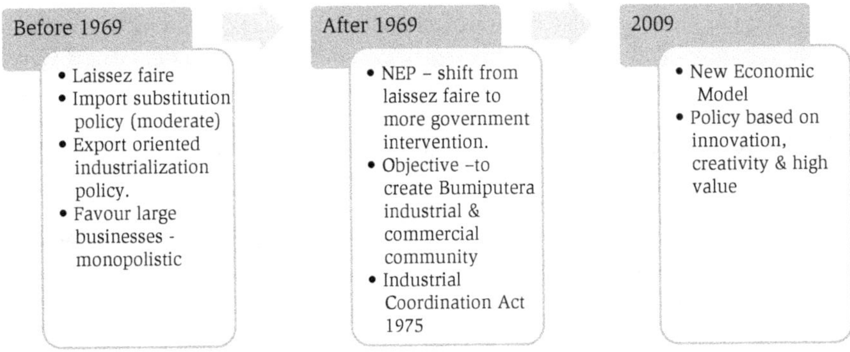

8. The three phases are:

(1) between 1957 and 1969;
(2) between 1969 and 2009; and
(3) 2010 and onwards.

9. The period after independence, but until 1969, saw much of the economy being run on laissez-faire. There was not much intervention into the economy by the Government except those concentrating on the provision of tariff protection, infrastructure facilities, tax exemption, etc.[9] Import substitution policy was introduced.[10] Large businesses and monopolistic set-up were very much favoured as a norm.[11]

10. In 1969, due to racial riots that shook the nation, Malaysia began to experience seismic changes to its economic policy.[12] What caused the racial riots was mired in political controversies, but the underlying facts included the dissatisfactions over the wealth gap between indigenous and non-indigenous communities. In response to these, the Government, who received advice from internationally renowned economists, introduced the National Economic Policy (NEP), marking a shift from laissez-faire to more intervention by the government.

11. The main objective of the NEP was to create Bumiputera industrial and commercial community but in the end, what the NEP sought to do was to bring the

---

9. Jomo Kwame Sundaram (ed.), *Malaysian Industrial Policy* 6 (NUS Press, 2007).
10. Samuel Bassey Okposin, Abdul Halim Abdul Hamid & Hway Boon Ong, *The Changing Phases of Malaysian Economy* (Pelanduk, 1999).
11. Nasarudin Abdul Rahman & Haniff Ahamat, *Competition Law in Malaysia* (Sweet and Maxwell, 2016).
12. Jomo Kwame Sundaram, *The New Economic Policy and Interethnic Relations in Malaysia* 1–2 (United Nations Research Institute for Social Development, 7 Sep. 2004).

indigenous Bumiputera and Malay communities out of poverty.[13] The Industrial Coordination Act was passed in 1975. Though the 1975 Act is concerned with the coordination of manufacturing activities in Malaysia, the procedures that must be complied with in the issuance of manufacturing licences were tallied with the national economic and social objectives which rather referred to the NEP.[14] Certain guidelines were laid down on corporate stock ownership that should reflect Malaysia's population make-up albeit more indirect and policy-oriented mechanism applied by Malaysia, rather than the direct and legislative-oriented mechanism used in other countries, such as India.[15]

12. The result was the emergence of public enterprises in various strategic sectors which came hand in hand with rapid industrialization during the era of Dr Mahathir Mohamad who became the Prime Minister of Malaysia for the first time in 1982. There was also a dramatic increase in foreign direct investment, manufacturing exports and activities of heavy industries. During this period, government-linked companies (GLCs) emerged as a tool to promote various objectives, such as national champion, as well as to further socio-economic goals, including to pursue the economic empowerment of indigenous ethnic groups.[16]

13. Thus, their performance may be judged by how economically efficient they are but more often than not, the relevance of GLCs in Malaysia is linked to promoting the interests of Bumiputera commerce and trade.[17] However, too much central planning and heavy market participation of GLCs have resulted in the slowing down of growth, low levels of innovation and value creation, bureaucracy and regulatory burden problems and low productivity.[18] Whether such claims are only confined to Malaysia or did they occur in other countries at the similar developmental stage is a question debated by many, but the bottom line is there was fear that Malaysia would fall into the income trap. Malaysia has not escaped from global trends, particularly those affecting middle-income countries, including the drive towards reducing subsidies and regulation and promoting competition and liberalization by governments.

14. In 2010, the Malaysian Government, under the leadership of Prime Minister Najib, launched the New Economic Model (NEM). It is argued that the NEM sought

---

13. Jomo Kwame Sundaram, *The New Economic Policy and Interethnic Relations in Malaysia 2–3* (United Nations Research Institute for Social Development, 7 Sep. 2004).
14. N. Yasuda, 'Malaysia's New Economic Policy and the Industrial Coordination Act', *The Developing Economies*, XXIX(4) (December 1991) 331.
15. E.T. Gomez, 'Targeting Horizontal Inequalities: Ethnicity, Equity, and Entrepreneurship in Malaysia', *Asian Economic Papers*, 11(2) (2012) 31–57.
16. E.T. Gomez, 'Targeting Horizontal Inequalities: Ethnicity, Equity, and Entrepreneurship in Malaysia', *Asian Economic Papers*, 11(2) (2012) 31–57.
17. C.Y. Whah, Chin Yee, & B.T.C. Guan, 'Malaysia's Protracted Affirmative Action Policy and the Evolution of the Bumiputera Commercial and Industrial Community', *SOJOURN: Journal of Social Issues in Southeast Asia,* 32 (2017) 336–373.
18. Wing Thye Woo, *Malaysia Is Falling into a Middle-Income Trap* (Channelnewsasia, 31 Mar. 2019), https://www.channelnewsasia.com/news/commentary/malaysia-falling-into-middle-income-trap-11376622 (accessed 3 Apr. 2019).

to steer Malaysia away from the middle-income trap by resorting to initiatives striving towards a market-led economy, a well-governed nation, a regionally-integrated country and an enterprising and innovative society.[19] The initiatives are re-energizing the private sector, developing quality workforce and reducing dependency on foreign labour, creating a competitive economy, strengthening the public sector, transparent and market-friendly affirmative action, building the knowledge base and infrastructure, enhancing the sources of growth and ensuring the sustainability of growth.[20]

15. The potency of the NEM in remedying the problems caused by previous policies, including the NEP, has been criticized, especially when there was a return to more populist measures, including those which revive the affirmative action objective of the NEP.[21] The market liberalization drive has produced results, including the passing of a competition legislation in 2010. Regional integration was also enhanced by Malaysia's connection with the ASEAN Economic Community (AEC) which was supposed to kick off in 2015. Deeper liberalization and regional integration were envisaged via the Trans-Pacific Partnership Agreement (TPPA) which, however, did not materialize, but there were others whose negotiations are still ongoing at the time of the writing of this book.

§3. Legal System

16. In order to understand the nature of the Malaysian legal system, one needs to relate to the history of such a system. Despite having been colonized by the same power, i.e., Britain, the essence of British colonialism with regards to each individual state within Malaysia differed. Such differences affected the application of English law to those states. The states can be divided into different categories. First, states which were under the direct colonial rule of Britain. They were Penang, Malacca, Sabah and Sarawak, which were Crown Colonies. The rest were the Malay States which were mere protectorates of the British, which were divided further into the Federated and the Unfederated Malay States.

17. The administrative control by the British over the Malay States was more limited, i.e., the Sultans were not asked to abdicate, but their powers were limited to Malay custom and Islam. The Sultans had to act on the advice of British appointed officials called residents.

---

19. Wan Saiful Wan Jan, *Malaysia's New Economic Model: Is the Malaysian Government Serious about Economic Liberalization?*, Friedrich Neumann Stiftung Background Paper No. 14/13 Sep. (2011).
20. Wan Saiful *Wan Jan, Malaysia's New Economic Model: Is the Malaysian Government Serious about Economic Liberalization?*, Friedrich Neumann Stiftung Background Paper No. 14/September 13 (2011) pp. 14–16.
21. Wan Saiful Wan Jan, *Malaysia's New Economic Model: Is the Malaysian Government Serious about Economic Liberalization?*, Friedrich Neumann Stiftung Background Paper No. 14/September 13 (2011) p. 21.

18. English law was introduced to all of those entities in stages and with other laws, particularly Muslim personal law and Natives' custom, being partially recognized.[22] More importantly, such colonial legacy continues even after Malaysia's independence. The Civil Law Act 1956 authorizes the importation of English common law, certain United Kingdom (UK) statutes and rules of equity to the states within Malaysia subject to certain cut-off dates which differ between West Malaysia (Peninsular Malaysia), Sabah and Sarawak.[23]

19. The 1956 Act also permits the application of English law to mercantile (commercial) cases in Malaysia, subject to certain cut-off dates for all states except Penang, Malacca, Sabah and Sarawak (as regards these mentioned states, English law can be applied as of today).[24] The application of English law in Malaysia (be it common law, rules of equity or statutes) is constrained by one important condition that is the common law, rules of equity or statutes shall not contradict the local circumstances that exist in Malaysia.

20. But what should be the sources of Malaysian law? This is a complex issue given the complex structure of Malaysia being a federation where powers are shared between federal and state entities. But generally, the sources of Malaysian law are the Federal and State Constitutions, legislations, judicial decisions, English law, Islamic law and customary law.[25]

21. Under the Federal Constitution, the term 'law' includes: (1) written law, (2) common law as it is in operation in Malaysia, and (3) custom or usage having the force of law in Malaysia.[26] Written law means statutes passed by both the Malaysian Federal Parliament and the state legislative assemblies. Also covered are UK statutes which are in operation in Malaysia subject to the limits prescribed by the Civil Law Act 1956.

22. Common law points to the recognition of English law as the law of the land. However, the term common law is not confined to English common law. It can be understood as law developed by judges. Hence, legal principles conceived as a result of judgment by a Malaysian court of law may fit into the definition of common law, but in cases not involving Islamic law or native custom, the judgment will be influenced by what the judges in England and other Commonwealth countries had decided.

23. Finally, custom and usage having the force of law indicate that customary law, particularly that of the natives also has legally binding effect in Malaysia.

---

22. *See* Ahmad Ibrahim, *Towards a History of Law in Malaysia and Singapore* (Dewan Bahasa dan Pustaka, Kuala Lumpur, 1992).
23. Section 3 of the Civil Law Act 1956.
24. Section 5 of the Civil Law Act 1956.
25. Wan Arfah Hamzah, *A First Look at the Malaysian Legal System* 27 (Oxford Fajar, 2009).
26. Article 160 of Federal Constitution 1957.

24. Islamic law, however, is not included in the definition of law in the Federal Constitution prompting debates as to whether Islamic law is a source of law in Malaysia.[27] Since Islamic law and native custom are under the competence of the state assemblies to enact a law, they may also fall within the definition of written law if they transform into legislation passed by such assemblies refer to unwritten Islamic Law which is referred in states' constitution as hukum shara and native custom whose principles are recognized by the courts of law in Malaysia.

25. As regards the branch of law which concerns commerce, as said, the Civil Law Act 1956 shows the importance of English law. At the same time, local statutes, particularly at the federal level (this is because commercial matters most fall under the jurisdiction of the Federal Government) play an important role to improve on the regulation of diverse and complex activities of commerce and trade.

§4. Historical Background of Antitrust Law

26. The mandate to implement a competition law was given in the Eighth Malaysia Plan (2001–2005).[28] The plan states:

> During the plan period, efforts will be made to foster fair trade practices that will contribute towards greater efficiency and competitiveness of the economy. In this context, a fair trade policy and law will be formulated to prevent anti-competitive behaviour, such as collusion, cartel price fixing, market allocation, and the abuse of market power. The fair trade policy will, among others, prevent firms from protecting or expanding their market shares by means other than greater efficiency in producing what consumers want. In addition, a national policy and master plan on distributive trade will be formulated to facilitate an orderly and healthy development of the sector.

27. The transformation of the policy into the law was a slow process. The plan to introduce a competition law was subsequently shifted to the Ninth Malaysia Plan, beyond the targeted year of 2005. In the Ninth Malaysia Plan, the Ministry of Domestic Trade and Consumer Affairs (MDTCA) proposed to establish the Fair Trade Practice Office (FTPO)[29] as an independent supervisory body responsible for ensuring the market functions effectively by preventing anticompetitive behaviours

---

27. Sharifah Suhanah Syed Ahmad, *Malaysian Legal System*, 2nd edn (Malayan Law Journal, 2007); Ahmad Ibrahim & Ahilemah Joned, *The Malaysian Legal System* 57–58 (Dewan Bahasa dan Pustaka, 1987).
28. *Eighth Malaysia Plan, Chapter 16: Distributive Trade,* https://www.pmo.gov.my/dokumenattached/RMK/RM8.pdf cl 16.32, 467.
29. The main functions of the Fair Trade Practices Office (FTPO) are to initiate and receive requests for investigations, conduct market monitoring and economic analysis, advise the government and sector regulators on the formulation of policies and legislation and conduct advocacy programmes. The FTPO will be transformed into an administrative arm of the Fair Trade Practices Commission within 3–5 years.

and unfair trade practices and the Malaysia Competition Network (MCN)[30] as a forum for private and public sector to deliberate issues under fair trade law.[31] The institutions were, however, never established.

28. In 2007, the Ministry decided to refocus on its competition law agenda. A dedicated team was formed to oversee competition matters, especially the drafting of the Bill. Competition law was listed as one of the Ministry's Key Performance Indicators. To achieve this, a capacity building was required, prompting officers to be sent for training locally and abroad. The Ministry also formed the CG-25, containing representatives of the key stakeholders: captains of industry, corporate giants, associations and government agencies. This was crucial for the team's understanding of the expectations of the interest groups and allowed them to plan how best to accommodate these interests in the drafting of the Bill.

29. After a series of discussions, the MDTCA submitted its Proposal to Introduce Competition Policy, which was approved by the Government on 26 October 2005. Below are the decisions made by the Government on 26 October 2005:

(i) A policy is introduced on competition law in Malaysia and will be known as the Fair Trade Practices Policy (FTPP).
(ii) The policy will not cover M&A through pre-merger notice and take-over.
(iii) The policy will not cover vertical business restraint to ensure the interests of the industry are protected in line with the country's socio-economic development objectives.
(iv) All sovereign functions of government, including those of encouraging socio-economic development and of generating efficiency and equity, are excluded from the scope of the policy.
(v) The formulation of a Fair Trade Practice Bill is proposed.
(vi) The establishment of a new division in the MDTCA to carry out early preparation before introducing the Fair Trade Policy is proposed.

30. The policies submitted to and approved by the Government on 26 October 2005 covered the following issues:

(i) Control of anticompetitive practices, such as cartels, tied selling, resale price maintenance (RPM) and bid-rigging.
(ii) Control of abuse of dominant position.
(iii) Control of unfair trade practices, such as misleading advertisement and unfair agreement between small and large enterprises.

---

30. The MCN consists of representatives from the main ministries and agencies, such as GLCs, Khazanah Nasional Bhd, Communications and Multimedia Commission, Securities Commission, Energy Commission, Financial Sector, Water Commission and Port Authority to streamline the enforcement of competition law and sectoral regulation. The MCN will determine Malaysia's stance in FTA negotiations. All actions taken in enforcing Trade Practices Policy must in line with the interests of other sectors under their respective supervision.
31. *Ninth Malaysian Plan 2006–2010: Thriving Distributive Trade,* http://www.epu.gov.my/html/themes/epu/html/rm9/english/Chapter9.pdf, cl 9.22, 215.

(iv) An Act to be entitled the Fair Trade Practices Act to be formulated to tackle the above issues, and a Fair Trade Practices Commission to be set up through the formulation of a Fair Trade Practices Commission Act.

31. Based on this mandate, the Ministry appointed legal consultants to formulate the Fair Trade Practices Act and Commission of Fair Trade Practices Act. The Government distributed a Public Consultation Document in 2008 containing the proposed provisions to be included in the Fair Trade Practice Act to CG-25.

32. Based on the comments and feedback submitted to the MDTCA, the Ministry, on 9 September 2009, submitted a second proposal to obtain a mandate from the Government for changes made to the scope of the law and the substantive provisions of the formulated Fair Trade Practices Law.

33. The proposals submitted on 9 September 2009 are as follows:

(i) Fair Trade Practices Bill was changed to Competition Bill, and Fair Trade Practices Commission Bill was changed to Competition Commission Bill.
(ii) Additional substantive provisions were included, such as control over Mergers & Acquisition (M&A).
(iii) Unfair Trade Practices was excluded from the Bill.
(iv) The Competition Bill is to be a single legislation dealing with competition issues across the board to ensure the consistent enforcement of competition legislation.

34. The proposal put forward in 2009 was not taken into consideration in its entirety. The MDTCA was instructed to undertake further discussion with the relevant parties before the final Act was finalized. Therefore, on 13 October 2009, the Ministry once again held a discussion with other ministries and agencies to discuss the amended version of the policy and law based on the opinion and clarification sought from the relevant stakeholders and based on the study undertaken by the MDTCA.

35. The main aspects of the policy were finally concluded to include the following:

(i) The Bill will exclude unfair trade practices provisions. Consequently, Fair Trade Practices Bill was re-titled to Competition Bill and Fair Trade Practices Commission Bill was re-titled to Competition Commission Bill.
(ii) The law will not include the provision on M&A. This proposal is in line with the government's goal of encouraging the development of the capital market and is in line with the government's policy of encouraging M&A among enterprises to strengthen the domestic economy and develop corporate competition globally. All activities of dominant players because of M&A shall only be controlled under the scope of the abuse of dominant position provision. A Special Competition Committee encompassing both the Competition

Commission and sector-specific regulators will be established. This institutional arrangement gives opportunity to the Competition Commission to express its view on the implication of M&A on competition before the Securities Commission or Central Bank allows and approves the M&A.

(iii) The Bill will not be a single legislation dealing with competition issues in which specific regulators have powers to oversee matters under their respective jurisdictions. However, the exclusion is only limited to the communications and multimedia and energy sectors. For the purpose of coordinating activities of all sector regulators and ensuring uniformity of competition provision in Malaysia, any competition issues will be resolved by a Special Competition Committee. Such a Committee would also be a forum for discussion and provide a platform through which to inform sector-specific regulators about the possibility of anticompetitive conduct occurring in their sectors.

Part I. Structure of Antitrust Law and Its Enforcement

Chapter 1. Sources of Antitrust Law

§1. National Sources

I. Fair Trade Practices Policy

36. The FTPP was approved on 26 October 2005 as a preparatory stage towards the enactment of the Competition Act (CA) 2010. The FTPP seeks the following policy objectives:

- promote and protect competition in the market;
- create dynamic and competitive entrepreneurs;
- provide fair and competitive market opportunities for businesses;
- prohibit anticompetitive practices including those originating from outside Malaysian and affecting the domestic territory;
- prohibit unfair trade practices in the economy;
- promote the rights of Small and Medium Enterprises (SMEs) to participate in the market place;
- promote consumer welfare; and
- encourage socio-economic growth, generate efficiency and equity.

37. However, the FTPP will not address:

(1) sovereign functions of the Government; and
(2) all actions and measures attributable to the state that seeks to encourage socio-economic growth to generate efficiency and equity.

II. Competition Act 2010

38. The Malaysian competition law was passed by the Parliament in 2010 in the form of CA 2010 (Act No.) but only came into force in 2012. The two years' grace period was given as a preparatory stage for the business entities to get familiar and ensure their activities are in conformity with the Act. The main objective of the CA 2010, as stated in the Preamble of the Act, is to promote economic development by promoting and protecting the process of competition in the Malaysia market. The protection of competition will, in turn, create economic efficiencies and benefits consumers in the form of lower price and increase in productivity.

39. The CA 2010 covers two important aspects, namely, prohibition against anti-competitive agreement and prohibition against abuse of dominant position. The Act does not regulate mergers activities that may result in or expected to result in substantial lessening competition in the market. In other words, this Act only focuses on the behavioural aspect rather than the structure of the market. Any anticompetitive conduct post-mergers activities will be regulated under section 10 if there is an abuse of dominant position in the market.

40. The CA 2010 contains six important parts. The crux of the competition law contains in Part II, i.e., anticompetitive practices. Part II consists of Chapter 1 Prohibition (anticompetitive agreement – section 4), Chapter 2 Prohibition (abuse of dominant position – section 10), Chapter 3 (Market Review), and Chapter 4 (Exclusion). Part III relates to investigation and enforcement powers and procedures. Part IV relates to the process of issuing a decision and imposing remedial measures by the Competition Commission and other compliance tools, such as undertaking, interim measures, leniency programme, etc. Part V relates to the establishment and functions of Competition Appeal Tribunal (CAT). Part VI relates to general provisions, including general penalty and right to private action.

III. Competition Commission Act 2010

41. The Malaysia Competition Commission (MyCC) was set up in 2011 pursuant to the Competition Commission Act (CCA) 2010. The main objective of the establishment of MyCC is to implement and enforce the CA 2010. MyCC also has other functions under the Act which are important in discharging its duties as a national competition authority including:

- to issue guidelines in relation to the implementation and enforcement of the competition law;
- to advise the government on various matters related to competition;
- to raise awareness among persons engaged in commerce or trade and among the public on the importance of competition laws and the manner in which the Commission will carry out its functions under the competition law;
- to educate the public regarding the ways in which competition may benefit consumers in, and the economy of Malaysia; and
- to carry out general studies in relation to issues connected with competition in the Malaysian economy, etc.

42. Under the CA 2010 and the CCA 2010, the MyCC has broader powers, including powers to carry out investigations, powers to decide and issue decisions and powers to impose penalties for any violation of any anticompetitive practices which are prohibited under the Act and the power to formulate procedures in conducting investigations and proceedings.

IV. Specific Legislations

43. Malaysia also adopts a sectoral approach to competition law. Several legislations regulating specific sectors, such as the Communication and Multimedia Act (CMA) 1998, Energy Commission Act (ECA) 2001 and Malaysian Aviation Commission Act (MACA) 2015 also incorporate competition provisions. All these sectors had been specifically excluded from the CA 2010 by virtue of the Second Schedule of the Act.

44. Brief competition provisions can also be found in the Financial Services Act (FSA) 2013 which oversees the financial services market. The competition provision in the FSA 2013 is, however, placed under the consumer protection regime. Section 124 of the FSA prohibits financial service providers from engaging in a certain type of conduct as stipulated in Schedule 7 of the Act.

45. There are six types of prohibited conduct listed under Schedule 7, including collusion and tied selling. The Central Bank had issued a Guidelines on Prohibited Conduct to inform how the consumer-competition-related provisions will be implemented. However, it is important to note that the financial services market is not excluded from the CA 2010. Therefore, competition provision of both the FSA 2013 and the CA 2010 may be implemented concurrently subject to the Memorandum of Understanding (MoU) entered into between MyCC and the Central Bank of Malaysia.

§2. International Sources

46. The CA 2010 adopted the UK legislation almost wholesale, while the UK, in turn, modelled its legislation after the European Union (EU) competition law regime. The reason for choosing the UK system as an anchor lies in the similarity between the laws and legal system of Malaysia and the UK. Malaysia has a long exposure to the English common law system and refers to the English courts' precedent as guidance to various legal issues. Since the CA is largely modelled after the UK's CA, the UK and EU case law has commonly been considered as influential and persuasive in the context of applying the CA in Malaysia.

47. The main objective of Malaysia's trade policy effort is to provide a more liberalizing and fair global trading environment. To achieve this objective, Malaysia continues its commitment to accord to a rule-based multilateral trading system under the World Trade Organization (WTO), participate in regional economic integration through ASEAN and strengthen bilateral economic and trading relations to complement the multilateral approach to trade liberalization. Malaysia is a party to various WTO agreements, such as General Agreement on Trade in Services (GATS) and Agreement on Trade-Related Aspects of Intellectual Property Rights (TRIPS) and plays an active role in ASEAN economic integration through AEC. Competition Policy forms part of the many multilateral or bilateral agreements to which Malaysia is a party. However, the competition policy under the multilateral or bilateral agreements is not a full-fledged competition law regime and often limited to international cooperation.

I. General Agreement on Trade in Services

48. GATS laid down principles and rules for trade in services. Article 1 defines 'services' to include 'any service in any sector except services supplied in the exercise of governmental authority'. 'A service supplied in the exercise of governmental authority' is further defined as 'any service which is supplied neither on a commercial basis, nor in competition with one or more service suppliers'.

49. Article VI of GATS states a general principle that 'in sectors where specific commitments are undertaken, each Member to ensure that all measures of general application affecting trade in services are administered in a reasonable, objective and impartial manner'.

50. Article VIII contains a provision related to monopolies and exclusive service suppliers. Paragraph 1 requires each Member State to ensure that 'any monopoly supplier of a service in its territory does not, in the supply of the monopoly service in the relevant market, act in a manner inconsistent with that Member's obligations under Article II and specific commitments'.[32]

51. Paragraph 2 further states that 'where a Member's monopoly supplier competes, either directly or through an affiliated company, in the supply of a service outside the scope of its monopoly rights and which is subject to that Member's specific commitments, the Member shall ensure that such a supplier does not abuse its monopoly position to act in its territory in a manner inconsistent with such commitments'.

52. However, Article IX of GATS states that 'Members recognize that certain business practices of service suppliers other than those falling under Article VIII may restrain competition and thereby restrict trade in services.' Therefore, 'each Member shall, at the request of any other Member, enter into consultations with a view to eliminating practices referred to in paragraph 1'.

32. Article II relates to Most-Favoured Nation Treatment. Under specific commitments Member may specify terms, limitations and conditions on market access, conditions and qualifications on national treatment and any additional commitments, the time-frame for the implementation of such commitments and the date of entry into force of such commitments.

II. Agreement on Trade-Related Aspects of Intellectual Property Rights

53. The TRIPS aims to 'promote effective and adequate protection of intellectual property rights, and to ensure that measures and procedures to enforce intellectual property rights do not themselves become barriers to legitimate trade'. It applies primarily to the seven categories of rights, namely, copyright and related rights, trademarks, geographical indications, industrial designs, patents, layout-designs (topographies) of integrated circuits, and protection of undisclosed information.

54. Article 40 recognizes that 'some licensing practices or conditions pertaining to intellectual property rights which restrain competition may have adverse effects on trade and may impede the transfer and dissemination of technology'.

55. Therefore, TRIPS does not 'prevent Members from specifying in their legislation licensing practices or conditions that may in particular cases constitute an abuse of intellectual property rights having an adverse effect on competition in the relevant market'.

56. A Member is free to 'adopt any appropriate measures to prevent or control such practices, which may include for example exclusive grant back conditions, conditions preventing challenges to validity and coercive package licensing, in the light of the relevant laws and regulations of that Member'.

III. Trans-Pacific Partnership Agreement and Free Trade Agreement

57. On 4 February 2016, the Ministers of the twelve Trans-Pacific Partnership countries, including Malaysia, announced the conclusion of their negotiations on TPPA. The result is a high-standard, ambitious, comprehensive, and balanced agreement that will promote economic growth, enhance innovation, productivity and competitiveness, promote transparency and good governance. The TPPA contains Competition Policy Chapter, which requires each country to establish a national competition authority and enforce its national competition law. The scope applies to all commercial activities regardless of ownership.

58. Competition Policy Chapter covers:

- Competition Law and Authorities & Anticompetitive Business Conduct.
- Procedural Fairness in Competition Law Enforcement.
- Private Rights of Action.
- Cooperation and Technical Cooperation.
- Consumer Protection.
- Transparency.
- Consultation.
- Non-Application of Dispute Settlement.

59. Under Article 16 of the TPPA, each Party to the agreement is required to 'adopt or maintain national competition laws that proscribe anticompetitive business conduct, with the objective of promoting economic efficiency and consumer welfare, and shall take appropriate action with respect to that conduct'. However, the agreement allows each Party to 'provide for certain exemptions from the application of its national competition laws provided that those exemptions are transparent and are based on public policy grounds or public interest grounds'.

60. With the withdrawal of the United States (US) from the TPPA on 23 January 2017, the remaining eleven countries had agreed to rename the TPPA as the Comprehensive and Progressive Agreement for the Trans-Pacific Partnership (CPTPP). On 9–10 November 2017, all eleven member countries reached an agreement on the core elements, the text of the agreement and the way forward to implement the CPTPP. The CPTPP was signed by all eleven participating countries on 8 March 2018 in Santiago, Chile pending the ratification of the agreement in order to bring the agreement into force.

61. Competition provisions in a bilateral Free Trade Agreement (FTA) are very limited. The competition chapters do not oblige the country to enact its own competition law, remaining limited to international cooperation.[33] With regard to competition provisions, the obligation is imposed on trading partners or parties to the agreement only.

62. For example, Article 105 of the *Japan–Malaysia Economic Partnership 2006* deals with monopolies and exclusive service suppliers. A country's monopoly supplier of a service cannot abuse its monopoly power when providing the service in the relevant market or when competing outside the scope of its monopoly rights. Article 124 (Unfair Competition) requires each country to formulate a mechanism to deter and remedy the effects of unfair trade practices.[34] The competition provisions are brief and included as part of the motivation to carry out national policy reform on the market economy and serve as a 'testing ground' and preparation for more complex multilateral agreements.[35]

33. , such as exchange of information and expertise from the trading partners, *see*, e.g., New Zealand Ministry of Foreign Affairs and Trade, *Malaysia–New Zealand Free Trade Agreement,* http://mfat.govt.nz/downloads/trade-agreement/malaysia/mnzfta-text-of-agreement.pdf, Art. 12.3.
34. Ministry of Foreign Affairs of Japan, *Malaysia–Japan Economic Partnership Agreement Malaysia–Japan Economic Partnership Agreement,* http://www.mofa.go.jp/region/asia-paci/malaysia/epa/content.pdf *See also Malaysia–New Zealand Free Trade Agreement*, Art. 8.11.
35. Vu Ba Phu and the Vietnam Competition Agency, 'Vision for an ASEAN Competition Regime' (Paper presented at the 2nd OECD–Southeast Asia Regional Forum: Enhancing Competitiveness through Regional Integration, Bangkok, Thailand, 27–28 Apr. 2009), www.oecd.org/dataoecd/29/9/42712787.pdf, p. 2.

IV. ASEAN Regional Guidelines on Competition Policy

63. The AEC 2015 was established with the aim to facilitate the creation of a single market and production base, and a legal rules-based framework towards a competitive ASEAN. The AEC Blueprint 2015 was formulated with the aims and visions of constructing an integrated and cohesive economy, enhancing competitiveness and dynamism through innovation and technology-oriented initiatives, ensuring a resilient, inclusive and people-oriented, people-centred ASEAN, promoting economic connectivity, enhancing sectoral integration and maintaining ASEAN's outward orientation. These noble missions were further reinforced under the new AEC framework beyond 2015 (AEC Blueprint 2025).

64. The ASEAN Expert Group on Competition (AEGC) was established in 2007 which 'serves as a forum for discussing and coordinating regional cooperation in competition policy, with the goal of promoting a healthy competitive environment in ASEAN'.[36]

65. For the purpose of policy discussion and coordination in ASEAN beyond 2015, the AEGC is committed to focusing its work on various matters including establishing a national law on competition in all ASEAN Member States (AMS) based on international best practices and identifying and establishing effective regional competition laws in ASEAN and working towards greater harmonization of competition policy and law in ASEAN.[37]

66. The AEGC had formulated a Regional Guidelines on Competition Policy (Regional Guidelines) which 'serve as a general framework guide for the AMS as they endeavour to introduce, implement and develop competition policy in accordance with the specific legal and economic context of each AMS'.[38]

67. Under the Regional Guidelines on Competition Policy, competition policy is defined as 'those governmental measures that directly affect the behaviour of enterprises and the structure of industry and markets. Competition policy basically covers two elements, the first element involves putting in place a set of policies that promote competition, and the second element, known as competition law, refers to legal acts (in the form of legislation, judicial decisions and regulations) aimed at controlling or prohibiting anticompetitive practices'.[39]

68. It is important to note that this Regional Guidelines 'are based on country experiences and international best practices with the view to creating a fair competition environment in ASEAN. It seeks to enhance and expedite the development

36. ASEAN Expert Group on Competition, available at, https://www.asean-competition.org/aegc.
37. ASEAN Expert Group on Competition, available at, https://www.asean-competition.org/about-aegc-asean-competition-action-plan-acap-2016-2025.
38. ASEAN Regional Guidelines on Competition Policy 2010.
39. ASEAN Regional Guidelines on Competition Policy 2010.

of national competition policy within each ASEAN Member State'.[40] The Guidelines cover the prohibition of anticompetitive (horizontal and vertical) agreements; abuse of dominant position (market power); anticompetitive mergers; and the prohibition of other restrictive trade practices.

§3. Secondary Sources

I. Guidelines

69. As of 1 April 2019, there are a total of seven Guidelines which have been issued pursuant to the powers conferred under the CA. The regulations and orders are:

- *MyCC Guidelines on Chapter 1 Prohibition*[41]
  These Guidelines explain the manner in which MyCC will interpret and enforce anticompetitive agreement provisions found in section 4(1) and section 4(2) of the CA 2010. The Guidelines provide guidance on how certain terms under the Act will be interpreted, how MyCC determines whether a particular conduct or agreement is anticompetitive and how a party to an agreement can release its liability based on section 5 of the CA 2010.
- *MyCC Guidelines on Chapter 2 Prohibition*[42]
  These Guidelines explain the manner in which MyCC will interpret and enforce the provision of abuse of dominant position under section 10(1) and section 10(2) of the CA 2010. The Guidelines provide guidance on how MyCC determines the dominant position, whether a particular conduct or agreement is abusive under the Act and any possible reasonable commercial justification.
- *MyCC Guidelines on Market Definition*[43]
  These Guidelines explain how MyCC defines and determines the relevant market when investigating possible infringements of Chapters 1 and 2 of the CA 2010.
- *MyCC Guidelines on Financial Penalties*[44]
  These Guidelines explain how MyCC determines the amount of financial penalty that will be imposed after an infringement decision has been made. The Guidelines provide guidance on various factors that will be taken into consideration in computing financial penalties for competition law purpose.

40. ASEAN Regional Guidelines on Competition Policy 2010.
41. http://www.mycc.gov.my/sites/default/files/handbook/MYCC-4-Guidelines-Booklet-BOOK1-10-FA-copy_chapter-1-prohibition.pdf.
42. http://www.mycc.gov.my/sites/default/files/handbook/MYCC%204%20Guidelines%20Booklet%20BOOK2-6%20FA%20copy.pdf.
43. http://www.mycc.gov.my/sites/default/files/handbook/MYCC-4-Guidelines-Booklet-BOOK4-10-FA-copy_market-defination.pdf.
44. http://www.mycc.gov.my/sites/default/files/handbook/Guildline-on-Financial-Penalties.pdf.

- *MyCC Guidelines on Leniency Regime*[45]

  These Guidelines explain how MyCC implements a leniency regime. The Guidelines provide guidance on among other factors that will be taken into consideration in granting leniency and determining the percentage of reduction from the financial penalties, conditions that a leniency applicant needs to fulfil before receiving leniency, the process of leniency application and how to be a marker under the Malaysian leniency regime.
- *MyCC Guidelines on Complaints Procedures*

  These Guidelines explain the process and procedure of lodging complaints about possible infringements of any of the prohibitions under the Act. The Guidelines also provide guidance on how MyCC responds to the complaints received, such as how MyCC treats confidential information and the procedures that MyCC needs to comply before closing any investigation.
- *MyCC Guidelines on Competition Law and Intellectual Property Right (IPR)*

  These Guidelines provide guidance on the application of competition law in the area of intellectual property (IP). The Guidelines explain on the interface between IP and competition law, market definition for conduct involving IP, various type of horizontal, vertical restraints and abuse of dominant position by IP right holders which may fall under the ambit of section 4 and section 10 of the CA 2010.

§4. Sources' Relation and Hierarchy

70. In enforcing the competition law, MyCC will rely on competition law cases from other countries, especially the UK and the EU and Singapore. However, MyCC views that all international cases are highly persuasive but not binding upon the Commission in interpreting the Act.

71. All guidelines issued by MyCC are not binding and only serve as guidance for MyCC to implement and enforce the competition provisions. The Guidelines are not a substitute for the Act and any regulations that are made pursuant to the Act. Any examples given in the Guidelines are for illustrative purposes only and are not exhaustive. They do not set a limit on the investigation and enforcement activities of the MyCC.

72. The CCA 2010 empowers the Minister to give to the MyCC directions of a general character relating to the performance of the functions and powers of the MyCC and MyCC is obliged to give effect to such directions. The direction should be given in writing and should be consistent with the provisions of the competition laws.[46]

73. All multilateral and bilateral trade agreements are binding on trading partners who are parties to the agreement. Trade agreements do not normally contain a

45. http://www.mycc.gov.my/sites/default/files/handbook/MyCC_Guildline-on-Leniency-Regime.pdf.
46. Section 18 of the Competition Commission Act 2010.

full-fledged competition law regime. However, most of the trade agreements require the trading partners to implement their own competition law regime and to comply with basic competition rules relating to national and non-discriminatory treatment, transparency, monopolies services and technical cooperation in the area of competition policy and law.

74. The regional guidelines 'are not intended to be a full or binding statement on competition policy'. However, the Guidelines 'will help to increase AMSs' awareness of the importance of competition policy, with a view to stimulating the development of best practices and enhancing cooperation between AMSs'. The non-binding nature of the Guidelines gives the AMS to 'take into account the varying development stages of competition policy in the AMSs. For example, the Regional Guidelines set out different measures that an AMS can adopt or maintain to proscribe anticompetitive business conduct, depending on its own stage of competition policy development'.[47]

§5. Role and Authority of Precedents

75. Unlike judges in the Malaysian courts, the MyCC is not bound by the doctrine of stare decisis (i.e., precedent), under which it is necessary for a court to follow the rules and principles laid down in previous decision when the same set of facts arise again in a new case or litigation. This means that in carrying out its assessment of whether an agreement or conduct in question is in breach of the CA, MyCC may but not be bound to consider its earlier decisions and reasoning if it considers such a conclusion to be inappropriate for the case at hand.

47. ASEAN Regional Guidelines on Competition Policy.

Chapter 2. Scope of Application

§1. Territorial Reach

76. The CA 2010 applies to any commercial activity which is transacted not only within Malaysia but also outside Malaysia, which has an effect on competition in any market in Malaysia.[48]

77. The extraterritorial approach applies to both the provision of the anticompetitive agreement under section 4 and abuse of dominant position under section 10 of the CA 2010.

78. The 'effect' doctrine was closer to the US practice rather than the EU or UK. The US Sherman Act 1890, by virtue of the Foreign Trade Antitrust Improvement Act 1982, only applies to conduct that has a direct, substantial and foreseeable effect in the US.

79. It is important to establish a local nexus through a 'direct, substantial and foreseeable' qualification to help reduce the burden of the competition authority in dealing with anticompetitive conduct that occurs outside Malaysia's territory and produces no substantial harm to Malaysia.

80. In addition to the 'effect' approach, the CA 2010 also incorporates a 'single economic unit' principle, which can be found in the EU competition law regime. Under this principle, anticompetitive conduct by a subsidiary company situated outside Malaysia may be imputed to its parent in Malaysia if the subsidiary company has no real autonomy in determining its action on the market but acted on its parent's instruction.

§2. Special Sectors

81. Initially, the CA 2010 excludes activities governed by two existing legislations, namely, the CMA 1998 and the ECA 2001. The two sectors have their own sector regulators overseeing competition issues in the respective sector long before the national competition authority was set up.

82. The CMA 1998 contains a very comprehensive competition law provisions that regulate competition in the multimedia and communication sectors. The CMA 1998 covers three important provisions, namely: (1) conduct that has the purpose of substantially lessening competition,[49] (2) conduct by a dominant licensee that has or may have the effect of substantially lessening competition,[50] and (3) hardcore

48. Section 2 of the Competition Act 2010.
49. Section 133 of the Communications and Multimedia Act 1998.
50. Section 139 of the Communications and Multimedia Act 1998.

restrictions, such as rate fixing, market sharing and boycott.[51] All activities regulated under the CMA 1998 must be subjected to this competition law regime.

83. Unlike CMA 1998, at the time the CA 2010 was enacted, the ECA 2001 had no comprehensive competition law regime. However, among the functions of the Energy Commission under the ECA is to promote and safeguard competition, fair and efficient market conduct, and to prevent misuse of market power in the electricity and energy sector. The Government had amended the Gas Supply (Amendment) Act (GSA) 2016 incorporating competition provisions which largely borrowed from the CA 2010, namely, an agreement that has the object or effect of significantly preventing, restricting or distorting competition in the market[52] and abuse of dominant position.[53] The ECAs as a regulator to implement and enforce the GSA 2016.

84. In 2013, the Second Schedule to the CA 2010 was amended to include the Petroleum Development Act (PDA) 1974 and Petroleum Regulations 1974 which exclude all commercial activities regulated under the Act and Regulations relating to upstream operations comprising the activities of exploring, exploiting, winning and obtaining petroleum either onshore or offshore of Malaysia.

85. In 2016, the Second Schedule to the CA 2010 was further amended to include the MACA 2015 which excludes activities regulated by the MACA 2015. The MACA 2015 contains three important competition provisions, namely, an anti-competitive agreement which has the object or effect of significantly preventing, restricting or distorting competition in any aviation service market,[54] abuse of dominant position[55] and mergers that have resulted or may be expected to result in a substantial lessening of competition (SLC) in any aviation service market.[56] All activities under the purview of MACA 2015 are subject to this competition law regime.

86. It should be noted that section 3(3) of the CA 2010 and the First Schedule put emphasis on 'activity' rather than 'entity'. Activities that are not regulated by the specific sector regulations will fall under the radar of the CA 2010. For example, the CMA 1998 only applies to operators licensed under the Act. The CA 2010 will still be applicable to non-licensees telecommunication providers, such as resellers of telecommunication products or services.

---

51. Section 135 of the Communications and Multimedia Act 1998.
52. Section 28C of the Gas Supply (Amendment) Act 2016.
53. Section 28G of the Gas Supply (Amendment) Act 2016.
54. Section 49 of the Malaysian Aviation Commission Act 2015.
55. Section 53 of the Malaysian Aviation Commission Act 2015.
56. Section 54 of the Malaysian Aviation Commission Act 2015.

87. Another example is that the Energy Commission's power in relation to competition is limited to the enforcement of Third-Party Access under the GSA.[57] Furthermore, the GSA only applies to the activity of delivery of liquefied natural gas or natural gas or the importation of natural gas through pipelines to the transmission and distribution pipelines or a piping system and to any gas appliance in the premises of a consumer.[58] Activities which are not within the power of the Energy Commission may fall under the purview of the CA 2010.

§3. State-Owned Enterprises and Public Utilities

88. Section 3 of CA 2010 defines 'enterprise' as entities carrying out commercial activity. Therefore, the concept of enterprise refers to an entity that carries out market activity for commercial considerations, including profit, regardless of the legal status of the entity and how it is financed.

89. The CA adopts the functional or fact-based approach in determining whether or not an entity is considered as an enterprise. The legal nature and the form of the entity are not relevant, but it is its activity that will be taken into account.[59]

90. The CA 2010 does not give an absolute exclusion from the Act to an entity just because the government owns some shares in it. Any individual, partnership, company, government agency, state-owned enterprise may be subject to the application and enforcement of the CA 2010 as long as they carry out activities which are commercial in nature.

91. For example, if a government agency or public body purchases drugs to be sold in pharmacies in competition with other market players, such a purchase will be a commercial activity. But if the agency purchases drugs to be used or dispensed in government hospitals, such a purchase will not be a commercial activity.[60]

92. Similarly, the purchase of rice by a government agency or a public body for the purpose of national stockpiling is not a commercial activity, but if rice goes to supermarket or groceries, such a purchase will be a commercial activity.[61]

93. Section 4 of the CA, however, provides a negative list in which certain activities are not considered a commercial activity, as given below.

---

57. Third-party access means access to the regasification terminal, transmission pipeline and distribution pipeline by a person other than the owner or operator of such facilities for purposes of delivery of gas to the consumers.
58. Section 1(3) of Gas Supply (Amendment) Act 2016.
59. H. Ahamat & N.A. Rahman, 'Defining "Government Authority" in the Malaysian Competition Act 2010: A Quest for Objectivity', *International Journal of Public Law and Policy*, 5(2) (2015) 194.
60. H. Ahamat & N.A. Rahman, 'Defining "Government Authority" in the Malaysian Competition Act 2010: A Quest for Objectivity', *International Journal of Public Law and Policy*, 5(2) (2015) 195.
61. H. Ahamat & N.A. Rahman, 'Defining "Government Authority" in the Malaysian Competition Act 2010: A Quest for Objectivity', *International Journal of Public Law and Policy*, 5(2) (2015) 195.

§4. NON-COMMERCIAL ACTIVITIES

I. Any Activity, Directly and Indirectly in the Exercise of Government Authority

94. The CA 2010 does not define clearly the word 'government authority'. The word 'government' includes 'government ministry or agency, and the government here covers the whole strata of governance which includes but is not limited to central/federal government, provincial government and local government. Additionally, companies which are owned, partly or wholly, by government, or controlled by it, or perform governmental functions can also be part of the government'.[62]

95. Activities in the exercise of government authority may cover any activities in the exercise of state function or state sovereignty, such as defence and military services, the administration of justice, maintenance of public order, collection of tax, protection of the environment, etc.

96. The activity in the exercise of a state function is something that a private entity is not capable of doing and does not have any private law content or character. The Commission will look at the nature of the function and the acts flowing from a discharge of that function.

97. Jacobson J. in *Australian Competition and Consumer Commission v. Malaysian Airline System Berhad*[63] stated that:

> [165] In Garuda, I came to the view that while the ambit of governmental functions may be difficult to define, governmental functions have a public character and depend upon their characterization as part of the machinery of the state: *Garuda* at [91]–[95].

98. The word 'indirectly' in section 3(4)(a) of the CA 2010 is also not clearly defined in the CA, but nonetheless has a significant meaning. The word intends to catch any governmental activity or function relating to public interests that had been delegated to a private entity.

99. In the book *Competition Law in Malaysia* by Nasarudin Abdul Rahman and Haniff Ahamat on page 58, it was stated that:

> The word *indirectly* is expected to protect entities that have been exclusively delegated by the government to carry out certain activities based on public

62. H. Ahamat & N.A. Rahman, 'Defining "Government Authority" in the Malaysian Competition Act 2010: A Quest for Objectivity', *International Journal of Public Law and Policy,* 5(2) (2015).
63. [2010] FCA 757.

interest or social objectives. This may include GLCs delegated by the government to carry out their activities, such as PETRONAS Bhd, for the purpose of exploring and extracting petroleum for the country's revenue. …[64]
[Emphasis added]

II. Any Activity Conducted Based on the Principle of Solidarity

100. The CA 2010 also excludes any entity including public authority and government agency which performs an exclusively social function and not for remuneration or profits, such as entities that provide social security, pensions and health insurance or healthcare services.

101. The principle of 'solidarity' is borrowed from the EU competition law regime. The principle of solidarity is described as 'the redistribution of income between those who are better off and those who, in view of their resources and state of health, would be deprived of the necessary social cover',[65] or 'designed as a matter of priority to assist those who are in a state of need'.[66] It was stated that 'the very essence of the system was to perform a social function which was inherently non-economic, i.e., the benefits did not depend on the contribution made nor the success of a particular investment'.[67]

102. In the case of *Christian Poucet v. Assurance Générales de France and Caisse Mutuelle Régionale du Languedoc-Roussillon*, the European Court of Justice decided that 'sickness funds, and the organizations involved in the management of the public social security system, fulfil an exclusively social function. That activity is based on the principle of national solidarity and is entirely non-profit-making'.[68]

103. In the case of *FENIN Federación Española de Empresas de Tecnología Sanitaria v. Commission of the European Communities,* the Court of First Instance found that the public that was responsible for the national health system had not infringed the competition law (abuse of its dominant position) due to the fact that it 'operates according to the principle of solidarity in that it is funded from social security contributions and other State funding and in that it provides services free of charge to its members on the basis of universal cover'.[69]

64. Nasarudin Abdul Rahman & Haniff Ahamat, *Competition Law in Malaysia* (Sweet & Maxwell, 2016).
65. *Christian Poucet v. Assurance Générales de France and Caisse Mutuelle Régionale du Languedoc-Roussillon* (C-159-160/91) [1993] ECR I-637, para. 18.
66. *Sodemare v. Regione Lombardia* (C-70/95) [1998] ECR I-3395, para. 29.
67. Jonathan Faull & Ali Nikpay, *The EC Law of Competition*, 2nd edn 194 (Oxford University Press, 2007).
68. (C-159-160/91) [1993] ECR I-637, para. 18.
69. (T-319/99) [2003] ECR II-357, para. 39.

III. Any Purchase of Goods and Services Not for the Purposes of Offering Goods and Services as Part of an Economic Activity

104. The CA 2010 excludes a certain type of purchasing activity from the ambit of the Act. It is not the purchasing of goods and services that the Commission will look into but rather the subsequent activity or use of the purchased goods or services. In *FENIN v. Commission of the European Communities,* the Court of the First Instance stated that:

> it is the activity consisting in offering goods and services on a given market that is the characteristic feature of an economic activity […] not the business of purchasing, as such […] it would be incorrect, when determining the nature of that subsequent activity, to dissociate the activity of purchasing goods from the subsequent use to which they are put. The nature of the purchasing activity must therefore be determined according to whether or not the subsequent use of the purchased goods amounts to an economic activity.[70]

105. The exclusion under section 3(4)(c) may be relevant to the procurement activity either by the federal government or state government in Malaysia. For instance, the act of purchasing drugs to be used in government hospitals will be excluded from the CA 2010. However, the exclusion will not be extended to the government's purchase of drugs to be supplied to private hospitals or pharmacies in competition with other market players.

106. By virtue of section 13 of the CA, activities falling under the Second Schedule will be excluded from the enforcement of the CA 2010.

§5. Excluded Activities

I. An Agreement or Conduct to the Extent to Which It Is Engaged in Order to Comply with a Legislative Requirement

107. Legislative requirement must be one which is imposed by or under an enactment in force in Malaysia. The word 'compliance' indicates that an enterprise must be required to act in a certain way, and section 13 does not apply to discretionary conduct of an enterprise. If the legislation merely encourages the enterprise to conduct in a certain way, the conduct in question may still be subject to the CA 2010.

108. The agreement or conduct in question must be specific to the legal requirement currently enforced. For example, if a legislation requires an enterprise to fix the price and any conduct or agreement to give the law full effect, it will be excluded from the ambit of the CA 2010.

---

70. Case T-319/99, para. 36.

109. An agreement or conduct that is engaged in pursuant to any instrument, such as licensing, directives or policy, will still be excluded from the CA 2010 provided that the said instrument is made under a legislation or enactment. For example, an agreement or conduct to fix a price in the fulfilment of licensing conditions will be excluded if the licence was issued in complying with a legislative requirement.

II. Collective Bargaining Activities or Collective Agreements in Respect of Employment Terms and Conditions

110. The CA 2010 does not apply to collective bargaining agreement relating to employment matters. Collective bargaining or collective agreement entered between employees and employers to fix wages or employment terms and conditions fall outside the purview of the CA 2010.

111. The very purpose of collective bargaining in the area of employment is to improve work condition and countervail the bargaining power of the employers *vis-à-vis* individual workers and prevent the exploitation of labour.

112. However, an agreement between employers to fix employment conditions and not to poach each other's employees may be prohibited under the CA 2010 as it reduces the ability of an enterprise to compete for highly skilled employees. The non-poaching agreement diminish competition in the labour market to the detriment of employees who were deprived of better salaries and job opportunities.

III. An Enterprise Entrusted with the Operation of Services of General Economic Interest or Having the Character of a Revenue: Producing Monopoly in So Far as the Prohibition under Chapter I and Chapter II of Part II Would Obstruct the Performance … of the Particular Tasks Assigned to Enterprise

113. The concept of 'Service of General Economic Interest' (SGEI) is borrowed from the EU competition law regime. The SGEI is defined as services that 'public authorities consider … need to be provided even where the market may not have sufficient incentives to do so'.[71]

114. The SGEI is relevant in the case of public sector activities which had been exposed to competition or economic regulation, such as postal services, electricity, water sewerage services, train, cargo, terminal operation and scheduled bus services.[72] These activities which were previously administrative or social in nature had become economic activities due to privatization undertaken by the Government.

---

71. *EU Communications from the Commission, Service of General interest in Europe* OJ (2001) C 17/4 para. 14.
72. Nasarudin Abdul Rahman & Haniff Ahamat, *Competition Law in Malaysia* 66 (Sweet & Maxwell, 2016).

115. The word 'entrusted' means that the task assigned must come from federal or state government. The task must not necessarily be assigned via legislation but can be via positive act, such as the award of concession to certain enterprise to undertake a project for general economic interests.

116. It is important to show that the application of the CA 2010 will obstruct the performance of the SGEI operator assigned with the tasks. Therefore, any derogation from the prohibition under the CA 2010 can only be allowed under 'economically acceptable condition' and when the obligation cannot be performed in a less restrictive manner.[73]

117. For example, while a large part of these sectors have been privatized and opened up to competition, some of the incumbent operators are also required to provide universal service obligation to the unprofitable part of the segment, i.e., the rural areas which involve large investment but minimum charges to consumers.

118. The non-application of the CA 2010 to the SGEI is important to resolve the issue of cherry-picking or cherry-skimming whereby competitors will normally focus on the profitable part of the segment leaving the unprofitable part to the incumbent operators. This empowers the State to award an exclusive right to an enterprise to perform the SGEI function and protect it from competition. In addition, the SGEI operator may also act in certain ways without fear of running afoul of the CA 2010. For instance, the operator entrusted with the SGEI may be allowed to increase price in one segment (urban areas) in order to cover losses incurred in another segment (rural areas) due to their social obligation.

§6. Sensible Effect and De Minimis

119. Section 4(1) of the CA 2010 states that:

> A horizontal or vertical agreement between enterprises is prohibited insofar as the agreement has the object or effect of *significantly* preventing, restricting or distorting competition in any market for goods and services.

120. The word 'significant' in section 4(1) indicates that the CA is only concerned with anticompetitive conduct that has a substantial effect on competition. In order to determine whether the effect is more than trivial, the Commission will look at the combined/individual market shares of the parties to the agreement.[74] This requires the determination of the relevant market.

---

73. *See,* for example, OFT, *Services of General Economic Interest Exclusion* (December 2004); *Guide to the Application of the European Union Rules on state aid, public procurement and the internal market to services of general economic interest, and in particular to social services of general interest* (Commission Staff Working Document 2013).

74. Paragraph 3.4, *MyCC Guidelines on Chapter I Prohibition.*

121. The *MyCC Guidelines on Chapter 1 Prohibition* set up a 'safe harbours' below which an anticompetitive agreement is not considered 'significant':

- the parties to the agreement are competitors who are in the same market, and their combined market share of the relevant market does not exceed 20%;
- the parties to the agreement are not competitors, and all of the parties individually have less than 25% in any relevant market. For example, an exclusive distribution agreement between a wholesaler and a retailer neither of whom has more than 25% of the wholesale market or retail market.

122. It is important to note that certain type of horizontal agreements, such as price-fixing and market sharing (or better known as a hardcore cartel) do not benefit from the 'safe harbour'. Section 4(2) of the CA 2010 is a 'deeming' provision and any conduct listed under section 4(2), such as price-fixing, output limitation, market sharing, and bid-rigging is *deemed to have the object of significantly* preventing, restricting and distorting competition in any market for goods or services.

123. This means that under section 4(2), the Commission is under no obligation to determine the relevant market and the enterprises participating in the hardcore cartel agreement may still be found liable even though the combined market shares of the enterprises are small or insignificant.

Chapter 3. Overview of Substantive Provisions

§1. Restrictive Agreements

124. Section 4(1) of the CA 2010 states that 'a horizontal or vertical agreement between enterprises is prohibited insofar as the agreement has the object or effect of significantly preventing, restricting or distorting competition in any market for goods or services'.

125. Note that section 4 of the CA 2010 applies to both legally and not legally enforceable agreement, oral or written, formal or informal agreement and whether or not a party to an agreement had the intention to comply with the agreement or otherwise. Conduct of two or more enterprises in the market who are acting in concert to restraint competition may fall under section 4 of the CA 2010, even though there is no express agreement between them.

126. Section 4 also applies to the decision made by a trade association and its members even though not all members of a trade association agreed and had no intention to abide by or implement the decision of the association.

127. Section 4 of the CA 2010 regulates various forms of business organizations including sole proprietors, partnership, company, state-owned enterprise or even government agencies as long as they carry out activities which are commercial in nature. Any social activities or activities in pursuant to government sovereignty shall not be covered under the CA 2010.

128. The prohibition under section 4 of the CA 2010 covers both agreements between enterprises operating on the same level of production or distribution chain (horizontal agreement) and agreements between enterprises not operating on the same level of production or distribution chain (vertical agreement). However, MyCC regards horizontal agreement to be more harmful than vertical agreement as it involves an agreement between competitors in the market.

129. Section 4(1) of the CA 2010 differentiates between restrictive agreement by 'object' and restrictive agreement by 'effect'. Restrictive agreement by 'object' refers to an agreement which has a clear aim of restricting competition in the market (such as an agreement between competitors to stop competing with each other in the market).

130. However, even though the anticompetitive object is not found (such as an agreement between producers and retailers), the agreement will still breach section 4 if it has an anticompetitive effect. It means that the latter's category of the restrictive agreement requires MyCC to undertake a more detailed economic analysis to unveil the effect of the agreement on the competition before deciding whether the agreement in question is in breach of the CA 2010.

131. Section 4 of the CA 2010 is concerned with an agreement that has 'significant' or more than a trivial effect on competition.[75] For the sake of certainty, *MyCC Guidelines on Chapter 1 Prohibition* provides a 'safe harbour' threshold below which an agreement will be considered as having an insignificant effect on competition. Market shares of parties to an agreement will be used as an indicator to determine whether a particular agreement falls under the purview of section 4 of the CA 2010.

132. The 'effect' on competition will be assessed in relation to the defined relevant market.[76] Anticompetitive agreement is not considered significant if:

- For an agreement between competitors (horizontal agreement), their combined market shares shall not exceed 20%.
- For an agreement between non-competitors (vertical agreement), all of the parties to an agreement individually have less than 25% market shares.[77]

§2. Dominant Enterprises

133. Section 10(1) states that: 'an enterprise is prohibited from engaging, whether independently or collectively, in any conduct which amount to an abuse of a dominant position in any market for goods or services'.

134. Section 10 does not prohibit an enterprise from being dominant in the market but rather put a special responsibility to a dominant enterprise not to do certain conduct which the law considers as abusive.

135. In assessing whether there is a breach of section 10 of the CA 2010, MyCC will conduct two important analyses as follows:

(1) the MyCC will ask whether the enterprise being complained about is dominant in a relevant market in Malaysia; and
(2) if the enterprise is dominant, then the MyCC will assess whether the enterprise is abusing that dominant position.

I. Dominance

136. An enterprise shall be dominant if it possesses significant market power in a relevant market. Defining a relevant market involves identifying which enterprises that compete in the market for goods or services under investigation.[78] The

75. Paragraph 3.4, *MyCC Guidelines on Chapter 1 Prohibition.*
76. Paragraph 3.4, *MyCC Guidelines on Chapter 1 Prohibition.*
77. Paragraph 3.4, *MyCC Guidelines on Chapter 1 Prohibition.*
78. Paragraph 2.6, *MyCC Guidelines on Chapter 2 Prohibition.*

relevant market includes both products as well as geographic market and in some situations depending on the dynamic of competition covers other dimensions, such as temporal and functional dimension.

137. The word 'dominant' indicates that an enterprise must have a strong market power to act without effective constraints from consumers and other competitors. For competition law purposes, even if only one enterprise is operating without any competitors (monopolist), this situation shall also be considered as a dominant position in the market.[79]

138. Dominant position can be held individually or collectively. Collective dominant is very much relevant when the market is controlled by a few enterprises (oligopoly). For example, few largest enterprises which dominate the market may form an alliance and act together in such a way that excludes or eliminates other competitors who are not within the alliance.

139. In the MyCC Guidelines on IPRs and Competition Law, it is stated that a collective dominant 'may be established when two or more undertakings, legally independent of each other, present themselves or act together from an economic point of view, in a particular market, as a collective entity. The economic link can be in the form of joint policies or activities, even in the absence of agreement or other links in law'.[80]

140. Dominant position may be determined by measuring the market share of an enterprise and its competitors. *MyCC Guidelines on Chapter 2 Prohibition* states that 'a market share above 60% to be indicative that an enterprise is dominant'[81] and 'an enterprise with 100% market share is likely to be dominant because there is no competition'.[82]

141. However, market shares shall not be considered as conclusive evidence of dominance.[83] For instance, even though an enterprise holds more than 60% shares, its behaviour in the market can be constrained by a potential new entrant if the entry into the market is relatively easy.

142. What is important in determining the dominant position is whether 'the enterprises ability to act without concerning the competitor's responses or ability to dictate the terms of competition in a market in Malaysia'.[84]

79. Paragraph 2.6, *MyCC Guidelines on Chapter 2 Prohibition.*
80. Paragraph 8.5, *MyCC Guidelines on Intellectual Property Rights and Competition Law.*
81. Paragraph 2.2, *MyCC Guidelines on Chapter 2 Prohibition.*
82. Paragraph 2.7, *MyCC Guidelines on Chapter 2 Prohibition.*
83. Paragraph 1.5, *MyCC Guidelines on Chapter 2 Prohibition.*
84. Paragraph 1.5, *MyCC Guidelines on Chapter 2 Prohibition.*

143. Whether an enterprise is dominant will depend on a range of competitive conditions in the relevant market and competitive constraints faced by the enterprise. Other factors that may be considered in assessing a dominant include the extent of entry barriers, countervailing buyer powers, the existence of economic regulation, such as price regulation, etc.

II. Abusive Conduct

144. The CA 2010 prohibits a dominant enterprise from engaging in certain conduct that its non-dominant competitors can do in the market. An enterprise which has significant market power may be able to distort the competitive process in the market. Therefore, regardless of the reason for which the dominant enterprise has its market power, the Act has put a special responsibility on the dominant enterprise not to allow its conduct to impair genuine competition in the market.

145. Section 10(2) of the CA 2010 lists down certain prohibited conduct which are considered as abusive. However, the list is not exhaustive and contains only some of the common anticompetitive conduct that may be potentially engaged by a dominant enterprise. Abusive conduct falling outside section 10(2) may be dealt with under section 10(1).

146. The list of prohibited conduct under section 10(2) contains both exploitative and exclusionary conduct. The CA 2010 does not only prevent conduct that may harm consumers (exploitative) but also those that impair or weaken the degree of competition by excluding or eliminating existing or potential competitors from effectively competing in the market (exclusionary). The list of conduct also covers both price and non-price behaviour. Conduct that is related to pricing policy includes excessive unfair price, price discrimination and predatory pricing. Non-price behaviour, on the other hand, includes tying, refusal to supply, output limitation, etc.

§3. CONCENTRATION

147. The CA 2010 does not contain merger provisions. This means that the MyCC is not able to block or prevent any merger that will be consummated in the Malaysian market. Any anticompetitive conduct arising after a merger has competed will be dealt with under section 10 of the CA 2010, which prohibits a dominant entity from abusing its dominant position (*ex post*-merger activities). Alternatively, the MyCC may invoke the provision of the anticompetitive agreement by virtue of section of 4 the CA if, during the merger process, the merging parties entered into an anticompetitive agreement, such as sharing sensitive information or collusion.

148. However, merger provisions can be found in two specific sectors, namely, aviation and multimedia and communications. The MACA 2015 empowers the

Malaysian Aviation Commission (MAVCOM) to regulate civil aviation industry, while the Communications and Multimedia Act (CMA) 1998 empowers the Malaysian Communications and Multimedia Commission (MCMC) to regulate activities in the communications market.

149. Section 54 of the MACA prohibits mergers that have resulted or may be expected to result, in an SLC in any aviation service market.

150. The CMA does not contain a clear merger provision. However, the word 'conduct' under sections 133 and 139 of the CMA capture a wide range of activities, including merger:

- Section 133 – the CMA prohibits licensees from engaging in 'any conduct which has the purpose of substantially lessening competition in a communications market'.
- Section 139 – the CMA gives the power to the Malaysia Communications and Multimedia Commission (MCMC) to 'direct a licensee in a dominant position in a communications market to cease a conduct in that communications market which has, or may have, the effect of substantially lessening competition in any communications market'.

151. The MCMC will be interested in assessing a merger if at least one of the parties to a merger is a licensee, and if the following scenario occurs:

(1) the merger occurs between parties operating in the communications market;
(2) the merger occurs between parties operating in the different communications market, and the merger enables the parties to leverage market power held in one communications market in another communications market; and
(3) where at least one of the parties to a merger is operating in a communications market, and the merger enables the said parties to leverage market power in a communications market.[85]

§4. Other Prohibitions

152. The main crux of the CA 2010 is the prohibition against anticompetitive agreement under section 4 and abuse of dominant position under section 10 of the Act. The CA 2010 omits merger control provision.

85. Paragraph 3.2, *Guidelines on Mergers and Acquisitions.*

§5. Tests of Illegality

I. Per Se Prohibitions and Naked Restraints

153. Section 4(1) of the CA 2010 prohibits any anticompetitive agreement which has the object or effect of significantly restricting, preventing or distorting competition in the market.

154. Section 4(2) of the CA 2010 laid down examples of conduct which are deemed to have the object of significantly restricting, preventing or distorting competition in the relevant market. These conducts are price-fixing, market sharing, limit of output, and bid-rigging. These conducts are also known as 'hardcore restriction' or classical cartel agreement where the anticompetitive object of the agreement is so obvious.

155. Section 4(2) is a deeming provision which has at least two legal implications. First, an agreement that falls under 4(2) is deemed to be anticompetitive under the Act, and MyCC is under no obligation to prove the actual effect of the agreement on competition. Second, an agreement under section 4(2) is presumed to have a significant effect on competition without the need on the part of MyCC to define the relevant market and determine the market powers of a party to an agreement.

156. Even though certain agreements are deemed to be anticompetitive, and the requirement to prove the actual effect of the agreement on competition is dispensed with, a party to an agreement may still ask for a relief of liability for the infringement under the section 4 prohibition. The burden of proof is shifted to the party to show that the agreement fulfils all four criteria laid down under section 5 of the CA 2010.

II. Balancing Tests

157. Section 5 of the CA 2010 states that an enterprise which is a party to an agreement may relieve its liability for the infringement of the prohibition under section 4 based on the following criteria:

(a) there are significant identifiable technological, efficiency or social benefits directly arising from the agreement;
(b) the benefits could not reasonably have been provided by the parties to the agreement without the agreement having the effect of preventing, restricting or distorting competition;
(c) the detrimental effect of the agreement on competition is proportionate to the benefits provided; and
(d) the agreement does not allow the enterprise concerned to eliminate competition completely in respect of a substantial part of the goods or services.

A. The First Criterion Is Related to the Possible Benefits That an Agreement May Bring About

158. A party is not required to prove each and every benefit as listed down under section 5(a). Efficiency and technological benefits may be overlapping as any improvement in technology may bring about efficiency benefits. Efficiency benefits include costs efficiency and qualitative efficiency.

159. Cost-efficiency may result, for example, from technological progress, synergies from economies of scale and scope, vertical integration, etc., whereas qualitative efficiency may result from, for example, research and development (R&D) and joint production. In the end, both cost and qualitative efficiencies may improve consumer welfare, in the form of lower price increased productivity and new or improved goods and services. The Commission had on many occasions rejected the argument that price-fixing was important due to various reasons, such as the newly revised electricity tariffs, the minimum wage policy, increase of diesel price, and the implementation of Good and Services Tax, etc.

160. The word benefit under section 5(a) includes social benefit. However, the CA does not explain on what amount to 'social benefit'.

B. The Second Criterion Is Related to the Indispensability Requirement

161. The benefits claimed must be specific to the agreement in question. A party to an agreement must prove that there is no other economically practical and less restrictive way of achieving the benefits. The agreement is indispensable if its absence would reduce the benefits that arise from the agreement. Hardcore restriction, such as price-fixing, is unlikely to be indispensable if there are other less restrictive means to achieve the claimed benefit.

C. The Third Criterion Is Related to 'Proportionality' Requirement

162. Even though section 5(c) uses the concept of 'proportionality', in practice, MyCC will assess whether the detrimental effect of the agreement on competition is outweighed by the benefits that flow from the agreement in question. Based on *MyCC Guidelines on Chapter 1 Prohibition*, the parties claiming for the benefits must prove that the benefits gained are passed on to consumers.[86] For example, if an agreement is likely to lead to a higher price, the parties must prove that consumer will be compensated with an increase of quality and other benefits. The balancing exercise will involve a value judgment on the part of MyCC.

86. Paragraph 5.2, *MyCC Guidelines on Chapter 1 Prohibition*.

D. The Fourth Criterion Is Related to Complete Elimination of Competition Requirement

163. A party to an agreement must show that the agreement in question preserves some form of competition in the market. For example, an agreement to share vessel in shipping liner industry may be allowed if the shipping liner operators can still be competing on price.

164. The criteria under section 5 can be used in several ways, as follows:

(1) It can be used by a party to an agreement as a defence when competition law action has been taken against the party. The party to a competition law proceeding must prove that the agreement in question satisfies all requirements under section 5.
(2) It can be used when a party applies for an individual exemption with respect to an agreement to MyCC under section 6 of the CA or when MyCC considers granting a block exemption to a particular category of the agreement under section 8 of the CA.
(3) An enterprise may use the criteria under section 5 as part of competition self-assessment on any proposed agreement or policy. This self-assessment programme will preliminarily assess whether any proposed agreement or policy is likely to comply with the CA 2010. The self-assessment programme itself may be used as a defence in competition enforcement or be part of mitigation to reduce the penalty imposed by MyCC in competition law action.

165. In *MyCC v. Containerchain & Four Container Depot Operators*, it was argued that 'the Containerchain system has proven efficiencies and brought significant improvements to the empty container logistic industry in Penang. The efficiencies of the system have been recognized in other jurisdictions'.[87] It was also submitted that 'the system was brought to Penang as a solution to the notorious problems and inefficiencies including delays and costs overruns caused by long queues by haulage trucks at depots'.[88] In this case, the party claiming for the efficiency benefits had failed to demonstrate how the fixing of depot gate charges (DGCs) and rebates to hauliers contribute to the efficiencies claimed. The party had also failed to prove that the agreement fulfils all four conditions under section 5 of the CA 2010.

166. In *MyCC v. MAS-Airasia,* the Commission stated that 'section 5 could have also been invoked as a valid defence for an infringement under section 4 (2) of the Act. MAS and AirAsia stated that the Collaboration Agreement's net economic benefit outweighs the anti- competitive effects. This defence would be available to any party in respect of any infringement of the Act. However, the burden to satisfy section 5 shifts to both MAS and AirAsia. Any party relying on section 5 would have

87. *MyCC v. Containerchain & Four Container Depot Operators* (No. 700.2.005.2013) para. 132.
88. *MyCC v. Containerchain & Four Container Depot Operators* (No. 700.2.005.2013) para. 134.

to satisfy All requirements of the section and the Commission is of the view that the parties did not satisfy the requirements of section 5 of the Act. This burden was not discharged by the parties'.[89]

III. Block Exemption on Shipping Liner

167. By virtue of section 8 of the CA 2010, the Commission may grant a block exemption to agreements which fall within a particular category of agreements to which section 5 of the CA 2010 applies. The Commission had granted a three-block exemption to shipping liner agreements starting from (2014–2017), (2017–2019) and (2019–2022). Liner shipping services are defined as 'any service provided by a liner operator to any transport user upon payment for the containerization of goods and scheduled transport of the containerized goods, or other scheduled transport of goods, by an ocean transport on a regular basis, through any particular route between ports, and in accordance with timetables and sailing dates which are made available and advertised in advance'.[90] The term of liner shipping service excludes full vessel chartering arrangements with any transport user, such as a tanker and bulk vessel services.

168. The first two Block Exemption sought to exempt two important shipping liner agreements, namely, Vessel Sharing Agreement (VSA)[91] and Voluntary Discussion Agreement (VDA).[92] However, the third Block Exemption is only applied to the VSA. In granting the block exemption, the Commission is satisfied that the four requirements under section 5 have been fulfilled.

A. There Are Significant Identifiable Technological, Efficiency or Social Benefits Directly Arising from the VSA

169. Since the shipping industry involves a very large investment and operating costs, the Commission is of the view that by entering into VSA, the liner shipping operators are able to provide shipping services at lower costs while maintaining the quality of the services. The agreements allow the liner operators to provide regular and scheduled service between various ports around the world. The nature of the

89. *MyCC v. MAS-AirAsia* (No. MyCC.0001.2012) para. 75.
90. Clause 2, Competition (Block Exemption for Vessel Sharing Agreements and Voluntary Discussion Agreements in Respect of Liner Shipping Services) Order 2014.
91. VSA is 'an agreement between liner operators in which the parties to such agreement shall only discuss and agree on operational arrangements relating to the provision of liner shipping services including the coordination or joint operation of vessel services', *see* Clause 2, Competition (Block Exemption for Vessel Sharing Agreements and Voluntary Discussion Agreements in Respect of Liner Shipping Services) Order 2014.
92. On the other hand, is 'an agreement between liner operators in which the parties to such agreement may exchange and review commercial issue relating to market data, demand and supply forecasts, international trade flows and industry trends, and voluntary and non-binding guidelines' Clause 2, Competition (Block Exemption for Vessel Sharing Agreements and Voluntary Discussion Agreements in Respect of Liner Shipping Services) Order 2014.

liner shipping industry requires cooperation among liner operators to maintain and observe the regularity and frequency of liner shipping services.

B. The Benefits Could Not Reasonably Have Been Provided by the Parties to the VSA Without the Agreement Having the Effect of Preventing, Restricting or Distorting Competition

170. The benefit of lower costs through regular and frequent service cannot be provided without agreements or cooperation in place between liner operators. The VSA encourages the liner operators to invest in ships, vessels and other facilities and infrastructures which are necessary for the continuous services in the liner shipping industry. The Block Exemption Order (BEO) only allows for the sharing vessels, joint operation of vessel services or exchange or charter of vessel space between liner shipping[93] and does not allow any element of price-fixing, price recommendation or tariff imposition and exchange of confidential information to be included in the VSA. The VSA shall not also contain any requirement to disclose confidential information relating to the shipping liner service arrangements to any transport user by any liner operator. It is unlikely that price-fixing is indispensable to achieving the efficiency benefits as there are other less restrictive means of achieving those benefits, namely, by sharing of vessels, exchange or charter of vessel space between liner operators.

C. The Detrimental Effect of the VSA on Competition Is Proportionate to the Benefits Provided

171. The Commission is satisfied that the detrimental effect of the agreements on competition is balanced by the efficiency benefits brought about by the agreements. The agreements entered into by liner operators to provide regularized and scheduled services ensure the stability in trade and regular services. The VSA is vital for the shipping liner operators to be able to meet the demand of shippers for the service regardless of size. It allows the shippers with small lots of cargoes to use the services to ship goods to various ports of destinations with lower costs.

D. The VSA Do Not Allow the Liner Operators to Eliminate Competition Completely in Respect of a Substantial Part of the Liner Shipping Services

172. Though VSA allow for regularized and scheduled services, they did not allow competition to be eliminated completely. The BEO prohibits any form of price-fixing and exchange of confidential information. Any party to the agreements is allowed to offer individual service arrangement, independently set rates and compete on pricing and level of service.

93. *See* Clause 4, Competition (Block Exemption for Vessel Sharing Agreements in Respect of Liner Shipping Services through Transportation by Sea) Order 2019.

IV. Reasonable Commercial Justification Defence

173. A dominant enterprise is not prevented 'from taking any step which has reasonable commercial justification or represents a reasonable commercial response to the market entry or market conduct of a competitor'.[94] The burden of proof justifying the conduct which would otherwise be abusive rests on the party claiming it.

174. Examples of reasonable commercial justification include:[95]

(1) refusing to sell to a buyer who has not paid for past purchases;
(2) refusing to grant access to a dominant enterprise's infrastructure that is already being used to capacity;
(3) offering a loyalty rebate that is related to the reduced costs of supplying a particular customer; and
(4) meeting a competitor's price even though the price may be below cost (in the short term).

94. Section 10(4) of Competition Act 2010.
95. Paragraph 5.5, *MyCC Guidelines on Chapter 1 Prohibition.*

Chapter 4. Overview of Main Notions

§1. Enterprise

175. Enterprise is defined as 'any entity carrying ton commercial activities relating to goods or services, and for the purpose of this Act, a parent and subsidiary company shall be regarded as a single enterprise if, despite their separate legal entity, both form a single economic unit within which the subsidiaries do not enjoy real autonomy in determining the actions of the subsidiaries on the market'.[96]

176. The CA emphasizes on the activity rather than the form of an entity. The word 'enterprise' includes individual operating as a sole proprietorship, partnerships, companies, cooperatives, societies, professional bodies, etc. This also includes government or government agencies or state-owned enterprises if they perform activities which are commercial in nature.

177. The word 'enterprise' also includes business chambers or trade associations. Even though some of these entities do not carry commercial activities, but the fact that they are groups of enterprise that carry out business activities for profits and become a platform to coordinate the activities of their members make them being regarded as enterprises in the eyes of the CA 2010.

I. Single Economic Unit

178. Generally, the CA does not apply to enterprises that form as a single economic unit within which the subsidiary does not enjoy real independence in its commercial decision and subject to the instruction of the parent company.

179. The adoption of 'single economic unit' has three main implications in the enforcement of the CA 2010:

(1) Agreement between two enterprises that form a single economic unit is not considered as an agreement but rather as an internal allocation of tasks between enterprises.
(2) The 'single economic unit' renders an enterprise liable for the conduct of another enterprise. For example, a parent company may be liable for anticompetitive conduct of its subsidiary if the later acted on the market based on the parent's instruction.
(3) The 'single economic unit' principle has a great influence on how the competition authority determines the amount of penalty for infringing the CA 2010. The competition authority may take into account the turnover of each enterprise within a corporate group and not just confine itself to the enterprise in breach.

96. Section 2 of the Competition Act 2010.

180. In *MyCC v. MAS-AirAsia*, the Commission has relied on the European Commission's decision in *Europemballage and Continental Can v. Commission* in 19736, where it was held that:

> the circumstances that this subsidiary company has its own legal personality does not suffice to exclude the possibility that its conduct might be attributed to the parent company. This is true in those cases particularly where the subsidiary company does not determine its market behaviour autonomously but in essential follows directives of the parent company.

181. The Commission has further elaborated that 'the applicable test is the test of control of which it is essential for the Commission to establish whether parties to the Collaboration Agreement are independent in their decision-making or whether one is able to exercise decisive influence over the other with the result that the latter does not enjoy "real autonomy" in determining its commercial policy on the market'.[97] In determining control, 'it is necessary to examine various factors such as the shareholding that a parent company has in the subsidiary company as well as the composition of the board of directors'.[98]

182. In *MAS-AirAsia*, AirAsia and AirAsia X (AAX) are companies with common shareholders and directors, and AirAsia owns majority shareholdings in AAX. The Commission of the view that 'AirAsia exercises decisive control over AAX, in a way that AAX is not independent in making its own decisions and therefore AirAsia and AAX is a single economic unit.'[99] For Malaysia Airlines System (MAS) and Firefly, the Commission finds that Firefly Sdn. Bhd. is a wholly owned subsidiary of MAS. Even though 'Fly Firefly Sdn. Bhd. is not a party to the Collaboration Agreement but being a wholly-owned subsidiary of MAS, the latter has the autonomous power to review Firefly's flight services operations.'[100]

183. In *MyCC v. My E.G. Services Bhd*, the Commission decided that 'My E.G. Commerce is a wholly-owned subsidiary of MyEG and despite their separate legal entity, they form a single economic unit. The fact that there are common directors also indicates that MyEG Commerce, as a subsidiary, does not enjoy real autonomy in determining its actions in the market.'[101] In the recent case of *MyCC v. Coca-Cola*, based on the fact that Coca-Cola Refreshments is a wholly owned subsidiary of Coca-Cola Bottlers, 'the Commission has made a legal presumption that Coca-Cola Bottlers exercised decisive influence over its subsidiaries and is therefore also liable for the conduct of the subsidiaries'.[102]

---

97. *MyCC v. MAS-AirAsia* (No. MyCC.0001.2012) para. 18.
98. *MyCC v. MAS-AirAsia* (No. MyCC.0001.2012) para. 19.
99. *MyCC v. MAS-AirAsia* (No. MyCC.0001.2012) para. 24.
100. *MyCC v. MAS-AirAsia* (No. MyCC.0001.2012) para. 13.
101. *MyCC v. MyEG Services Bhd* (MyCC (ED) 700-1/1/2/2015) para. 8.
102. *MyCC v. Coca-Cola Bottlers (Malaysia) Sdn Bhd & Coca-Cola Refreshments Malaysia Sdn Bhd* (No. 700-1/3/3/2018).

§2. Relevant Market

184. Market is defined as 'market in Malaysia or in any part of Malaysia, and when used in relation to any goods or services, includes a market for those goods or services and other goods or services that are substitutable for, or otherwise competitive with, the first-mentioned goods or services'.[103]

185. Market definition is one of the important economic concepts under the Malaysian competition law. It is typically the first crucial step in a competition analysis to developing a framework for identifying 'all close substitutes for product under investigation'.[104] It helps the Competition Commission to find out any competitive constraint faced by a supplier or producer for a product that is being complained of.

186. Market definition allows the Commission to:

(1) identify all enterprises which compete against the enterprise against whom the complaint has been made (i.e., who compete in the same market);
(2) determine whether an agreement violates the Chapter 1 Prohibition because it has the 'effect of significantly preventing, restricting or distorting competition in any market for goods or services'. Market definition is important to determine whether there is a significant anticompetitive effect in a market;
(3) determine whether conduct by a dominant enterprise violates Chapter 2 Prohibition by engaging in conduct which 'amounts to an abuse of a dominant position in any market for goods and services'. To be dominant in a market requires assessing whether a firm has substantial market power in a market; and
(4) take into account the turnover of the firm in the relevant market in assessing the amount of penalty.[105]

187. Defining the relevant market is useful in determining whether an agreement has an effect on competition and whether a firm is occupying a dominant position. From the enforcement perspective, the process of defining market helps the Competition Commission to quickly respond to an agreement that has no significant effect on competition or when an enterprise clearly does not possess market power. For instance, when anticompetitive agreement involves competitors with small market shares, MyCC may not need to define precisely the relevant market or may close the investigation as the potential effect of the agreement is insignificant.[106]

188. However, it is important to note that certain horizontal agreements are deemed to be anticompetitive without the need on the part of MyCC to determine

103. Section 2 of the Competition Act 2010.
104. Paragraph 1.5, *MyCC Guidelines on Market Definition.*
105. Paragraph 1.6, *MyCC Guidelines on Market Definition.*
106. Paragraph 1.8, *MyCC Guidelines on Market Definition.*

the relevant market and market powers of the parties to the agreement. It is also important to note that defining the relevant market sometimes involves a practical judgment which means that in some cases, it may not be even necessary to define the relevant market precisely.[107]

I. Product Market

189. Product market involves the identification of 'the smallest group of products (in a geographical area) that a hypothetical monopolist controlling that product group (in that area) could profitably sustain a price above the "competitive" price i.e. a price that is at least a small but significant amount above the competitive price'.[108]

II. Geographic Market

190. Geographic market involves the identification of 'the area over which consumers can substitute the products under consideration and the area over which sellers can competitively sell the relevant products'.[109]

III. Other Types of Market

A. Temporal Market

191. Temporal dimension involves the analysis of the possible introduction of new products and services in the future and the extent to which these products will be substitutable for the existing products and services.[110] For example, 'if customers can defer the purchase of an existing product because a new product may be introduced in the future, it will be necessary to consider whether the new product and the existing product form part of the same market'.[111] Temporal market analysis also considers the time characteristic of the market. 'For example, if services have differences in the level of demand during peak and off-peak times, it will be necessary to consider whether services supplied during peak times are in a separate market to services supplied during off peak times.'[112]

107. Paragraph 1.10, *MyCC Guidelines on Market Definition.*
108. Paragraph 2.2, *MyCC Guidelines on Market Definition.*
109. Paragraph 3.5, *MyCC Guidelines on Market Definition.*
110. MCMC, *Market Definition Analysis* (24 Sep. 2014) para. 3.12.
111. MCMC, *Market Definition Analysis* (24 Sep. 2014) para. 3.11.
112. MCMC, *Market Definition Analysis* (24 Sep. 2014) para. 3.11.

B. Functional Market

192. Functional market refers to 'the level of the supply chain at which products and services are supplied (for example, the wholesale or retail levels of the supply chain)'.[113] 'In determining the relevant functional market, the key issue for consideration is whether the behaviour of firms operating at one functional level of the market is constrained by substitution between products or geographic sources of supply at another functional level.'[114]

IV. The Hypothetical Monopolist Test

A. Product Market

193. In identifying the relevant market, MyCC will use the Hypothetical Monopolist Test (HMT). Using the HMT, MyCC will assess whether a hypothetical monopoly could profitably sustain a small but significant increase in price (SSNIP). MyCC will normally use a price range of 5%–10% above competitive level to represent SSNIP.[115] Defining the relevant market based on HMT involves three important steps:[116]

Step 1: MyCC will start off with a focal product of a hypothetical monopolist (the product that is under investigation).
Step 2: MyCC will ask 'would a hypothetical monopolist of a market for focal product find it profitable to sustain the increase of price for the focal product of 5%–10% above the competitive level?':

(a) If the answer is YES – then the market definition is the market for the focal product for competition purposes as all products that compete with the focal product around that price have been identified.
(b) If the answer is NO – then MyCC will identify the closest substitute for the focal product and the later will be included in the definition of the relevant market.

Step 3: The question in step 2 will be repeated: would the hypothetical monopolist for the focal product plus the closest substitutes profitably increase the price between 5% and 10% above competition level? If the answer is YES, then the definition of the relevant market is the focal product plus the close substitutes. If the answer is NO, then MyCC will identify other closest substitutes until it reaches the stage where a hypothetical monopolist could maintain the price of 5%–10% above the competitive level.

194. Economic evidence used in determining the relevant market:[117]

113. MCMC, *Market Definition Analysis* (24 Sep. 2014) para. 3.10.
114. MCMC, *Market Definition Analysis* (24 Sep. 2014) para. 3.10.
115. Paragraph 2.3, *MyCC Guidelines on Market Definition.*
116. Paragraph 2.4, *MyCC Guidelines on Market Definition.*
117. Paragraphs 2.6 & 2.7, *MyCC Guidelines on Market Definition.*

- Market survey on consumers' willingness to switch product as price changes.
- Interviews with an industry association to understand the market trend and consumers' behaviour.
- Interviews with the initial complainant to provide more information, especially on their own marketing strategies.
- Interview with competitors to provide information on the competition dynamics.
- Interview with customers on their decision and response to a price increase.
- Evidence of switching costs that buyers may face in switching to other products and services.
- Similar price changes which may indicate the products are in the same market as they are subject to the same competitive pressures.
- Own or cross-price electricity: evidence of change in demand for a product arising from a change in its price or a change of demand for a product in response to a change in the price of another product.
- Peak and off-peak services: the ability of consumers or producers to switch demand or supply between the two periods.
- Innovation/inter-generalization products: the consumers' decision to defer expenditure on the belief that new innovation will soon be produced.

B. *Geographic Market*

195. The framework applied to define the product market is also used to define the geographic market. Defining the relevant geographic market starts with identifying a narrow geographic area known as the focal area.[118] MyCC will ask a question: could a hypothetical monopolist operating in a focal area profitably increase the price between 5% and 10% above competitive level?

196. If the answer is YES – then the geographic market is the focal area as any increase in price will not trigger consumers to switch to other areas.

If the answer is NO – then the geographic market will include any neighbouring areas to which the consumers will switch in response to a price increase of 5%–10% above competitive level by the hypothetical monopolist.[119]

C. *Demand-Side Substitutability*

197. The definition of the relevant market and the test that is used to define the relevant market is very much related to the concept of 'substitutability'. The most important consideration in defining the relevant market is 'whether consumers themselves see the products as substitutes as the price of the focal product changes'.[120] This is called as 'demand substitutability' or switching behaviour of the consumers. A product does not have to be identical to or have similar functions as

118. Paragraph 3.3, *MyCC Guidelines on Market Definition.*
119. Paragraph 3.3, *MyCC Guidelines on Market Definition.*
120. Paragraph 2.9, *MyCC Guidelines on Market Definition.*

other products to be substitutable by consumers. MyCC will look at how quick consumers can switch from one product to another and 'the more quickly buyers can switch products, the greater the constraint on the exercise of seller market power'.[121]

198. Generally, a twelve-month period will be used to assess consumers' switching behaviour depending on the type of market. For instance, if consumers switch from focal product to another product within twelve months, they later will be included in the relevant market, and MyCC considers that any period longer than twelve months does not provide an effective constraint on the behaviour of the hypothetical monopolist.[122]

199. In defining the relevant geographic market, MyCC will take into consideration an additional factor, i.e., the transportation costs relative to the price. 'The higher the costs of transportation, the smaller the geographic market is likely to be'[123] as consumers facing high transportation costs may be unwilling to travel further to buy cheaper supplies.[124]

D. Supply-Side Substitutability

200. In addition to demand-side substitutability, MyCC may also take into account supply-side substitutability in defining the relevant product or geographical market. MyCC will ask whether 'other enterprises currently not supplying the product in question could easily switch production or otherwise supply the focal product and its substitutes within a short time period'.[125] In other words, supply-side substitutability focuses on the possibility of entry into a market in the event of a price increase and MyCC will only consider supply-side substitutability 'when entry is reasonably likely to occur and is a factor that existing producers take into account in making their decisions'.[126]

201. In considering whether an entry is possible, MyCC will look at several factors, such as whether the entry can occur quickly (less than one year), whether the entry is effective enough to affect prices (normally in large scale) and whether the entry does not involve substantial sunk investment.[127]

121. Paragraph 2.10, *MyCC Guidelines on Market Definition.*
122. Paragraph 2.10, *MyCC Guidelines on Market Definition.*
123. Paragraph 3.5, *MyCC Guidelines on Market Definition.*
124. Paragraph 3.5, *MyCC Guidelines on Market Definition.*
125. Paragraph 2.11, *MyCC Guidelines on Market Definition.*
126. Paragraph 2.14, *MyCC Guidelines on Market Definition.*
127. Paragraph 2.12, *MyCC Guidelines on Market Definition.*

V. Other Important Issues

A. Competitive Price

202. The HMT very much relies on competitive price as the base price to assess the switching behaviour of consumers or suppliers. MyCC acknowledges the difficulty in determining a competitive price. This problem is better known as the 'Cellophane Fallacy'. For example, most of the time, a monopolist has already imposed a monopoly price. A monopolist who increases the price by 5%–10% above this price will lose the sales and profits to other substitutes. Therefore, incorrectly identifying substitutes based on price above competitive level may result in the market being defined widely than it is supposed to be.[128] However, MyCC may take into consideration other evidence to determine whether the prices are above the competitive level, such as excess profits or past price movement.[129]

B. Product Differentiation

203. The process of defining the relevant market becomes a more complex exercise in the existence of product differentiation. Products offered in the market may have differentiated features in terms of brand, location, quality, etc. For the purpose of HMT, MyCC may sometimes ignore product differences in its competition analysis.[130] However, if the degree of product differentiation is so high, MyCC may not define the market precisely. MyCC may instead focus on whether consumers view other products as substitutable for the differentiated products without going through the process of HMT and whether other products or producers act as constraints to the exercise of market power directly.[131] If a producer sells distinct products in the bundle, MyCC may assess whether consumers prefer to buy the distinct products separately or view the bundle as a group of products that they prefer to buy together.[132]

§3. Dominant Position

204. Dominant position is 'a situation in which one or more enterprises possess such significant power in a market to adjust prices or outputs or trading terms, without effective constraint from competitors or potential competitors'.[133]

128. Paragraph 4.2, *MyCC Guidelines on Market Definition.*
129. Paragraph 4.4, *MyCC Guidelines on Market Definition.*
130. Paragraph 5.1, *MyCC Guidelines on Market Definition.*
131. Paragraphs 5.2 & 5.3, *MyCC Guidelines on Market Definition.*
132. Paragraph 5.5, *MyCC Guidelines on Market Definition.*
133. Section 2 of the Competition Act 2010.

205. In determining whether an enterprise is in a dominant position, MyCC will take into consideration the following constraints that the enterprise may be facing in the market:[134]

(1) Constraints imposed by existing competitors – by assessing market shares of the parties and other competitive factors.
(2) Constraints imposed by potential competitors – the possibility of a new entry into the market.
(3) Other constraints, including buyers' power or economic regulation, imposed by the government, such as price regulation.

I. Constraints Imposed by Existing Competitors: Market Shares

206. The most important task in determining whether an enterprise under investigation is dominant is to assess whether the enterprise has significant market power and the ability to affect competition in the market without effective constraint from other competitors or consumers.

207. Market power can be assessed through market shares of an enterprise under investigation in the relevant product or geographical market. Market share is a good starting point or a screening device for MyCC in assessing whether an enterprise holds a dominant position in the market. Generally, market share above 60% would be considered as an indicator that an enterprise is dominant.[135] The set threshold allows MyCC to focus on an enterprise that has clear substantial market power when dealing with a complaint on abuse of a dominant position.

208. However, market share is not conclusive as to whether an enterprise occupies or does not occupy a dominant position.[136] MyCC may also take into consideration other factors, such as the level of entry barriers to the market. For example, a producer who sells a new product that is protected by the IPRs may be dominant even though the market share of the producer is below 60%. Market shares may be calculated based on several methods, such as value of sales, volume of units and production capacity.[137]

A. Degree of Product Differentiation

209. MyCC may also consider product differentiation in assessing dominance. A producer selling a distinct or differentiated product may be occupying a dominant position. In this situation, market share is no longer a good indicator to describe the

134. Paragraph 2.9, *MyCC Guidelines on Chapter 2 Prohibition* (abuse of dominant position).
135. Paragraph 2.14, *MyCC Guidelines on Chapter 2 Prohibition* (abuse of dominant position).
136. Section 10(4) of the Competition Act 2010.
137. Paragraph 2.17, *MyCC Guidelines on Chapter 2 Prohibition* (abuse of dominant position).

state of competition in the market. MyCC will decide whether a differentiated product forms a separate market from the others on a case-to-case basis.[138]

B. *Likely Response by Buyers to Price Increases*

210. Some products may have a 'sought after' or 'must have' status in the eyes of consumers. Sellers of these products may be enjoying a dominant position in the relevant product market. The sellers may be able to raise the price easily as the consumers are technically locked in to these products and will not switch to others due to this perceived status.[139]

C. *The Degree to Which Innovation Drives Competition*

211. Some markets may be featured with innovative products which are subject to continual improvement and evolution. The existing producers who are currently enjoying large market shares may no longer be in a dominant position when other producers enter into the market and produce new products with a new patented technology which the formers do not have access to. The existing products can simply be replaced by other products with the latest innovation and technology.[140]

II. Constraints Imposed by Potential Competitors: Barriers to New Entry

A. *Economies of Scale and Scope*

212. Economies of scope occur when 'the average costs of production fall as output increases' whereas economies of scope occur 'when fixed costs can be shared over greater range of products'.[141,142] A new entrant incurring high fixed costs may delay or decide not to enter into a market as it takes a long time to reach sufficient outputs or to offer a range of products to further reduces the costs.

B. *Regulated Entry*

213. Market which is heavily regulated, such as through licensing requirement, may limit the number of new entrants to enter into the market. An existing enterprise which has obtained the licence may enjoy a monopoly or dominant position in the market and may act in the market without any constraints.[143]

138. Paragraph 2.18, *MyCC Guidelines on Chapter 2 Prohibition* (abuse of dominant position).
139. Paragraph 2.18, *MyCC Guidelines on Chapter 2 Prohibition* (abuse of dominant position).
140. Paragraph 2.18, *MyCC Guidelines on Chapter 2 Prohibition* (abuse of dominant position).
141. Paragraph 2.19, *MyCC Guidelines on Chapter 2 Prohibition* (abuse of dominant position).
142. Paragraph 2.20, *MyCC Guidelines on Chapter 2 Prohibition* (abuse of dominant position).
143. Paragraph 2.20, *MyCC Guidelines on Chapter 2 Prohibition* (abuse of dominant position).

C. Limited Access to Necessary Inputs or Distribution Outlets

214. Existing distribution arrangement may also confer market power to an exclusive distributor and prevent other enterprises from competing for important inputs which are necessary to produce other products.[144]

D. Network Effects

215. A product's value to the users increases if it is widely used by other users.[145] For example, in the case of payment system, such as credit card, the value of a credit card increases when the users of the credit card grow. More users using the credit card will eventually attract more merchants to be part of the said payment system giving the credit card operator a dominant position in the payment system market. In this situation, new entrants will be facing difficulty to persuade consumers to switch to their products.[146]

High Sunk Cost

216. Sunk cost is defined as irrecoverable costs, such as advertising cost, which cannot be recovered if the business marketing is unsuccessful. In a certain consumer product market, the advertising cost is relatively high. If new entrants are faced with high advertising cost, they may decide not to enter into the market at all. In this situation, the dominant enterprise may act in the market without effective constraints.[147]

E. Conduct of Incumbent

217. Conduct of incumbent dominant enterprise may pose a potential threat to new entrant so that the incumbent may strengthen its dominant position in the market. For example, an incumbent enterprise may impose predatory pricing to drive competitors out of the market.[148]

III. Other Constraints

218. Buying or purchasing power may be taken into consideration in assessing dominance. Purchasers who have a bargaining power may offset the seller's power. For example, certain hypermarkets or supermarkets may have purchasing power

144. Paragraph 2.20, *MyCC Guidelines on Chapter 2 Prohibition* (abuse of dominant position).
145. Paragraph 2.20, *MyCC Guidelines on Chapter 2 Prohibition* (abuse of dominant position).
146. Paragraph 2.20, *MyCC Guidelines on Chapter 2 Prohibition* (abuse of dominant position).
147. Paragraph 2.20, *MyCC Guidelines on Chapter 2 Prohibition* (abuse of dominant position).
148. Paragraph 2.20, *MyCC Guidelines on Chapter 2 Prohibition* (abuse of dominant position).

over grocery suppliers which enable them to prevent the suppliers from imposing excessive price or setting unfair trading conditions.[149]

§4. Collective Dominance

219. Dominance is not only the conduct of a single enterprise but can also be the conduct of two or more enterprises holding and exercising market power together.[150] However, coordinated activities of independent enterprises in the market, such as collusion will normally be dealing with under Chapter 1 Prohibition (anticompetitive agreement). However, 'there may be a breach of the Chapter 2 Prohibition if two or more separate enterprises, which have significant market power, act similarly in a market and that conduct excludes equally efficient competitors'.[151]

§5. Agreements and Concerted Practices

I. Agreement

220. Agreement means 'any form of contract, arrangement or understanding, whether or not legally enforceable, between enterprises, and includes a decision by an association and concerted practices'.[152]

221. Agreement under the CA 2010 is very wide, which covers both oral and written agreement.

222. The word 'agreement' under section 2 of the CA 2010 intends to catch an agreement that is not binding or legally enforced. The word 'arrangement or understanding' means that it is sufficient to have a broad framework without a detailed agreement and a mechanism to enforce and ensure compliance with the agreement provided it influences parties to stop operating independently.

223. Agreement under the CA 2010 includes gentlemen agreement, partial or conditional agreement, circulars, warnings, guidelines, standard form of contract, exchange of correspondence, etc.

224. Agreement covers various forms of communication including telephone conversation, email, letters or mere presence in a meeting with other competitors. *MyCC Guidelines on Chapter 1 Prohibition* states that:

> An agreement could also be found whereby competitors attending a business lunch listen to a proposal for a price increase without objection' and 'mere

149. Paragraph 2.20, *MyCC Guidelines on Chapter 2 Prohibition* (abuse of dominant position).
150. Paragraph 2.23, *MyCC Guidelines on Chapter 2 Prohibition* (abuse of dominant position).
151. Paragraph 2.24, *MyCC Guidelines on Dominant Position* (abuse of dominant position).
152. Section 2 of the Competition Act 2010.

presence with competitors at an industry association meeting where an anti-competitive decision was made may be sufficient to be later implicated as a party to that agreement.[153]

225. In *MyCC v. Cameron Highlands Floriculturist Association (.G.)*, the Commission has relied on a copy of the Minutes of the Meeting on the Price Increase of Cameron Highlands Cut Flowers held on 28 February 2012 submitted by the CHFA to the MyCC as evidence of an agreement between CHFA members to fix the price of cut flowers.[154] The minutes of the meeting also showed that 'all the members present then decided to increase the prices of Cameron Highlands cut flowers by 10% and the increase shall come into force on 16 March 2012 for flowers sold in Malaysia and abroad, except Japan'.[155] Furthermore, the Commission has also considered that 'whether or not all the CHFA members complied with the decision made was of no relevance. Likewise, whether or not the decision made by the CHFA was applicable to all its members'.[156]

226. In *MyCC v. 15 Sibu Confectionery and Bakery*, the Commission found that 'an agreement arose between the Target Enterprises when they collectively decided to increase prices during the AGM. The Target Enterprises agreed unanimously by a show of hands to the proposal to increase the prices of confectionery and bakery products by 10% to 15% in Sibu, Sarawak'.[157] The Commission has stated in paragraph 48 of its Final Decision that 'the fact that an enterprise may have played only a limited part in the setting up of the agreement, or may not be fully committed to its implementation, or participated only under pressure from other parties does not mean that it is not a party to the agreement'. In this case, six of the target enterprises argued that they did not agree with the decision made in the annual general meeting (AGM) and five enterprises argued that they had increased their prices independently despite their attendance to the AGM. The Commission found that they are liable together with the other four target enterprises who admitted liability. However, the Commission found that enterprises who did not participate in the meeting and did not implement the outcome of the meeting were not liable.[158]

227. In *MyCC v. 24 Ice Manufacturers*, the agreement to increase the price of edible tube ice 'was reached between the enterprises (including Atlas) through a number of telephone conversations'[159] and/or through a meeting held on 17 December 2013.[160] In this case, thirteen enterprises admitted liability while twelve others contested the Commission's decision with some of them argued that they have

153. Paragraph 2.2, *MyCC Guidelines on Chapter 1 Prohibition.*
154. *MyCC v. Cameron Highlands Floriculturist Association* (MyCC/0003/2012(ACA)) para. 2.4.
155. *MyCC v. Cameron Highlands Floriculturist Association* (MyCC/0003/2012(ACA)) para. 2.7.
156. *MyCC v. Cameron Highlands Floriculturist Association* (MyCC/0003/2012(ACA)) para. 2.5.
157. *MyCC v. 15 Members of Sibu Confectionary and Bakery Association* (No. MyCC.0045.2013) para. 39.
158. *MyCC v. 15 Members of Sibu Confectionary and Bakery Association* (No. MyCC.0045.2013), *see* paras 29 & 30.
159. *MyCC v. 24 Ice Manufacturers* (No. MyCC.700.2.0001.2014) para. 11.
160. *MyCC v. 24 Ice Manufacturers* (No. MyCC.700.2.0001.2014) para. 12.

increased their prices independently[161] and some argued that 'they have yet to increase their prices hence they had not implemented the price increase announcement'.[162] However, the Commission found that the twelve enterprises had actually participated in the meeting, and thus, they were party to the agreement. The Commission has decided that one enterprise was not liable as there was no evidence that it had participated in the meeting to increase the price and had implemented the decision of the meeting.[163]

228. In *Seven Tuition and Daycare Centres*, the Commission decided that the enterprises had entered into a price-fixing agreement during the first meeting conducted on 12 May 2017 to discuss the standard service fees of tuition and daycare, even though, at that particular time, the enterprises had not signed any agreement to adjust and standardize the tuition fees.[164] The fact that some enterprises did not implement the agreement, or partially implement the agreement or had stopped implementing the fee scale does not mean that they are not parties to the agreement. Furthermore, the Commission is satisfied that none of the enterprises had publicly distanced itself from the agreement.[165] The Commission has also come to a conclusion that the conduct of the enterprises discussing standard service fees of tuition and daycare is still considered as an agreement even though the notice to adjust and standardize the fees only served guidelines and not all target enterprises distributed the said notice to the parents of their students.

II. Decision of a Trade Association

229. Agreement also includes a decision of a trade association. The CA 2010 recognizes the importance of a trade association in promoting the mutual interests of its members. However, a trade association may be used as a platform to coordinate the activities of their members, such as facilitating collusion to fix prices which may infringe the CA.[166] In *MyCC v. Cameron Highlands Floriculturist Association,* the Commission had emphasized that 'it is the intention of the Competition Act to widen the meaning of an agreement to also cover all the decisions made by an association without limiting to just an ordinary agreement'.[167]

230. Agreement under the CA 2010 covers both horizontal and vertical agreement.[168] According to *MyCC Guidelines on Chapter 1 Prohibition*, 'contractual

161. *MyCC v. 24 Ice Manufacturers* (No. MyCC.700.2.0001.2014) para. 24.
162. *MyCC v. 24 Ice Manufacturers* (No. MyCC.700.2.0001.2014) para. 19.
163. *MyCC v. 24 Ice Manufacturers* (No. MyCC.700.2.0001.2014) para. 27.
164. *MyCC v. Seven Tuition and Daycare Centre* (No. 700.1.1.43.2017) para. 105.
165. *MyCC v. Seven Tuition and Daycare Centres* (No. 700.1.1.43.2017) para. 107.
166. Paragraph 2.3, *MyCC Guidelines on Chapter 1 Prohibition.*
167. *MyCC v. Cameron Highlands Floriculturist Association* (MyCC/0003/2012(ACA)) para. 2.3.
168. Horizontal agreement is defined as 'an agreement between enterprises each of which operates at the same level in the production or distribution chain'. While vertical agreement is defined as 'an agreement between enterprises each of which operates at a different level in the production or distribution chain'.

restrictions could apply at any stage of the production chain, including between manufacturer and wholesaler or wholesaler and retailer'.[169]

III. Concerted Practices

231. Concerted practice is defined as 'any form of coordination between enterprises which knowingly substitutes practical co-operation between enterprises for the risks of competition and includes any practice which involves direct or indirect contact or communication between enterprises, the object or effect of which is either:

(a) to influence the conduct of one or more enterprises in a market; or
(b) to disclose the course of conduct which an enterprise has decided to adopt or is contemplating to adopt in a market, in circumstances where such disclosure would not have been made under normal conditions of competition'.[170]

232. A concerted practice could normally arise when there is an informal communication or cooperation between competitors or when the conduct of competitors is influenced 'in some ways following contact or communication between them'.[171]

233. Information arrangement or cooperation can take place in the form of conscious parallel behaviour or tacit collusion, where a market leader sets a price for the other competitors to follow suit without any reasonable commercial justification.

234. Parallel behaviour can be considered as a 'concerted practice' and falls under the definition of agreement unless 'the decision was made completely independently from all other competitors and there is a reasonable explanation for following each other, such as an increase in price of an important input'.[172]

235. The 'concerted practice' is 'designed to cater for a looser form of collusion falling short of an agreement'[173] where there is an absence of evidence, such as e-mails, faxes and correspondence to prove the existence of an agreement. It allows MyCC to pursue a wider range of anticompetitive behaviour.

236. In *MyCC v. Counterchain and Four Container Depot Operators*, the Commission found that Containerchain had engaged in concentrated practices with four Container Depot Operators (CDOs) 'which have the effect of influencing their conduct to increase their depot gate charge (DGC) from RM5 to RM25 in the market

169. Paragraph 2.4, *MyCC Guidelines on Chapter 1 Prohibition.*
170. Section 2 of the Competition Act 2010.
171. Paragraph 2.6, *MyCC Guidelines on Chapter 1 Prohibition.*
172. Paragraph 2.6, *MyCC Guidelines on Chapter 1 Prohibition.*
173. Nasarudin Abdul Rahman & Haniff Ahamat, *Competition Law in Malaysia* 80 (Sweet & Maxwell, 2016).

for the provision of empty container storage, maintenance and handling services within a 5–15km radius of the Penang port'[174] and had engaged with four CDOs 'in which it recommended, facilitated, influenced and coordinated their conduct in agreeing to a RM5 rebate to hauliers in respect of the DGC in the market for the provision of empty container storage, maintenance and handling services within a 5–15km radius of the Penang port'.[175]

237. For the four target CDOs, the Commission found that all target CDOs had engaged in an agreement to increase the DGC and to fix the rebate to be paid to the hauliers. All CDOs had engaged in the following conduct:

- participated in a meeting to communicate and discuss their intention to increase the DGC;
- contacted each other, discussed and exchanged information about the revised DGC;
- announced the proposed increase in DGC and the MYR 5 rebate in or about the same time through flyers and CCA; and
- implemented the increase in DGC and the MYR 5 rebate in or about the same time.[176]

§6. Restriction of Competition

238. Section 4(1) prohibits anticompetitive agreement that has the object or effect of preventing, restricting and distorting competition in the market.

239. In determining the 'object', 'the MyCC will not just examine the actual common intention of the parties to an agreement but also assess the aims pursued by the agreement in light of the agreement's economic context. If the "object" of the agreement is highly likely to have a significant anti-competitive effect, then the MyCC may find the agreement to have an anti-competitive "object"'.[177] When the object of an agreement is obvious limiting competition, MyCC is under no obligation to prove the effect of the agreement on competition.[178] The anticompetitive by 'object' is only applicable to a serious anticompetitive agreement where the actual or potential negative effect of the agreement on competition and consumers are obvious and significant without sound justification. For example, price-fixing agreement relaxes price competition, remove uncertainty as to future conduct to be adopted in future and artificially limits the independent commercial negotiation among market participants. The consumers will be worse-off as they would not be enjoying a variety of choices in relation to prices. In determining the 'object', the

174. *MyCC v. Containerchain & Four Container Depot Operators* (No. 700.2.005.2013) para. 150(i).
175. *MyCC v. Containerchain & Four Container Depot Operators* (No. 700.2.005.2013) para. 150(ii).
176. *MyCC v. Containerchain & Four Container Depot Operators* (No. 700.2.005.2013) para. 189.
177. Paragraph 2.13, *MyCC Guidelines on Chapter 1 Prohibition.*
178. Paragraph 2.14, *MyCC Guidelines on Chapter 1 Prohibition.*

MyCC may take into account, for example, the nature of the products the real conditions and structure of the market in question (economic context).

240. Generally, both anticompetitive by object and effect under section 4(1) of the CA 2010 are subjected to a 'safe-harbour' threshold laid down in Guidelines on Chapter 1 Prohibition. MyCC is only concerned with the anticompetitive agreement that has a significant effect on competition. An agreement which involves parties with small market shares (below the threshold) will automatically be excluded from the ambit of the section.

241. However, section 4(2) of the CA 2010 lists down horizontal agreement which deemed to be anticompetitive. Agreements which fall under section 4(2) will automatically be regarded as anticompetitive by object and do not enjoy the benefit of the 'safe-harbour'. The agreement includes:

- Price fixing agreement.
- Market sharing agreement.
- Agreement to limit production, investment, technological development and market access.
- Bid-rigging.

242. In *Seven Tuition and Daycare Centres*, the Commission stated that 'the nature of the infringement particularly s. 4(2)(a) of directly or indirectly fixing prices are by their very nature restrictive of competition negates the need for a market definition for the purposes of determining whether there is a significant anti-competitive effect in a market'.[179]

243. In *MyCC v. 15 Sibu Confectionery and Bakery,* the Commission found that 15 Sibu Confectionary and Bakery have infringed section 4(2)(a) of the Act by entering into an agreement that has as its object to fix, directly or indirectly, the selling price of confectionery and bakery products in Sibu, Sarawak. The Commission has further argued that:

> Price fixing is a major concern of the Commission as the restriction of competition is obvious in any price fixing cases. The agreement to fix price leaves no room for individual enterprises to assess their own operating costs and determine for themselves the cost-pass-through effects and how much should the price increase be and also whether the price increase should be borne by themselves or by the consumers.[180]

244. In *MyCC v. 24 Ice Manufacturers,* the Commission found that twenty-four enterprises have infringed section 4(2)(a) of the Act by entering into an agreement that has as its object to fix, directly or indirectly, the selling price of edible tube ice

---

179. *MyCC v. Seven Tuition and Daycare Centres* (No. 700.1.1.43.2017) para. 80.
180. *MyCC v. 15 Members of Sibu Confectionary and Bakery Association* (No. MyCC.0045.2013) para. 51.

and the price of block ice within Malaysia. The Commission considers that 'an agreement such as this, where there are different sizes of enterprises allows the parties to increase prices across the board by a standard amount and to maximise profitability without any competition'.[181] The Commission has rejected the argument that the price increase is necessary 'to prevent their agents from making excessive profits from their edible tube ice and block ice',[182] thus, protecting their customers. The Commission accepted their justification that the price increase 'was made due to various reasons such as the newly revised electricity tariffs, the minimum wage policy, increase of diesel price as well as maintenance of vehicles'.[183]

245. In *Seven Tuition and Daycare Centres*, the Commission stated that:

> By colluding to adjust and standardise the tuition and daycare fee charged by their respective centres, the Enterprises had the objective of reducing competition in the market by impeding the ability of the enterprises to independently determine their fees based *inter alia* on their operational costs, which in turn may result in the fees charged being artificially inflated to the detriment of consumers. The collusion by the Enterprises also has as its objective of depriving parents with school-going children around the SS19 in Subang Jaya area the opportunity of switching to other tuition and daycare centres that may offer a more competitive fee for similar services offered by the Enterprises.[184]

246. In *MyCC v. MAS-AirAsia*, the Commission stated in its Final Decision that:

> the restriction of competition here is obvious; MAS and AirAsia have agreed not to compete with each another, either themselves or through their subsidiaries thus eliminating any possibility of competition between the parties. The Collaboration Agreement allows both airlines to operate freely within separate market segments and it provides them the freedom to impose higher prices to maximise profitability without any competition. This will eventually leave consumers to face the increased likelihood of higher airfares and fewer choices.[185]

247. The Commission has further stated that:

> There is no doubt that MAS and AirAsia are competitors and the Collaboration Agreement is a horizontal agreement between competitors which clearly has the object of sharing markets. The Act stipulates that any agreement between competitors to share the market would be an infringement of section

181. *MyCC v. 24 Ice Manufacturers* (No. MyCC.700.2.0001.2014) para. 42.
182. *MyCC v. 24 Ice Manufacturers* (No. MyCC.700.2.0001.2014) para. 14.
183. *MyCC v. 24 Ice Manufacturers* (No. MyCC.700.2.0001.2014) para. 19.
184. *MyCC v. Seven Tuition and Daycare Centres* (No. 700.1.1.43.2017) para. 73.
185. *MyCC v. MAS-AirAsia* (No. MyCC.0001.2012) para. 58.

4 (2) of the Act. Section 4 (2) which was reproduced earlier is a deeming provision and therefore, it is not necessary for the Commission to conduct any 'effect' analysis.[186]

248. However, when the parties appeal to the CAT, the CAT had set aside the decision made by the Commission. The CAT had a conclusion that:

> The Commission did not give any reason or analysis for its decision concluding that the purported object of the CA is market sharing. Even if it is a deeming provision the onus is on the Commission to establish that the object of the CA is to share the market. It is observed that in the Final Decision, the Commission did not or failed to identify the relevant market. Identification of relevant market is integral in any competition inquiry.[187]

249. The CAT also stated in paragraph 90 that 'it is pertinent to note that the Malaysian competition law uses a deeming provision to establish cases of anti-competition while many other jurisdictions use market impact cases to do the same. A simplistic use of the deeming provision upon airlines business may not be proper'.

250. The CAT further stated at paragraph 111 that 'we are therefore, of the considered view that based on the terms and conditions of the CA, it is crystal clear that the CA is a conditional agreement and would only be enforceable if detailed anti-trust analysis is conducted and all the legal requirements are complied with'.

251. The decision of the CAT was quashed by the High Court on 20 December 2018. The High Court concluded that 'in determining whether the Collaborative Agreement has anti-competitive object, it is pertinent not only to examine the terms of the Collaboration Agreement but also the factual background before both MAS and AirAsia entered into this Collaboration Agreement'.[188]

252. The High Court found that based on the Collaboration Agreement entered between the two parties especially clauses 1.2, 5 and 7 together with the factual ground before the conclusion of the agreement including the discussion and resolution made in MAS and AirAsia's board of directors 'there will no longer be any competition between MAS and AirAsia. MAS will concentrate as a full service premium carrier (FSC). AirAsia will focus on regional low-cost carrier (LCC) while AirAsia X will focus on medium to long haul LCC'.[189] The effect of this Collaborative Agreement is that both parties are able 'to control the pricing of the airlines business such as ticket price which is to the disadvantage of the consumers'.[190]

---

186. *MyCC v. MAS-AirAsia* (No. MyCC.0001.2012) para. 63.
187. Decision of Competition Appeal Tribunal (Appeal No. TRP 1-2014, TRP 2-2014, 18 Feb. 2016) para. 89.
188. Judgment, Application for Judicial Review (No. WA-25-82-05/2016) para. 73.
189. Judgment, Application for Judicial Review (No. WA-25-82-05/2016) para. 82.
190. Judgment, Application for Judicial Review (No. WA-25-82-05/2016) para. 83.

Therefore, 'the deeming provision of subsection 4 (2) (b) is applicable, that the Collaboration agreement has the object of significantly preventing, restricting or distorting competition in airlines services which MAS and AirAsia has not shown to the contrary'.[191]

253. With regard to the requirement to define the relevant market, the High Court further stated that 'the imposition to identify the relevant market is not the prerequisite in invoking the deeming provision under subsection 4 (2)' and 'by imposing the requirement to identify the relevant market, the Tribunal is putting words in the clear wordings of the statute, particularly under subsection 4 (2) of the Competition Act 2010'. This, according to the High Court 'have the effect of usurping the powers of the Parliament'.[192]

254. The High Court was also of the view that the CAT's observation with regard to the application of 'deeming provision' to the airlines' industry, is misplaced and concluded that 'the deeming provision must be invoked if the prerequisite facts has been proven irrespective of any business parties are involved without exception including the airlines business'.[193]

255. The High Court also dismissed the CAT's argument that the Collaborative Agreement is only conditional agreement and would only be enforced if the detailed antitrust analysis is conducted and legal requirements are complied with. The High Court emphasized that 'by having a clause in the Collaboration Agreement that the terms in the agreement are subject to antitrust analysis and fulfilment of other legal requirements, does not alter the fact that if it has anti-competitive object, it is still an infringement of subsection 4 (1)'.[194]

§7. Abuse of Dominance

256. The CA 2010 does not prohibit an enterprise from being a monopoly or dominant in the market. The Act only prohibits a dominant enterprise from abusing its dominant position in the market.

257. An enterprise holding a dominant position in one market in Malaysia may abuse its dominant position in a separate market.[195] For example, a dominant enterprise in one market may use its profits in that market to price below cost in a separate market or a dominant enterprise in one market may tie its product in the market with other product in a separate market to foreclose competitors in the tied product market.

191. Judgment, Application for Judicial Review (No. WA-25-82-05/2016) para. 90.
192. Judgment, Application for Judicial Review (No. WA-25-82-05/2016) para. 94.
193. Judgment, Application for Judicial Review (No. WA-25-82-05/2016) para. 98.
194. Judgment, Application for Judicial Review (No. WA-25-82-05/2016) para. 108.
195. Paragraph 4.1, *MyCC Guidelines on Chapter 2 Prohibition* (abuse of dominant position).

258. Abusive conduct can be divided into two categories, namely, exploitative and exclusionary conduct.

I. Exploitative Conduct

259. Exploitative conduct refers to 'the ability of an enterprise to maintain price above the competitive level for some time without worrying about whether consumers will switch to other products or worrying that new competitors will enter the market'.[196]

260. Exploitative conduct may be the outcome of the structural condition of a market. When there is no effective competition in the market, a dominant enterprise has the incentive to raise price above the competitive level, which exploits the consumers.[197]

261. MyCC is only concerned with the imposition of excessive price by a dominant enterprise especially when there is no likelihood that market forces will reduce the dominance and the dominant enterprise reaps excessive profits out of anticompetitive behaviour not the reward for innovation.[198]

262. There is no definite or single economic tool to determine the excessive price. Generally, MyCC will consider 'the actual price set in relation to the costs of supply and other factors, such as the dominant enterprises profitability'.[199]

II. Exclusionary Conduct

263. Exclusionary conduct refers to 'the ability of an enterprise to dictate the level of competition in a market by preventing efficient new competitors from entering or significantly harming existing equally efficient competitors – either by driving them out of the market or preventing them from effectively competing'.[200]

264. In *MyCC v. MyEG Bhd*, the Commission stated that:

> The appointment of MyEG as a sole concession holder in the provision and management of PLKS renewals is not by itself a breach of the Act. The Commission takes a strong position that a dominant enterprise such as MyEG should abide by the Act to comply fully with the provisions of the Act. The fact that MyEG is now an agent for other insurance companies raised greater

196. Paragraph 2.4, *MyCC Guidelines on Chapter 2 Prohibition* (abuse of dominant position).
197. Paragraph 3.2, *MyCC Guidelines on Chapter 2 Prohibition* (abuse of dominant position).
198. Paragraph 3.3, *MyCC Guidelines on Chapter 2 Prohibition* (abuse of dominant position).
199. Paragraph 3.4, *MyCC Guidelines on Chapter 2 Prohibition* (abuse of dominant position).
200. Paragraph 2.4, *MyCC Guidelines on Chapter 2 Prohibition* (abuse of dominant position).

concerns as MyEG is also gaining more market share which could potentially allow it to also be in a dominant position in the downstream market.[201]

265. MyEG is a monopoly company in the provision and management of foreign workers permit renewals. Since the purchase of mandatory insurance is required for the online renewals, MyEG has become an agent for RHB Insurance (through MyEG Commerce) and is competing against other insurance agents including agents representing RHB Insurance and other insurers in the sale of mandatory insurances for online Pas Lawatan (Kerja Semenentara) (PLKS) renewal applications. The data shows that: 'RHB Insurance has been gaining market share in the sales of Mandatory Insurances for PLKS renewals whilst other competing insurance companies are losing their market share in the same market. This was caused by the agency agreement entered into between MyEG Commerce and RHB Insurance.'[202]

266. The Commission has come to the conclusion that:

> MyEG had been abusing its dominant position as the sole concession holder in the provision and management of online PLKS renewal services in Peninsular Malaysia (upstream market) in the market for the sale of the Mandatory Insurances for online PLKS renewal application (downstream market), by imposing different conditions to equivalent transactions with its competitors to an extent that it has harmed competition in the downstream market in which MyEG Commerce is participating.[203]

267. In assessing whether an exclusionary conduct is anticompetitive, MyCC will adopt an 'effect-based' approach.[204]

268. In assessing the effect of exclusionary conduct, MyCC will use two main tests for assessing anticompetitive effects:

- 'firstly, does the conduct adversely affect consumers?'.
- 'secondly, does the conduct exclude a competitor that is just as efficient as the dominant enterprise?'.[205]

269. The effect-based approach focuses on protecting the competitive process, not protecting individual competitor. The word 'equally efficient' means MyCC is not concerned with the well-being of inefficient enterprises in the market. A dominant enterprise should not be prohibited from engaging in pro-competitive conduct

201. *MyCC v. MyEG Services Bhd* (MyCC (ED) 700-1/1/2/2015) para. 47.
202. *MyCC v. MyEG Services Bhd* (MyCC (ED) 700-1/1/2/2015) para. 55.
203. *MyCC v. MyEG Services Bhd* (MyCC (ED) 700-1/1/2/2015) para. 59.
204. Paragraph 3.7, *MyCC Guidelines on Chapter 2 Prohibition* (abuse of dominant position).
205. Paragraph 3.9, *MyCC Guidelines on Chapter 2 Prohibition* (abuse of dominant position).

which benefits consumers even if the inefficient enterprises need to leave the market.[206] The definition of 'equally efficient' is best illustrated in the case of a margin squeeze. In assessing whether a dominant enterprise has engaged in 'margin squeeze', the Commission will adopt the 'equally efficient competitor' test as it assesses whether the dominant enterprise would have been sufficiently efficient to offer its downstream product, otherwise than at a loss, if it had been obliged to pay its own price for the input.

270. A margin squeeze can be demonstrated by showing that the dominant enterprise's own downstream business could not operate profitably based on the upstream price that it has charged, or is charging, its rivals in the downstream market. In *MyCC v. Megasteel*, the Commission has considered the question whether Megasteel could have offered its Cold Rolled Coil (CRC) product, otherwise than at a loss, if Megasteel had been obliged to pay for its own Hot Rolled Coil (HRC) at the same price as that was charged on other CRC producers.

Other Examples of Abusive Exclusionary Conduct

- Predatory
- Price discrimination
- Exclusive dealing
- Loyalty rebates
- Refusal to supply and access to essential facilities
- Bundling and tying
- Buying up scarce intermediate goods or resources.

§8. CONCENTRATIONS

I. Aviation Service Market

271. Section 54(2) of the MACA 2015 defines a merger to include:

(1) Two or more independent enterprises merge, including:
   - two or more independent enterprises merge into a new enterprise; or
   - an enterprise is absorbed by and into another enterprise causing the former to cease to exist as a separate legal entity.

(2) One or more persons or enterprises acquire direct or indirect control of the whole or part of one or more other enterprises.

(3) One enterprise (acquiring) acquires the assets of another enterprise (acquired) putting the acquiring enterprise in a position to substantially replace the acquired enterprise.

206. Paragraph 3.6, *MyCC Guidelines on Chapter 2 Prohibition* (abuse of dominant position).

272. Control refers to the ability of an enterprise to exercise decisive control over another enterprise by reason of rights, contracts or any combination of rights, contracts or other means regardless of whether such control is actually exercised.[207]

273. Control exists when:[208]

(1) A person or enterprise owns assets of another enterprise.
(2) A person or enterprise has the right to use all or part of the assets of another enterprise.
(3) A person or enterprise has acquired the rights or contracts which enable the said person or enterprise to exercise decisive influence regarding the composition, voting or decisions of the enterprise.

274. Direct and indirect control:

(1) Direct control – A person or enterprise becomes a holder of the rights or contract or entitled to use other means.[209]
(2) Indirect control – A person or enterprise acquires the power to exercise the rights derived from the rights, contracts or any other means. For example, indirect control may be established if there are links between an acquiring enterprise and an enterprise enjoying indirect control. The link may be established through, for instances the source of funding and family relations between the acquiring person or enterprise and the person or enterprise that allegedly has the actual power to exercise the control over the acquired enterprise.[210]

275. The following situations do not constitute a merger:[211]

(1) The person acquiring control is a receiver or liquidator acting as such or is an underwriter acting as such.
(2) Control is acquired solely as a result of testamentary disposition intestacy or the right of survivorship under a joint tenancy.
(3) All of the merger parties are under the direct and indirect control of the same enterprises, for example, a merger between parent and subsidiary which form a single economic unit. Control is required by an enterprise whose normal activities is holding or dealing with securities for its own account or for the account of others. The control acquired through the holding of securities in the acquired enterprise must be on a temporary basis for the purpose of arranging the disposal of all or part of the acquired enterprise, its assets or securities within the specified period and not for the purpose of determining the manner in which any activity of the acquired enterprise should be carried on.

207. Section 54(3) of the MACA; Paragraph 3.2, *Guidelines on Substantive Assessment of Mergers.*
208. Paragraph 3.2, *Guidelines on Substantive Assessment of Mergers.*
209. Paragraph 3.4, *Guidelines on Substantive Assessment of Mergers.*
210. Paragraph 3.5, *Guidelines on Substantive Assessment of Mergers.*
211. Section 54(6) of the MACA.

II. Communications Market

276. The Guidelines on Mergers and Acquisitions issued by the Malaysian Communications and Multimedia Commission (MCMC) defines a merger as follows:[212]

(1) Two or more previously independent firms merge by:
  - combining into a new firm, which each firm ceasing to exist as separate legal entities; or
  - one firm being absorbed into another, where the former firm ceases to exist as a legal entity and the latter firm retaining its legal identity.

(2) One or more firms acquire direct or indirect control of the whole or part of one or more of other firms.

(3) A firm acquires assets (including goodwill) of another firm which results in the former firm replacing the latter in the business it was engaged in immediately before the acquisition.

277. In determining 'control', the Commission will consider whether one firm can exercise decisive influence over the activities of another firm by reason of rights, contracts or other means.[213]

278. Control can be divided into two:[214]

(1) Legal control – which is determined by ownership control, such as having more than 50% ownership of all voting rights in a firm.

(2) De facto control – where there exists a relationship between two parties which allows one party to have influence over another's activities. The following circumstances may suggest that de facto control exists:
  - An agreement in which one party agreed to cease all production and only source its requirement from another.
  - The existence of financial/lending arrangements, which allows one firm to gain decisive influence over another firm's activities.
  - The ability of minority shareholders to veto decisions essential for the strategic commercial behaviour of the undertaking through additional rights (e.g., decision relation to budgets and business plan).

§9. Joint Ventures

I. Aviation Service Market

279. The definition of merger under section 54(2) of the MACA also includes a joint venture (JV) which is created to perform, on a lasting basis, all functions of an autonomous economic entity.

212. Paragraph 3.10, *Guidelines on Mergers and Acquisitions.*
213. Paragraph 3.16, *Guidelines on Mergers and Acquisitions.*
214. Paragraph 3.16, *Guidelines on Mergers and Acquisitions.*

280. A JV must be able to perform functions carried out by normal enterprise in the aviation service market. This requires support in terms of management and resources to carry out its daily operation.

281. A JV is intended to operate on a lasting basis:[215]

(1) When the parent provides dedicated resources for the JV to operate as an autonomous entity.
(2) The period of JV is long enough to cause a lasting change in the structure of the JV enterprise. This excludes a JV which is established to complete a specific project within a short period of time. The fact that a JV provides for an opportunity for dissolution does not prevent the JV from being considered as operating on a lasting basis.
(3) Two or more enterprises formed a JV with joint control and are able to exercise a decisive influence on the activities of the JV.

II. Communications Market

282. Pursuant to the Guidelines on Mergers and Acquisitions, a merger includes a JV which is created to perform, on a lasting basis, all the functions of an autonomous economic entity and involves changes in the shareholding structure of the firm.[216] Lasting basis means 'the joint venture is intended to, and can, operate for such a length of time that the joint venture involves a lasting change in the structure of the parent company, the structure of the market and competition in the market'.[217]

215. Paragraph 3.1(d), *Guidelines on Substantive Assessment of Mergers.*
216. Paragraph 3.10, *Guidelines on Mergers and Acquisitions.*
217. Paragraph 3.11, *Guidelines on Mergers and Acquisitions.*

Chapter 5. Consequences of Violations and Enforcement Institutions

§1. ADMINISTRATIVE ENFORCEMENT

283. The CA 2010 mandates the establishment of a regulator to oversee competition issues in Malaysia. The MyCC was then set up in 2011 as a competition authority whose main function is to implement and enforce cross-sector competition law in the country. Generally, MyCC has three important powers, namely, investigative, adjudicative and administrative powers.

I. Antitrust Authorities

A. *Formation, Composition*

284. The MyCC is a corporate body established under the CCA 2010. The Commission shall have perpetual succession and may sue and be sued in its name, enter into a contract, acquire or dispose of movable and immovable property.

285. The Commission can exercise all the powers and to perform all things necessary or expedient for or in connection with the performance of its functions under the competition laws.[218] This includes the power to impose a penalty for the infringement of the competition law, to impose fees or charges for services rendered by the Commission, to formulate and implement programmes for the proper and effective performance of the Commission's functions, and to co-operate with any corporate or government agencies for the purpose of performing the Commission's functions.[219]

286. The Commission shall consist of members who must be appointed by the Prime Minister upon the recommendation of the Minister. The members include:

(a) a Chairman;
(b) four members representing the Government, one of whom shall be a representative of the Ministry for the time being responsible for matters concerning domestic trade and consumer affairs; and
(c) not less than three but not more than five other members, who have experience and knowledge in matters relating to business, industry, commerce, law, economics, public administration, competition, consumer protection or any other suitable qualification as the Minister may determine.[220]

218. Section 17(1) of the Competition Act 2010.
219. Section 17(2) of the Competition Act 2010.
220. Section 5 of the Competition Commission Act 2010.

287. A member of the Commission shall hold office for a term not exceeding three years[221] but shall be eligible for reappointment, but no member shall hold office for more than two consecutive terms.[222] A chairman is entitled to remuneration and allowances as determined by the Minister after consultation with the Minister of Finance.[223] Other members of the Commission are entitled to allowances as determined by the Minister after consultation with the Prime Minister.[224]

288. The Commission may set up any committee which it thinks necessary to assist in the performance of its functions under the competition laws.[225] A committee set up by the Commission must be chaired by any member of the Commission, must conform to and act in accordance with any direction given to it by the Commission and may determine its own procedure.[226]

289. The appointment of any member of the Commission can only be revoked by the Prime Minister on the ground that the revocation is 'necessary in the interest of the effective and economical performance of the functions of the Commission'.[227] The revocation of appointment must be supported with reason in writing.[228] Any member of the Commission may also, at any time, resign his office by a written notice addressed to the Prime Minister.[229]

B. Investigating Powers

290. The Commission has the power to launch an investigation if it has 'reason to suspect that any enterprise has infringed or is infringing any prohibition under this Act or any person has committed or is committing any offence under this Act'.[230]

291. The power to conduct an investigation of any offence under the Act is delegated to Commission officer who 'shall have all or any of the powers of a police officer in relation to police investigation in sizeable cases as provided for under the Criminal Procedure Code [Act 593]'.[231]

221. Section 9(1) of the Competition Commission Act 2010.
222. Section 9(2) of the Competition Commission Act 2010.
223. Section 10(1) of the Competition Commission Act 2010.
224. Section 10(2) of the Competition Commission Act 2010.
225. Section 14(1) of the Competition Commission Act 2010.
226. Section 14(2) of the Competition Commission Act 2010.
227. Section 11(1) of the Competition Commission Act 2010.
228. Section 11(2) of the Competition Commission Act 2010.
229. Section 11(3) of the Competition Commission Act 2010.
230. Section 14(1) of the Competition Act 2010.
231. Section 17(2) of Competition Act 2010.

C. Adjudicating Powers (Ascertaining and Sanctioning)

292. One of the unique features of MyCC is it has an adjudicative or quasi-judicial function which empowers it to decide on competition matters just like a court of law.

293. Upon the completion of the investigation, the Commission will issue a proposed decision if it found out that one of the prohibitions under Part II (anticompetitive agreement and abuse of dominant position) has been or is being infringed.[232]

294. The proposed decision is not a final decision but rather the Commission's initial finding after the investigation is completed. Before finalizing the decision, the infringing enterprise has the right to defend themselves by submitting a written representation to the Commission.[233] The Commission has the power to conduct an oral representation upon request by the infringing enterprises.[234] At this stage, the infringing enterprise will be given an opportunity to present their argument based on the proposed decision and written submission previously submitted. MyCC may, at its discretion, conduct a proper hearing for the purpose of determining whether an enterprise has infringed or is infringing competition law provisions.[235]

295. After taking into consideration the enterprises' argument and defence, the Commission may decide whether to issue a final infringement decision[236] or non-infringement decision.[237] If the Commission decides to issue a final infringement decision, the Commission will take any administrative action to remedy the anti-competitive effect, including imposing a financial penalty on the infringing enterprise.[238]

296. The Commission had issued non-infringement decisions to the following enterprises (after a proposed decision had been issued):

No	*Enterprise*	*Date*
1.	Finding of Non-Infringement under section 39 of the CA 2010 – 1 Ice Manufacturer	30 January 2015
2.	Finding of Non-Infringement under section 39 of the CA 2010 – 9 Members of the Sibu Confectionery and Bakery Association	12 February 2015

232. Section 36 of Competition Act 2010.
233. Section 36(c) of Competition Act 2010.
234. Section 37 of Competition Act 2010.
235. Section 38 of Competition Act 2010.
236. Section 40 of Competition Act 2010.
237. Section 39 of Competition Act 2010.
238. Section 40 of Competition Act 2010.

No	*Enterprise*	*Date*
3.	Finding of Non-Infringement under section 39 of the CA 2010 – Wood Sellers	7 February 2017
4.	Finding of Non-Infringement under section 39 of the CA 2010 – Label Stock Makers	7 February 2017

D. Other Institutional Tasks (Consultancy to Parliament/Government)

297. MyCC has the power to advocate on competition matters to the government. This includes:

(a) to advise the Minister or any other public or regulatory authority on all matters concerning competition;
(b) to alert the Minister to the actual or likely anticompetitive effects of current or proposed legislation and to make recommendations to the Minister, if appropriate, for the avoidance of these effects;
(c) to advise the Minister on international agreements relevant to competition matters and to the competition laws.

298. As far as the accountability is concerned, the Commission is required to furnish the Minister the important documents, such as returns, reports, accounts, and information with respect to its activities and finances as the Minister may, from time to time, require or direct.[239] The documents or reports must contain information relating to the proceedings and policy of the Commission and any other matter as the Minister may, from time to time, specify.

II. Government Direct Enforcement Activities

299. The Commission shall be responsible to the Minister.[240] The Minister may, in writing, give to the Commission directions of a general character, consistent with the provisions of the competition laws, relating to the performance of the functions and powers of the Commission and the Commission shall give effect to such directions.[241]

300. As far as investigation is concerned, the Commission must launch an investigation against any suspected infringement of any of the prohibition or commission of an offence under the CA 2010 based on the direction of the Minister.[242]

239. Section 19 of Competition Commission Act 2010.
240. Section 18(1) of Competition Commission Act 2010.
241. Section 18(2) of Competition Commission Act 2010.
242. Section 14(2) of Competition Act 2010.

301. The Minister may direct the Commission regarding interworking arrangements between the Commission and any other authority in Malaysia or in a foreign jurisdiction or any international organization and determine the arrangements for such interworking or membership of international organizations.[243]

302. The Minister who is in charge of the competition law has the power to make regulations which may be necessary or expedient for:

(a) giving full effect to the provisions of the CA 2010;
(b) carrying out or achieving the objects and purposes of the CA 2010; and
(c) providing for any supplemental, incidental or consequential matters in relation to the CA 2010.[244]

III. Other Administrative Agencies Applying Antitrust Rules

303. The CA 2010 by virtue of section 3 and First Schedule of the Act excludes any commercial activity regulated by some sector regulations, namely, the ECA 2001, the CMA 1998, the MACA 2015, and the PDA 1975. All these legislations except for PDA contain rules governing competition in the respective sectors. All specific sectors other than those that listed in the First Schedule are subjected to the CA 2010. For example, the FSA 2013 is still subjected to the CA 2010 even though the FSA contains rules on collusion and tied selling.[245]

304. The CA 2010 also establishes the CAT under Part V of the Act. The CAT has the exclusive jurisdiction to review any decision made by MyCC under sections 35 (interim measures, 39 (non-infringement decision) and 40 (infringement decision).[246] Any party who was aggrieved or whose interest was affected by a decision of MyCC under the said section may appeal to CAT. The CAT may confirm or set aside the decision of MyCC or part of it and may also:

(a) remit the matter to the Commission;
(b) impose or revoke, or vary the amount of, a financial penalty;
(c) give such direction, or take such other step as the Commission could itself have given or taken; or
(d) make any other decision which the Commission could itself have made.

305. A decision of the CAT is final and binding on the parties to appeal.

243. Section 39 of Competition Act 2010.
244. Section 65 of Competition Act 2010.
245. *See* s. 124 of Financial Service Act 2016.
246. Section 44 of Competition Act 2010.

IV. Administrative Fines

306. The competition has the power to impose on infringing enterprise a financial penalty which shall not exceed 10% of the worldwide turnover of an enterprise over the period during which infringement occurred.[247] In imposing the penalty, MyCC will consider the following objectives:

(1) the penalty should reflect the seriousness of the infringement; and
(2) the penalty should serve as a deterrent effect on anticompetitive practices leading to an infringement of a prohibition under the CA 2010.[248]

307. The use of 'worldwide' turnover in this particular section has two implications. First, in determining the penalty to be imposed, MyCC will take into consideration both the turnover of the product market which is and is not subjected to infringement. Second, in calculating the financial penalty, MyCC will take into consideration the turnover of the infringing parties together with those of its related companies within a corporate group.

308. However, for a starting point, MyCC will consider the turnover of the market involved, i.e., a market that is subjected to the infringement during the period of infringement (the relevant turnover). If the period of infringement is less than six months, such a period will be counted as half a year and if the period is longer than six months but less than a year, such period will be counted as a full year.[249] MyCC will then take into account any aggravating or mitigating factors which may further increase or decrease the basic penalty. The final amount should not exceed 10% of the enterprises' worldwide turnover.

309. The aggravating factors may include:

(1) the role of the enterprise as an instigator or leader or having engaged in coercive behaviour with others;
(2) obstruction of or lack of cooperation in the investigation;
(3) the enterprise has a record of committing similar infringement or other infringements;
(4) continuance of the infringement after the start of investigation; and
(5) involvement of board members or senior management in the infringement.[250]

310. The mitigating factors include:

(1) low degree of fault;
(2) playing a minor role in the infringement especially if involvement is secured by threats or coercion;

247. Section 40(4) of Competition Act 2010.
248. Paragraph 3.1, *MyCC Guidelines on Financial Penalties*.
249. Paragraph 3.2, *MyCC Guidelines on Financial Penalties*.
250. Paragraph 3.4, *MyCC Guidelines on Financial Penalties*.

(3) cooperation by the enterprise in the investigation;
(4) existence of a corporate compliance programme that is appropriate having regard to the nature and size of the business of the enterprise; and
(5) any compensation made to victims of the infringement.[251]

311. In *MyCC v. Cameron Highlands Floriculturist Association* (CHFA),[252] the Commission decided not to impose any financial penalty on the CHFA and its members since it was the first case that the Commission had ever decided since its inception. Instead, the Commission had taken non-monetary remedial actions including instructing CHFA and its member to cease and desist the infringing act of fixing the price of flowers and imposing a financial penalty in the event that the CHFA fails to comply with the remedial action stipulated by the Commission.[253]

312. In *MyCC v. MAS-AirAsia*, the Commission laid down the following steps in determining the financial penalty:

Step 1: Determine the basic amount of financial penalty as a proportion of the flight turnover earned between January and April 2012.
Step 2: Increase the financial penalty by taking into account aggravating factors (if any), and decrease the financial penalty by taking into account mitigating factors (if any).
Step 3: Enhance the specific and general deterrence effects of the financial penalty by adjusting it further (as necessary).
Step 4: Verify that the financial penalty is no more than 10% of the enterprise's worldwide turnover over the period of infringement.[254]

313. In this case, the Commission considered that the period of infringement began on 1 January 2012 since MAS and AirAsia entered into the Collaboration Agreement prior to the enforcement of the CA 2010. The Commission also considered the infringement was ended on 2 May 2012 when the parties dropped the market sharing agreement through a Supplemental Agreement.[255] The Commission has calculated the financial penalties based on the turnover of both MAS and AirAsia that were earned between 1 January 2012 and 30 April 2012 from their respective flights on the routes of Kuala Lumpur-Kuching; Kuala Lumpur-Kota Kinabalu, Kuala Lumpur-Sandakan; and Kuala Lumpur-Sibu.[256] The Commission has stated in its Final Decision the reasons for focusing on these routes at paragraphs 83 & 84:

> Under the current Government's policy on air transport (which is based on an internationally accepted 'cabotage policy'), only locally-owned airline operators are permitted to carry passengers between any two points within Malaysia

251. Paragraph 3.5, *MyCC Guidelines on Leniency Regime*.
252. *MyCC v. Cameron Highlands Floriculturist Association* (CHFA) (No. MyCC/0003/2012(ACA).
253. *MyCC v. Cameron Highlands Floriculturist Association* (CHFA) (No. MyCC/0003/2012(ACA) para. 3.1.
254. *MyCC v. MAS-AirAsia* (No. MyCC.0001.2012) para. 86.
255. *MyCC v. MAS-AirAsia* (No. MyCC.0001.2012) para. 78.
256. *MyCC v. MAS-AirAsia* (No. MyCC.0001.2012) para. 85.

(including any two points between Peninsular Malaysia and both Sabah and Sarawak. Furthermore, flights between Peninsular Malaysia and both Sabah and Sarawak cannot be substituted by other forms of transport (namely, sea transport by boat or ferry, or road transport). For this reason, consumers who travelled between Peninsular Malaysia and both Sabah and Sarawak were directly affected following the market exit of Firefly.

314. In *MAS-AirAsia* case, the Commission did not consider any aggravating factors. However, the Commission had considered that both parties had given full cooperation, especially in the provision of requested data and information and voluntarily removed market sharing clauses in the Collaboration Agreement as part of the mitigating factors.[257]

315. In *MyCC v. 15 Members of the Sibu Confectionery and Bakery Association*, the Commission has decided to impose financial penalties on fourteen of the target enterprises that have infringed section 4(2)(a) of the CA 2010 by agreeing to increase the prices of confectionery and bakery products in Sibu. The Commission had set that duration of the infringement starts from 17 November 2013 at the time when the target enterprise participated in the AGM at which they agreed to increase prices until 18 September 2014 at the time when the target enterprises ceased from the decision made during the AGM.[258] The Commission has determined the financial penalties based on the target enterprise's turnover generated from the monthly sales of bakery and confectionery products in Sibu throughout the infringement period.[259] The Commission has decided to reduce the financial penalties for ten enterprises for not implementing the decision to increase prices even though they had participated in the meeting.[260] The Commission has decided not to apply any mitigating factors on four target enterprises 'who implemented the decision made at the AGM and did not take any step to cease the conduct prior to the Commission's Proposed Decision'.[261] However, the Commission has decided not to impose any financial penalty on one sole proprietor as 'he has become bankrupt and only generated a very insignificant amount of total turnover during the infringement period'.[262]

316. In *MyCC v. 24 Ice Manufacturers*, in determining the amount of financial penalty, the Commission took into consideration 'the nature of the product, the structure of the market and the seriousness of the infringement in determining the

257. *MyCC v. MAS-AirAsia* (No. MyCC.0001.2012) para. 91.
258. *MyCC v. 15 Members of the Sibu Confectionery and Bakery Association* (No. MyCC.0045.2013) paras 63 & 64.
259. *MyCC v. 15 Members of the Sibu Confectionery and Bakery Association* (No. MyCC.0045.2013) para. 65.
260. *MyCC v. 15 Members of the Sibu Confectionery and Bakery Association* (No. MyCC.0045.2013) para. 68.
261. *MyCC v. 15 Members of the Sibu Confectionery and Bakery Association* (No. MyCC.0045.2013) para. 67.
262. *MyCC v. 15 Members of the Sibu Confectionery and Bakery Association* (No. MyCC.0045.2013) para. 66.

basic amount of the financial penalties'.[263] The Commission decided to increase the basic amount of the financial penalties for three enterprises as they did not provide full cooperation to the Commission.[264] On the other hand, the Commission has decided to decrease the basic amount of the financial penalties for the eleven enterprises as they have fully cooperated with the Commission throughout the investigation by providing additional information during the investigation period.[265]

317. In *MyCC v. Containerchain and Four Container Depot Operators*, in determining the level of financial penalty, the Commission stated in its final decision that 'the infringements caused a wide impact within the industry as majority of the CDOs in Penang increased their DGC regardless of their respective cost structures and/or whether or not they implemented the Containerchain system'.[266] In this case, the financial penalty was calculated based on 'the Containerchain's turnover generated from the fixed fee of RM 5.00 per transaction which was imposed on the target CDOs throughout the infringement period' and 'the target CDO's turnover generated from the RM15.00 DCG'.[267] The infringement period started when the target CDOs signed Implementation, Support and License Agreements (ISLAs) with the Containerchain and the cut-off date is when the Commission served its Proposed Decision to the target CDOs.[268] The Commission did not consider any aggravating factors on the target enterprises. However, the Commission had considered a mitigating factor and reduced the financial penalty on one of the four target CDOs for its significant cooperation throughout the investigation process by providing additional relevant facts and evidence.[269]

318. In *MyCC v. My E.G. Services Bhd,* the Commission had considered that 'the infringement by MyEG has distorted competition in the market of the sale of the Mandatory Insurances for online PLKS renewal applications (downstream market)'.[270] The infringement period started 'when MyEG imposed different conditions to equivalent transactions during the period when JIM's manual counters were closed and no alternative channel was available for permit renewals',[271] and the cut-off date is the date of the Proposed Decision being served on MyEG. The financial penalty was calculated based on the MyEG's turnover generated from the commission gained for the sale of Mandatory Insurances throughout the infringement periods.[272] The Commission had further imposed the daily penalty since 'the abusive conduct still subsists and MyEG has yet to provide an efficient gateway for all its

263. *MyCC v. 24 Ice Manufacturers* (No. MyCC.700.2.0001.2014) para. 49.
264. *MyCC v. 24 Ice Manufacturers* (No. MyCC.700.2.0001.2014) para. 50.
265. *MyCC v. 24 Ice Manufacturers* (No. MyCC.700.2.0001.2014) para. 51.
266. *MyCC v. Containerchain & Four Container Depot Operators* (No. 700.2.005.2013) para. 199.
267. *MyCC v. Containerchain & Four Container Depot Operators* (No. 700.2.005.2013) para. 203.
268. *MyCC v. Containerchain & Four Container Depot Operators* (No. 700.2.005.2013) para. 202. ISLA or Implementation, Support and License Agreement is an agreement between Containerchain and the CDOs for the use of Containerchain system for the management of empty container at their respective depots.
269. *MyCC v. Containerchain & Four Container Depot Operators* (No. 700.2.005.2013) para. 204.
270. *MyCC v. MyEG Services Bhd* (MyCC (ED) 700-1/1/2/2015) para. 176.
271. *MyCC v. MyEG Services Bhd* (MyCC (ED) 700-1/1/2/2015) para. 177.
272. *MyCC v. MyEG Services Bhd* (MyCC (ED) 700-1/1/2/2015) para. 179.

competitors in the market of the sale of the Mandatory Insurances and allows the other competitors to compete at the same level'.[273] In MyEG case, the Commission also imposed a daily penalty due to the fact that 'MyEG failed to adhere to the directions imposed by the Commission in its Proposed Decision which is to provide an efficient gateway for all of its competitors at the downstream market.'[274] The power to impose a daily penalty drives from section 40(1)(d) of the CA 2010 which empowers the Commission to give any direction as it deems appropriate.

319. In *MyCC v. Seven Tuition and Daycare Centres*, the Commission took into consideration several factors in determining the financial penalties to be imposed on the infringing enterprises including the degree of fault, the extent to which the enterprises implemented the agreement and the degree of involvement with the price-fixing. In determining the degree of fault, 'the Commission will look at whether the infringement has been intentionally or negligently committed'.[275] The Commission rejected the argument that some enterprises are unaware that their conduct had infringed the CA 2010. The Commission stated that:

> the Enterprises were fully aware that the objective of the 'Notice' was to negate the likelihood of customers or potential customers negotiating the fees with individual tuition and daycare centres located within the SS19 Subang Jaya, Selangor area. With the fixing of prices, customers will have no option but to accept the prices offered by the colluding Enterprises. As such, the Enterprises ought to have known and could not have been unaware that the nature of the agreement to fix the tuition and daycare fees had the objective of restricting, preventing and distorting competition in the relevant market. Thus, the Commission is of the view that infringement was intentional regardless of the fact that the Enterprises argued that they were unaware that their conduct had infringed the prohibitions of the Act.[276]

320. In *MyCC v. Seven Tuition and Daycare Centres*, the Commission also considered steps taken to implement the revised fee scale as an aggravating factor while 'for Enterprises who had implemented the agreement but thereafter took steps to cease the infringing conduct prior to the Commission's Proposed Decision, the Commission concludes that no aggravating factor applies in this situation'.[277] The Commission also concluded that the active involvement of all seven enterprises in the conduct leading to the price-fixing by attending the first and second meeting to standardize and increase the tuition fee would be considered as an aggravating factor.

---

273. *MyCC v. MyEG Services Bhd* (MyCC (ED) 700-1/1/2/2015) para. 180.
274. *MyCC v. MyEG Services Bhd* (MyCC (ED) 700-1/1/2/2015) para. 171.
275. *MyCC v. Seven Tuition and Daycare Centre* (No. 700.1.1.43.2017) para. 121.
276. *MyCC v. Seven Tuition and Daycare Centre* (No. 700.1.1.43.2017) para. 124.
277. *MyCC v. Seven Tuition and Daycare Centre* (No. 700.1.1.43.2017) para. 135.

V. Leniency

321. The determination of the financial penalty is also subjected to any leniency granted by MyCC to the applicant. Section 41 of the CA 2010 provides:

> There shall be a leniency regime, with a reduction of up to a maximum of one hundred per cent of any penalties which would otherwise have been imposed, which may be available in the case of any enterprise which has –
>
> (a) admitted its involvement in an infringement of any prohibition under subsection 4 (2); and
> (b) provided information or other forms of cooperation to the Commission which significantly assisted, or is likely to significantly assist, in the identification or investigation of any finding of an infringement of any prohibition by any other enterprises.

322. The leniency programme is only available in relation to the financial penalty that may otherwise be imposed by the MyCC. The leniency is only applicable to the admission of the involvement in the hardcore cartel as laid down under section 4(2) of the CA 2010. In order to qualify for the leniency, the applicant must provide the Commission with any information or form of cooperation that would 'significantly' assist MyCC in its investigation on possible anticompetitive conduct. The word 'significantly' is not defined in the Act but MyCC will consider 'the facts of the case in hand, the stage of investigation as well as the state of knowledge of the MyCC about the cartel in question'.[278] The type of information or form of cooperation includes both the one that relates to the admission of involvement or any other cartel information.[279]

323. MyCC has the discretion to determine the amount of reduction of the financial penalty. The percentage of reduction depends on the following:

(a) whether the enterprise was the first person to bring the suspected infringement to the attention of the Commission;
(b) the stage in the investigation at which:
  (i) any involvement in the infringement was admitted; or
  (ii) any information or other cooperation was provided; or
(c) any other circumstances which the Commission considers appropriate or have regard to.[280]

324. As noted above, MyCC may grant up to 100% reduction of the financial penalty to the successful leniency applicant provided that:

(a) the applicant has admitted its involvement in a cartel; and

278. Paragraph 2.5, *MyCC Guidelines on Leniency Regime.*
279. Paragraph 2.6, *MyCC Guidelines on Leniency Regime.*
280. Section 41(a) of Competition Act 2010.

(b) the applicant offers to provide information or other forms of cooperation about the same cartel in which MyCC has no knowledge.[281]

325. The likelihood to get 100% reduction is higher for the first applicant who obtained the marker (refer paragraph 3.28), and the information was given before the Commission discovers the cartel activities. However, the leniency applicant is not entitled to 100% reduction of the financial penalty if the applicant is the initiator of the cartel or has taken any steps to coerce another enterprise to take part of the cartel activity.[282]

326. The amount of reduction for subsequent leniency application depends 'on the stage of investigation, the nature and the "value-added" of the information and other cooperation to be provided by the applicant which has already been received by the MyCC'. Since MyCC will assess the leniency application in the light of information that has already in its possession including the information that received from leniency applicants, an applicant is more likely to receive greater reduction if the application is submitted at the early stage of investigation. Similarly, the first applicant is more likely to receive a greater reduction than the subsequent applicants.

327. The Malaysia leniency regime provides for a system of the marker in which the potential leniency applicant may ask for a marker in order to preserve its priority in receiving a reduction of penalty pending the submission of the application. In applying for the marker, the applicant is required to provide details of the suspected infringement.[283] The marker will record the priority, date, time, possible infringement, and date by which the enterprise must complete the application. An applicant with an earlier marker in terms of date and time will be given priority in the reduction of financial penalty over other applicants, with a marker, with a later date and time for the same matter. The leniency application must be submitted within thirty days from the date of the marker is granted failing which, the first applicant will lose its priority position.[284]

328. Initially, MyCC will issue a conditional leniency, and the final (unconditional) leniency can only be granted if the applicant fulfils all conditions stipulated in the conditional leniency and when the Commission has made an infringement decision. If MyCC decides to grant a conditional leniency to an applicant, the applicant is required to enter into an agreement to fulfil all conditions in order to be entitled to unconditional leniency. The conditions include the undertaking by the applicant to stop the infringement, to provide full disclosure on its participation in

281. Paragraph 3.4, *MyCC Guidelines on Leniency Regime.*
282. Paragraph 2.7, *MyCC Guidelines on Leniency Regime.*
283. Paragraph 6.4, *MyCC Guidelines on Leniency Regime.*
284. Paragraph 5.9, *MyCC Guidelines on Leniency Regime.*

the admitted or other cartels, to provide continuous cooperation, not to destroy any relevant documents, not to disclose confidential information to anyone on any aspect of the grant of leniency, etc.[285]

329. In deciding whether or not to grant a leniency, MyCC will consider whether the applicant will provide information about a cartel of which MyCC has no or little knowledge. MyCC may at any time revoke the conditional leniency if the applicant fails to fulfil any condition stipulated or provides misleading or false information to MyCC. MyCC can even revoke the final leniency if it discovers that the applicant has not fulfilled one or more conditions of the conditional leniency.[286]

330. In *MyCC v. Seven Tuition and Daycare Centres*, one of the infringing enterprises formally applied for a leniency under section 41 of the Act ('the Application'). However, the application was duly dismissed on the grounds that the applicant failed to give information which is significantly assisting the Commission in its investigation as the application 'was made at an advanced stage of investigation and the Commission had by that time already obtained most of the evidence required for the purposes of investigations' and 'the evidence shows that the role of the leniency applicant as an instigator to the price fixing agreement was obvious and significant'.[287]

331. In *AG v. Commission of the European Communities*,[288] the Court held that:

> It should be noted that in order to be classified as an instigator of a cartel, an undertaking must have persuaded or encouraged other undertakings to establish the cartel or to join it. By contrast, it is not sufficient merely to have been a founding member of the cartel. Thus, for example, in a cartel created by two undertakings only, it would not be justified automatically to classify those undertakings as instigators. That classification should be reserved to the undertaking which has taken the initiative, if such be the case, for example by suggesting to the other an opportunity for collusion or by attempting to persuade it to do so.

332. In *Shell Petroleum NV v. European Commission,*[289] the Court held that 'it should be noted that, in order to be classified as an instigator of a cartel, an undertaking must have persuaded or encouraged other undertakings to establish the cartel or to join it'.

333. The Court further stated that:

285. Paragraph 8.4, *MyCC Guidelines on Leniency Regime.*
286. Paragraph 10.1, *MyCC Guidelines on Leniency Regime.*
287. *MyCC v. Seven Tuition and Daycare Centres* (Case No. 700-2.1.003.2015) para. 136(a) & (b).
288. Case T-15/02, *BASF,* para. 321.
289. Case T-343/06, para. 155.

In order to be classified as a leader in a cartel, an undertaking must have been a significant driving force for the cartel and have borne individual and specific liability for the operation of the cartel. That factor must be assessed in the light of the overall context of the case (*BASF v Commission*, paragraph 140 above, paragraphs 299, 300, 373 and 374, and Case T-410/03 *Hoechst v Commission* [2008] ECR II-881, paragraph 423). It may, inter alia, be inferred from the fact that the undertaking, through specific initiatives, voluntarily gave a fundamental boost to the cartel (*BASF v Commission*, paragraph 140 above, paragraphs 348, 370 to 375 and 427, and *Hoechst v Commission*, paragraph 426). It may also be inferred from a combination of indicia which reveal the determination of the undertaking to ensure the stability and success of the cartel (*BASF v Commission*, paragraph 140 above, paragraph 351).[290]

VI. Administrative Injunctions and Other Restrictive Orders

334. If the Commission decides that there is an infringement of a prohibition under Part I of the CA 2010, the Commission shall require that the infringement be ceased immediately. In addition, the Commission may take the following actions:

(a) specify appropriate steps which are required to be taken by the infringing enterprise for bringing the infringement to an end; and
(b) give any other direction as it deems appropriate.

335. In *MyCC v. 15 Sibu Confectionery and Bakery* (SCBA), the Commission has directed the target enterprises to cease and desist the fixing of prices of confectionery and bakery products in Sibu, Sarawak. The Commission has also directed the members of the Sibu Confectionary and Bakery Association (SCBA) to provide the Commission with a signed undertaking not to be involved in any future conduct contrary to the CA 2010.

336. In *MyCC v. My E.G. Services Bhd*, the Commission had required MyEG to cease and desist immediately from imposing different conditions to equivalent transactions in the processing of Mandatory Insurances for online PLKS renewal applications. In addition, MyEG is required to provide an efficient gateway for all its competitors in the market for the sale of the Mandatory Insurances and allows the other competitors to compete at the same level.[291]

337. In *MyCC v. Containerchain & Four Container Depot Operators*, in addition to financial penalties imposed on the infringing enterprises, the Commission had also directed the target CDOs to cease and desist from implementing the agreed rate for the DGCs and rebates which arose from their anticompetitive behaviour; to remove clause 7 of the Carrier Access Agreement (CAA) which contains the DGC

290. Case T-343/06, para. 198.
291. *MyCC v. MyEG Services Bhd* (MyCC (ED) 700-1/1/2/2015) para. 173.

or rebates or any similar clauses and to ensure that the CCA uploaded in the Containerchain's website does not contain any clause which allows the CDOs to share confidential information. The Commission had also directed the Containerchain to provide an undertaking to reconfigure the Containerchain system to ensure that it is not being used for anticompetitive behaviour.[292]

338. In *MyCC v. 7 Tuition and Daycare Centres*, one of the remedial action imposed by the Commission on 7 Tuition and Daycare Centres is the infringing enterprises are required to 'enrol and complete the MyCC's e-Learning Course on Competition Compliance for Small and Medium Enterprises (SMEs) within one (1) month from the issuance of this Decision and produce to the Commission, the certificate of completion thereof'.[293]

VII. Interim Measures

339. The Competition may give any direction to any person before the completion of an investigation if the Commission has reasonable grounds to believe that any prohibition under the CA 2010 has been infringed or is likely to be infringed and it is necessary for the Commission to act based on the urgency to:

(a) prevent serious and irreparable damage, economic or otherwise, to a particular person or category of persons; or
(b) protect the public interest.[294]

340. An interim measure can only be imposed if the Commission has commenced but not completed an investigation under section 14.[295] A direction may include requiring any person to:

(a) suspend the effect of, and desist from acting in accordance with, any agreement which is suspected of infringing any prohibition under Part II;
(b) desist from any conduct which is suspected of infringing any prohibition under Part II; or
(c) do or refrain from doing, any act, but which shall not require the payment of money.

341. Before giving the direction, the Commission must serve a written notice to the person to whom the Commission proposes to give the direction. The notice sets

292. *MyCC v. Containerchain & Four Container Depot Operators* (No. 700.2.005.2013) para. 197. CAA is an agreement between the CDOs and the hauliers which stipulates terms and conditions before the hauliers enter into a depot. CAA refers to the imposition of an increased DGCs of RM25 and a term providing for a common rebate.
293. *MyCC v. Seven Tuition and Daycare Centres* (Case No. 700-2.1.003.2015) para. 143(c).
294. Section 35(1) & (2) of Competition Act 2010.
295. Section 35(1) of Competition Act 2010.

out the nature of the direction and reasons for giving the directions. The Commission must give that person an opportunity to make written representations. The Commission may at any time withdraw a direction given under subsection (2) of section 35 of the CA 2010.

342. In *MyCC v. 24 Ice Manufacturers,*[296] the Commission then issued Notice of Proposed Interim Measures under section 35 of the CA 2010 to all enterprises to suspend the effect of, and desist from acting in accordance with the announcement made in local newspapers to collectively raise the price of edible tube ice by MYR 0.50 per bag and the price of block ice by MYR 2.50 per big block respectively with effect from 1 January 2014. The Commission took this decision as a matter of urgency and as provided for under section 35 of the Act to prevent serious and irreparable damage, economic or otherwise, to a particular person or category of persons or protecting the public interest.

VIII. Undertaking

343. The CA 2010 also empowers the Commission to accept undertakings from an enterprise to do or refrain from doing anything as the Commission considers appropriate.[297] If the Commission decides to accept the undertaking, the Commission is bound to close the investigation without making a finding of infringement and shall not impose a penalty on the enterprise.[298] The undertaking must be offered during an investigation or assessment and before the issuance of a proposed decision.

344. The list of undertakings:

Undertaking Given By	*Date*
Barbers Association	30 January 2014
Pan Malaysia Lorry Owners Association (PMLOA)	7 May 2014
Giga Shipping Sdn Bhd & Nexus Mega Carriers Sdn Bhd	1 October 2014
Malaysia Heavy Construction Equipment Owners' Association (MHCEOA)	12 October 2015
Containerchain Malaysia Sdn. Bhd	30 June 2016
Sand Traders for the four Districts namely Kota Bahru, Pasir Mas, Tanah Merah and Machang in Negeri Kelantan	25 September 2017

296. *MyCC v. 24 Ice Manufacturers* (No. MyCC.700.2.0001.2014).
297. Section 43 of Competition Act 2010.
298. Section 43(2) of Competition Act 2010.

IX. Malaysian Indian Hairdressing Saloon Owners Association

345. On 1 February 2013, the former Chairman of Malaysian Indian Hairdressing Saloon Owners Association (MIHSOA) issued a statement which was published in major newspapers in Malaysia that the members of MIHSOA in a meeting dated 30 January 2013 decided to increase the price of haircut services by MYR 2.00 effective from 1 February 2013. The MIHSOA also informed that it would not hesitate to take action against those members who fail to follow the decision of the meeting. Based on this information, the Commission conducted an investigation on this matter and found that the MIHSOA and its members had engaged in horizontal agreement that had the object to fix the price of haircut services offered by them. The MIHSOA and its member had given an undertaking to the Commission that it will conduct an Emergency General Meeting with an agenda to withdraw decision made to raise the price of haircut services by MYR 2.00 and will direct and ensure that all its members to not engage in anticompetitive behaviour in the future.[299]

X. Malaysia Heavy Construction Equipment Owner's Association

346. The MHCEOA made an announcement in a local newspaper to increase the machinery rental charges by 1 February 2014. The Commission found that clause 3.6 of the MHCEOA's Constitution mandates the Association 'to draw up and maintain code of ethics and guidelines for hiring fees and tender of contracts by the members'. The Commission has agreed to accept the MHCEOA's undertakings, including to remove the Clause 3.6 of the MHCEOA's Constitution, to refrain from reinstating a similar clause in the Constitution, to refrain from making similar press statements in relation to selling or hiring fees and to refrain from entering into any agreement or decision in contravention of the CA 2010.[300]

XI. Undertaking by Sand Operators

347. The Commission received a complaint that sand traders mainly based in Kota Bharu, Pasir Mas, Tanah Merah and Machang had increased the price of sand per lorry from MYR 70.00 to MYR 110.00. The price was allegedly set through an association. During the course of the investigation, it was also found that there had been a meeting among the sand traders on 10 January 2017 to discuss among others the operational and management costs of each trader (such as the price of the sand, docket, diesel, the lorry driver daily salary, and the type transportation, etc.) During the meeting, the participants shared their own operational and management costs.

---

299. Undertaking by Malaysian Indian Hairdressing Saloon Owners Association (MIHSOA) dated 30 Jan. 2014.

300. Undertaking Malaysia Heavy Construction Equipment Owner's Association (MHCEOA) dated 12 Oct. 2015.

348. Based on the information, they prepared a table of pricing according to their districts stating the reasonable selling price so that they may sustain their business and are able to compete with one another. The Commission found that the price list prepared was used as a focal point for the traders to form a cartel to fix the price.[301] However, the Commission took into account that most of the representatives of the sand traders are not highly educated as they are from rural areas. The Commission took into consideration that none of the trades had complied with the price lists as they charged different prices for the sale of sands based on their management and operational costs.[302] The Commission also found the sand traders were actually obliged to comply with the price list issued by the State Authority on the 18 January 2017.[303]

349. All sand traders gave an undertaking to abolish the price lists for the sale of sands according to their district issued on 19 January 2017 and to cease any anti-competitive behaviour based on the price lists. The sand traders were also required to issue a press statement to apologize for their anticompetitive behaviour.

XII. Giga Shipping Sdn Bhd and Nexus Mega Carriers Sdn Bhd

350. The Commission had launched an investigation under section 15(1) of the CA 2010 against *Giga Shipping Sdn Bhd* and *Nexus Mega Carriers Sdn Bhd* for possible infringement of section 4(1) and section 10(1) of the CA 2010 in relation to the provision of logistic and/or shipment services by sea for motor vehicles from ports in Peninsular Malaysia to ports in Sabah, Sarawak and Labuan. The two enterprises admitted that sometimes in the year 2010 they had entered into certain agreements that contain exclusive clauses which stipulate that the enterprises shall be the exclusive provider of the services to such customers for up to three years, in consideration of which the enterprises had agreed to give such customers a lower price arising from the volume of businesses generated from such agreements. The enterprises had offered an undertaking 'with a view to addressing the Commission's preliminary competition concerns and to avoid the time, inconvenience, and expense of further proceedings or actions between the parties'.[304]

351. The enterprises had given undertaking to cease to include in any of the agreements with customers or potential customers any exclusivity clause or clauses which have the same effect as exclusivity clauses unless such agreements have been or are entered into following an open tendering process carried out by the customers or potential customers and such agreements containing exclusivity clauses are for a duration of two years or less. The enterprises had also agreed to inform their

301. Undertaking by Sand Operators dated 25 Sep. 2017, para. 65.
302. Undertaking by Sand Operators dated 25 Sep. 2017, para. 67.
303. Undertaking by Sand Operators dated 25 Sep. 2017, para. 66.
304. Undertaking by Giga Shipping Sdn Bhd and Nexus Mega Carriers Sdn Bhd dated 1 Oct. 2014, para. 4.

customers on the matters, to publish the undertaking in five major newspapers, to continue their competition law compliance programme and to conduct training for their senior management and directors.

XIII. Containerchain (Malaysia) Sdn Bhd

352. Pursuant to paragraph 197(iv) and 197(v) of the Commission's infringement decision against Containerchain and four Container Depot Operators (CDOs), Containerchain had given an undertaking to reconfigure the Containerchain system in order to ensure that it is not used for any competitive conduct. The Containerchain undertakes to reconfigure its system so that CDOs are able to publish their own DGCs and determine rebates that will be given to hauliers without the involvement of the Containerchain. In order to ensure that the CDOs are able to set their own CDOs, each CDOs will be given a unique individual login credential to log into the system and are able to set or revise the DGCs once they enter into the system. The system will automatically and instantaneously send a notification to hauliers (when they log into the system) about the DGC or revised DGC. If a haulier uses more than one CDO, the haulier should be able to view the DGCs of all CDOs it uses.

353. In relation to rebates that will be given to hauliers for early payment, the rebates will be removed from the Containerchain system. The invoice generated by the system will not make reference or taken into account any rebates given by CDOs to the hauliers. The Containerchain also undertakes to inform the CDOs by a written notice that any rebates should be managed and given independently by the CDOs outside the Containerchain system.[305]

354. The Commission has the power to issue a warning letter to any enterprise based on the Commission's power to do anything incidental to any of its functions and powers.[306] However, the warning can be only during the assessment and investigation before the issuance of the proposed decision. The Commission had issued warning letters to following companies for their anticompetitive behaviour:

Warning Letters Given To	*Date*
Nursery Association and Babysitters in: Selangor, Wilayah Persekutuan, Kedah, Pulau Pinang, Kelantan, Pahang, Terengganu, Johor, Melaka, Sabah, and Sarawak	14 July 2015
Perak Fish Breeders Association	27 August 2015
Persatuan Penternak Ikan Tawar Temerloh	27 August 2015
Kuching Bakery Association	17 August 2015

305. Undertaking by Containerchain (Malaysia) Sdn Bhd dated 30 Jun. 2016.
306. Section 17(2)(j) of Competition Commission Act 2010.

Warning Letters Given To	*Date*
Sarawak Restaurant Association	11 April 2015
Federation of Goldsmith & Jewellers Association of Malaysia	25 February 2016
Federation of Livestock Farmers' Association of Malaysia	22 February 2016
Malaysia Corrugated Carton Manufacturers Association	10 March 2016
Avery Dennison Materials Sdn. Bhd. and UPM Raflatac Sdn Bhd	7 February 2017

§2. Civil Enforcement

I. Competent Civil Courts

355. The Commission may bring proceedings before the High Court against any person who fails to comply with a direction given by the Commission under section 35 (interim measures) or a decision under section 40 (infringement decision). The High Court may make an order requiring the person to comply with the Commission's direction or decision. If a person fails to pay the penalty within the specified period, the High Court may order the person to pay interest on top of the initial penalty at the normal judgment rate starting from the day following that on which the payment was due. Any person who fails to comply with the order of the High Court shall be liable for contempt of court.

356. A decision given by the CAT may, by leave of the High Court, be enforced in the same as a judgment and where the leave is so given, judgment may be entered in terms of the decisions.[307]

357. The decision of the CAT or any administrative body can be appealed to the higher court (e.g., High Court, Court of Appeal) for judicial review. The application of judicial review is governed by Order 53 of the Rules of Court 2012. The court will review the decision of the administrative body to determine the lawfulness of the decision, actions or omission.

358. The CA allows any person who has suffered direct loss or damage because of infringement by an enterprise to bring a private action in civil court against such an enterprise providing the latter is a party to such infringement.[308] The action may be brought by any person irrespective of whether such person involves directly or indirectly with the enterprise.[309]

307. Section 59 of Competition Act 2010.
308. Section 64(1) of Competition Act 2010.
309. Section 64(2) Competition Act 2010.

II. Sanctions

A. *Nullity*

359. Judicial review: the remedies available for judicial review can be divided into two: private and public remedies. Public remedies include certiorari, prohibition and mandamus. Certiorari is an order by the court that a decision of an administrative body to be quashed if, for example, there has been an error of law or the administrative body exceeded its power in issuing a decision, while prohibition is an order to quash the decision that is going to be made or to prevent the judicial body to proceed with the trial of a case. Mandamus, on the hand, is an order by the court which commands an administrative body to perform a specific act required by the law.

B. *Damages*

360. Private action – remedies available in general private action include damages and other equitable remedies.

361. Private action – damages are subjected to the principles enunciated in section 74 of the *Contract Act 1950*. However, the entitlement to damages arises from the breach of the contract itself. With regard to damages in tort, Malaysia applies the common law principles; namely, the plaintiff must prove the loss and damage suffered and the foreseeability on the part of the defendant. The apportionment of damages among claimants is a matter of the judge's discretion, and there is no clear rule governing it.

C. *Interim Measures*

362. Private action – the court may grant equitable remedies, such as injunctions, specific performance, declarations, rectification, and rescission. However, the granting of equitable remedies is subjected to the provisions in the *Specific Relief Act 1950* (SRA) and remedies, such as specific performance and injunction subject to the discretion of the court. For example, section 21 of the SRA provides for specific performance while section 50 the SRA provides for preventive relief, such as injunctions.

363. Judicial review – the court may provide private remedies in the form of damages, injunctions, and declarations.

§3. CRIMINAL ENFORCEMENT

I. Criminal Sanctions for Antitrust Violations

364. The CA 2010 does not provide a criminal sanction for breaching the competition law rules under Part II (Chapter 1 and Chapter 2) of the CA 2010. The Commission can only take administrative action and sanction against the infringing enterprise for engaging in anticompetitive behaviour.

II. Other Application of Criminal Law to Relevant Conducts

365. However, the CA 2010 provides criminal sanctions for violation of other general offences under the Act including:

(a) Giving false or misleading information, evidence or document in response to a direction issued by the Commission.[310]
(b) Destructing, concealing, mutilating or altering records with intent to defraud the Commission or to prevent, delay or obstruct the carrying out of an investigation or the exercise of any power by the Commission.
(c) Obstructing any Commission officer from performing his duties under the CA 2010.
(d) Tipping off by information or any other matter which is likely to prejudice that investigation or proposed investigation.
(e) Threat and reprisal against any person who is making a complaint to the Commission or cooperating with the Commission in its investigation.
(f) Disclosing or making use of any confidential information with respect to a particular enterprise or the affairs of an individual obtained by virtue of any provision of the CA 2010.[311]

366. Any person who commits the general offences under the CA 2010 shall on conviction be liable:

(a) if such person is a body corporate, to a fine not exceeding MYR 5 million, and for a second or subsequent offence, to a fine not exceeding MYR 10 million; or
(b) if such person is not a body corporate, to a fine not exceeding MYR 1 million or to imprisonment for a term not exceeding five years or to both, and for a second or subsequent offence, to a fine not exceeding MYR 2 million or to imprisonment for a term not exceeding five years or to both.[312]

310. Section 23 of Competition Act 2010.
311. Section 21 of Competition Act 2010.
312. Section 61 of Competition Act 2010.

III. Role of Prosecutors

367. The Attorney General shall be the Public Prosecutor and shall have the control and direction of all criminal prosecutions and proceedings under the Criminal Procedure Code.[313] Based on the Malaysian Federal Constitution, 'the Attorney General shall have power, exercisable at his discretion, to institute, conduct or discontinue any proceedings for an offence, other than proceedings before a Syariah court, a native court or a court-martial'.[314]

368. Under the CA 2010, any criminal offence cannot be instituted without the consent in writing of the Public Prosecutor.[315] Every criminal prosecution before any Court and every inquiry before a Magistrate shall be conducted by the Public Prosecutor, a Senior Deputy Public Prosecutor, a Deputy Public Prosecutor or an Assistant Public Prosecutor.[316] However, criminal prosecution can be conducted by any other person, such as an advocate, an officer of any government department, or any local authority or statutory body who is authorized in writing by the Public Prosecutor.[317]

IV. Competent Criminal Courts

369. Criminal offences under the CA 2010 will be tried in either Magistrate or Sessions Court. For example, a First Class Magistrate has jurisdiction to try all offences for which the maximum term of imprisonment provided by law does not exceed ten years imprisonment or which are punishable with fine,[318] while a Second Class Magistrate only has jurisdiction to try offences for which the maximum term of imprisonment provided by the law does not exceed twelve months of either description or which are punishable with fine only.[319] On the other hand, a Sessions Court shall have jurisdiction to try all offences other than offences punishable with death.[320]

313. Section 376 of Criminal Procedure Code 2012.
314. Article 145(3) of the Federal Constitution (Malaysia) 1957.
315. Section 40 of Competition Act 2010.
316. Section 377(a) of Criminal Procedure Code 2012.
317. Section 377(b) of Criminal Procedure Code 2012.
318. Section 85 of the Subordinate Courts Act 1948.
319. Section 88 of the Subordinate Courts Act 1948.
320. Section 63 of the Subordinate Courts Act 1948.

Part II. Application of the Prohibitions

Chapter 1. Restrictive Agreements

§1. Horizontal Agreements

370. Section 4(1) of the CA 2010 prohibits a horizontal or vertical agreement which has the object or effect of significantly restricting, preventing or distorting competition in the market. Horizontal agreement is defined as 'an agreement between enterprises each of which operates at the same level in the production or distribution chain'.

371. Section 4(1) of the CA 2010 involves two-step analyses: First, the Commission will determine whether an agreement has as its object the restriction, prevention or distortion of competition. The Commission 'will not only examine the actual common intentions of the parties to an agreement but also assess the aims pursued by the agreement in light of the agreement's economic context'.[321] Second, if an anticompetitive 'object' is proven, the Commission is not required to prove the actual effect of the agreement on competition.

372. Section 4(2), on the other hand, is a deeming provision. It laid down certain types of horizontal agreements between enterprises which are deemed to have the object of significantly restricting, preventing competition. The conduct listed in section 4(2) is also known as hardcore cartel or hardcore restrictions. The deeming provision means that a mere fact that an enterprise is entering or has entered into an agreement listed down in section 4(2) is a prima facie evidence of anticompetitive conduct which runs afoul the CA 2010. The Commission is also under no obligation to examine the anticompetitive effect of such agreement[322] including to determine the relevant market and market powers of the parties to the agreement.

373. The agreements which are deemed to be anticompetitive include:

(a) Fix, directly or indirectly, a purchase or selling priced or any other trading conditions.
(b) Share market or sources of supply.
(c) Limit or control of:

321. Paragraph 2.13, *MyCC Guidelines on Chapter 1 Prohibition.*
322. Paragraph 3.25, *MyCC Guidelines on Chapter 1 Prohibition.*

(i) production;
(ii) market outlets or market access;
(iii) technical or technological developments; or
(iv) investment.
(d) Perform an act of bid-rigging.

I. Cartels

A. Price Fixing

374. Section 4(2)(a) prohibits not only an agreement to fix the selling price but also purchasing price. The latter is known as a buyer's cartel. The term of 'price-fixing' from the perspective of competition law is not limited to the fixing of the final price but also the component of the price, such as setting the price of transport charges (such as fuel charges), credit interest rate term, commission, etc. Price-fixing also includes fixing a discount, a percentage of price increase or setting the permitted range of prices between competitors.[323]

375. In *MyCC v. Cameron Highlands Floriculturist Association (CHFA)*, the MyCC has come to a conclusion that the action of CHFA and its members to increase the prices of cut flowers by 10% in Malaysia and abroad except for Japan, effective from 16 March 2012, is an infringement of a prohibition under section 4(2) of the CA 2010 and constituted a horizontal agreement between enterprises to fix, directly or indirectly, a purchase or selling price.[324]

376. In *MyCC v. 15 Sibu Confectionery and Bakery Association,*[325] the Commission found that the 15 members of the SCBA had infringed section 4(2)(a) of the CA 2010 for their agreement to increase the prices of confectionery and bakery products by 10%–15% in the Sibu area effective from 1 December 2013.

377. In *MyCC v. 24 Ice Manufacturers,*[326] the Commission concluded that 24 ice manufacturers had infringed section 4(2) of the CA 2010 for their agreement to collectively raise the price of edible tube ice by MYR 0.50 per bag and the price of block ice by MYR 2.50 per big block effective from 1 January 2014 have infringed section 4(2)(a) of the Act.

378. In *MyCC v. Containerchain & Four Container Depot Operators,*[327] the Commission had taken action against four CDO for their anticompetitive behaviour by not only agreeing to increase the DGCs from MYR 5 to MYR 25 but also to fix

323. Paragraph 3.27, *MyCC Guidelines on Chapter 1 Prohibition.*
324. *MyCC v. Cameron Highlands Floriculturist Association* (No. MyCC/0003/2012(ACA) p. 1.
325. *MyCC v. 15 Sibu Confectionary and Bakery Association* (No. MyCC.0045.2013).
326. *MyCC v. 24 Ice Manufacturers* (No. MyCC.700.2.0001.2014).
327. *MyCC v. Containerchain & Four Container Depot Operators* (No. MyCC. 700.2.005.2013).

the discount to be offered to hauliers in respect of the DGCs. The Commission concluded that the conduct had infringed section 4(2) which is deemed to have the object of significantly preventing, restricting or distorting competition in the market for the provision of empty container storage, maintaining and handling services within a 5–15km radius of Penang Port. In this case, the CDOs are providing services to restore, maintain and clean empty containers. The hauliers are transporters who transport empty containers from the port to the shippers and vice versa. The haulier will be engaged by either shipper (who export and import goods) or shipping line (shipping company) to pick up empty containers from a CDO at an assigned depot. The hauliers will be charged with DGC for every access to the CDO's sites to either collect or store empty containers. Rebates will be given to the hauliers for making a prompt payment within fourteen days. Out of MYR 25, as agreed by the target CDOs, MYR 5 will be paid to Containerchain Sdn Bhd as a service for using the latter's system and another MYR 5 will be returned to the hauliers for their early payment.[328]

379. In *MyCC v. Seven Tuition and Daycare Centres*, the Commission has come to a conclusion that seven tuition and daycare centres 'have infringed the prohibition imposed by section 4(2)(a) by participating in a price-fixing agreement to adjust and standardise tuition and daycare fees paid by the parents of students with effect from July 2017'.[329]

380. The term of price-fixing also covers an arrangement that facilitates collusion to fix price, including price recommendation, an agreement between competitors to share price lists before increasing prices either directly or indirectly through a trade association, or an agreement between competitors to consult each other before making a decision on price[330] or conscious parallelism where when a market leader increases or lowers the price, other competitors will follow suit without an express agreement between them. The word 'purchasing price' means that section 4(2)(a) also condemns anticompetitive behaviour by buyers or better known as buyers' cartel.

381. In *Dongwha Fireboard and Evergreen Fireboard*,[331] the Commission received a complaint alleging that two largest Medium Density Fireboard (MDF) manufacturers in Malaysia had entered into a pact to set the purchase price for rubberwood small logs. In this case, MDF manufacturers are operating in the downstream market and are considered as consumers of rubberwood small logs while the smallholders and contractor of the rubberwood are operating in the upstream market as they supply the rubberwood to the MDF. As a result of the agreement, one of the MDF manufacturers had lowered the purchase price of the wood small logs in oppressing smallholders and contractor of rubberwood. It was alleged that the

328. *MyCC v. Containerchain & Four Container Depot Operators* (No. MyCC. 700.2.005.2013) para. 51.
329. *MyCC v. Seven Tuition and Daycare Centres* (No. 700.1.1.43.2017) para. 72.
330. Paragraph 3.27, *MyCC Guidelines on Chapter 1 Prohibition.*
331. Finding of Non-Infringement under s. 39 of the Competition Act 2010 of Dongwha Fibreboard Sdn. Bhd. and Evergreen Fibreboard Bhd, 7 Feb. 2017 (No. MyCC(ED)700-1/2/6/2015).

agreement to collude to fix the purchase price eliminates competition between MDF at the downstream level of the market, to the detriment of the contractor, loggers as well as small rubber estate holders in the upstream market.[332]

382. However, the evidence gathered by the Commission during the investigation did not suggest or indicate that the price imposed was due to an anticompetitive agreement between the producers.[333] For example, the Commission finds that 'the price of rubber wood small logs are directly affected by the supply and demand in the market, whereas when there is lower supply of the small logs and high demands, the price of the small logs will increase. Conversely, when there is a higher supply of small logs and low demands, the price of small logs will decrease'.[334] Other factors that influenced the prices of small logs identified include weather, location and transportation costs, and the volume of supply (the higher the volume of supply, the better the rates).

B. Market/Client Allocation

383. Market allocation involves an agreement between competitors to share or allocate customers or geographic territory with understanding that they will stay out of each other's allocated territory or customer base. Market allocation of market sharing includes an agreement between competitors to buy only from certain suppliers or to specialize in certain products or ranges or products or in particular technologies only.[335]

384. In *MyCC v. MAS-AirAsia,*[336] the Commission has come to a decision that:

> MAS and AirAsia by entering into the Collaboration Agreement to share the market have infringed section 4(2)(b) of the CA 2010. The Collaboration Agreement is clearly an agreement entered into by the parties to share the market in relation to aviation services.[337] The Commission viewed that Clause 5 of the Collaboration Agreement is a market sharing agreement between competitors where each of the parties agreed to focus on separate sectors in the airlines industry. Under the agreement, MAS was mandated to focus on being a Full Service Premium Carrier (FSC) while AirAsia was mandated to focus on being a regional low-cost carrier and AirAsia X was mandated to focus on being a medium-to-long haul low-cost carrier respectively. The Commission

---

332. Finding of Non-Infringement under section 39 of the Competition Act 2010 of Dongwha Fibreboard Sdn. Bhd. and Evergreen Fibreboard Bhd, 7 Feb. 2017 (No. MyCC(ED)700-1/2/6/2015) para. 25.
333. Finding of Non-Infringement under s. 39 of the Competition Act 2010 of Dongwha Fibreboard Sdn. Bhd. and Evergreen Fibreboard Bhd, 7 Feb. 2017 (No. MyCC(ED)700-1/2/6/2015) para. 17.
334. Finding of Non-Infringement under s. 39 of the Competition Act 2010 of Dongwha Fibreboard Sdn. Bhd. and Evergreen Fibreboard Bhd, 7 Feb. 2017 (No. MyCC(ED)700-1/2/6/2015) para. 60.
335. Paragraph 3.27.2, *MyCC Guidelines on Chapter 1 Prohibition*, para. 3.27.2.
336. *MyCC v. MAS-AirAsia* (No. MyCC.0001.2012).
337. *MyCC v. MAS-AirAsia* (No. MyCC.0001.2012) para. 49.

found that 'the agreement also resulted in an outcome whereby Firefly (a wholly owned subsidiary of MAS) withdrew from the Kuala Lumpur-Kuching, Kuala Lumpur-Kota Kinabalu, Kuala Lumpur-Sandakan and Kuala Lumpur-Sibu routes (Sabah and Sarawak routes) leaving AirAsia to be the sole low cost carrier'.[338]

C. Production/Innovation Limitation

385. Section 4(2)(c) of the CA 2010 covers the following conduct:

– *Limit production*: for example, an agreement between competitors to set production quotas with an intention to push upward during an economic downturn or during specific seasons.[339]
– *Market outlets or market access*: for an agreement between competitors to determine where retail outlets to be allocated or to limit the numbers of retail outlets in certain areas or an agreement to prevent or restrict new players to enter into a particular market.[340]
– *Technical or technological development*: for an example, an agreement between competitors not to introduce new innovative products into the market or to set technological standards collectively with the view of preventing other competitors from selling a particular product or not to buy certain technologies from certain suppliers.[341]

386. In My Egg Consortium Sdn Bhd ('the My Egg'), the Commission had received complaints that the My Egg was set up by members of the Federation of Livestock Farmers Associations of Malaysia in 2010 with the objective to reduce the supply of chicken eggs in the local market to ultimately push up the egg prices. It was alleged that 'My Egg procured eggs from major producers representing more than 75% of the total production of eggs in West Malaysia. The My Egg was said to export chicken eggs in huge quantities to the international market, such as Hong Kong and Angola, thus reducing supply and increasing the demand, which will eventually drive up egg prices.'[342] However, after the assessment of all evidence obtained, the Commission found that there is no compelling evidence 'to support the allegation that the My Egg was created with the object of reducing egg supply in Malaysia in order to raise the prices of eggs'.[343] In fact, the evidence shows that there was an excess supply of eggs in the local market for years 2003–2014 and the

338. *MyCC v. MAS-AirAsia* (No. MyCC.0001.2012) para. 9.
339. Paragraph 3.27.3, *MyCC Guidelines on Chapter 1 Prohibition.*
340. Paragraph 3.27.3, *MyCC Guidelines on Chapter 1 Prohibition.*
341. Paragraph 3.27.3, *MyCC Guidelines on Chapter 1 Prohibition.*
342. Finding of Non-Infringement under s. 39 of the Competition Act 2010 – My Egg Consortium Sdn. Bhd (May 2015, No. MyCC/0004/2012) para. 3.
343. Finding of Non-Infringement under s. 39 of the Competition Act 2010 – My Egg Consortium Sdn. Bhd (May 2015, No. MyCC/0004/2012) para. 33.

excess supply was greater than export.[344] The Commission also finds that 'although the price of eggs kept fluctuating and also increased over time, the price of eggs fell in 2012, the year the allegation was made'.[345]

D. Group Boycott

387. The CA 2010 and its guidelines do not contain any provision on boycott or group boycott. An agreement not to buy from a particular supplier may have the object of preventing, restricting or distorting competition. However, the conduct of boycotting certain enterprises may fall under section 4(1) of the CA 2010.

E. Bid-Rigging

388. Bid-rigging is a collusion in a tender process whereby competitors are taking turns to win the otherwise competitive tender. Bid-rigging includes cover bids, bid suppression or bid rotation. There may be more than one bid-rigging practices that can occur at one time[346] the purpose of which to allow a predetermined bidder to win a particular tender. All competitors may have the chance of winning the subsequent tenders. Examples of bid-rigging include:

- *Cover bids* – an agreement between bidders to submit artificially high bid price in order to allow a predetermined party to win the tender. Normally, the unsuccessful bidders may get kickbacks in the form of commission or subcontracts.[347]
- *Bid suppression* – an agreement between bidders that only one of the bidders will submit a bid for a particular tender. The others will refrain themselves from submitting their bids or withdraw themselves from the bidding right before the close of the tender.[348]
- *Bid rotation* – an agreement between bidders to take turns to win a particular tender.

F. Fixing of Trading Conditions

389. Section 4(2)(a) prohibits not only price fixing arrangement but also the fixing of trading conditions. Standard terms and conditions are generally good for consumers by making it easier for consumers to make an informed choice and to compare various products or services offered in the market. However, standards

344. Finding of Non-Infringement under s. 39 of the Competition Act 2010 – My Egg Consortium Sdn. Bhd (May 2015, No. MyCC/0004/2012) para. 20.
345. Finding of Non-Infringement under s. 39 of the Competition Act 2010 – My Egg Consortium Sdn. Bhd (May 2015, No. MyCC/0004/2012) para. 25.
346. Paragraph 3.27.4, *MyCC Guidelines on Chapter 1 Prohibition.*
347. Paragraph 3.27.4, *MyCC Guidelines on Chapter 1 Prohibition.*
348. Paragraph 3.27.4, *MyCC Guidelines on Chapter 1 Prohibition.*

terms and conditions which lead to the uniformity of prices is equivalent to the price-fixing arrangement. Standard terms and conditions may become a platform to coordinate on non-price behaviour and reduce the ability of enterprises to compete on non-price factors.

390. Standardization agreement may have an adverse effect on competition if it restricts the ability of enterprises to set new standards, to introduce new products or to serve as an entry barrier for new competitors.[349]

II. Information Exchange Practices

391. Information sharing may be anticompetitive or pro-competitive depending on the nature and characteristic of the information shared. Whether information sharing falls within the conduct deemed to have the object of significantly preventing, restricting and distorting competition in the market must be decided on a case-to-case basis:

- *Price and non-price information* – sharing price information is more harmful to competition than sharing non-price information. Sharing non-price information, such as standards, new technologies, market trends, etc., in fact, improves competition in the market.[350] Sharing sensitive information on the price may, on the other hand, facilitate collusion to fix prices among competitors and reduce uncertainty that competitors will face.[351]
- *Future information and historical data* – sharing information is likely to be problematic when it involves the disclosure of future prices as it reduces uncertainty on the prices that will be imposed and commercial strategy that will be embarked on by the competitor.
- *Aggregate and individual data* – the sharing of aggregate data where the identification of individual data is not possible is unlikely to have an effect on competition. The more individualized the data, the more likely it is to be problematic.
- *Frequency of information exchange* – the frequent exchange of information is more likely to have a significant effect on competition than the infrequent exchange depending on the characteristic of the market. For example, in a concentrated market, even a one-off exchange of information may increase the chance of collusion among a few competitors.
- *Availability of information* – genuinely public information which is equally accessible by both competitors and consumers is less likely to be problematic. Exchange of information between competitors that is not provided to consumers is likely to have an adverse effect on competition.

---

349. Paragraph 3.10, *MyCC Guidelines on Chapter 1 Prohibition.*
350. Paragraph 3.6, *MyCC Guidelines on Chapter 1 Prohibition.*
351. Paragraph 3.7, *MyCC Guidelines on Chapter 1 Prohibition.*

III. Cooperation Agreements

392. Enterprises may enter into a cooperation agreement between each other to jointly produce, sell, distribute, purchase or even market their products and services together. Cooperation agreement allows enterprises to share business risks, reduce costs of business operation and increase productivity and innovation. At the end of the day, consumers may enjoy many benefits from the cooperative agreement, such as lower price, a product of good quality and variety of choices.

393. In assessing whether a cooperation agreement is anti-competitive, normally the competition authority will consider the extent to which the agreement restricts actual and potential competition and how far does the agreement foreclose the market for competitors and the third party. Generally, cooperation agreement is only a matter of concern if one or both parties to the agreement have significant market power. Cooperation agreement which involves a hardcore cartel, such as price-fixing, market sharing and limit of output, will be considered as anticompetitive 'by object'.

A. *Research and Development*

394. R&D agreement involves a collaboration between two or more enterprises to undertake R&D to improve the existing products or technologies or to produce a totally new product or process. Parties may limit their collaboration to purely R&D stage or extend it to the manner in which they exploit the result of R&D, such as joint production and joint marketing of products or processes under their R&D programme. Pure R&D collaboration where the parties are free to exploit the fruit of the R&D or R&D collaboration between non-competitors is not likely to have an adverse effect on competition. However, R&D agreement may also raise competitive concerns if, for example, it limits the freedom of parties to carry out R&D independently or in collaboration with third parties in a field outside the subject matter of the R&D agreement, or if it limits the number of products that may be manufactured or sold using the contract technology or process or fixes the selling price of the contract product to a third party.[352]

B. *Specialization*

395. Specialization agreement is an agreement between enterprises active in the same product market where one party agrees to cease production and agrees to buy

352. Guidelines on the applicability of Article 101 of the Treaty on the Functioning of the European Union to horizontal cooperation agreements, https://eur-lex.europa.eu/LexUriServ/LexUriServ.do?uri=OJ:C:2011:011:0001:0072:EN:PDF; *see also* Slaughter & May, The EU competition rules on horizontal agreements: A guide to the assessment of horizontal agreements (including the European Commission's guidelines on horizontal cooperation and the block exemption regulations on R&D and specialization agreement) June 2016.

the product from the other party. It may also involve a reciprocal agreement between enterprises where they agree on a reciprocal basis to cease production or supply of certain different products and agree to obtain them from the other(s). Specialization agreement may generate economic efficiency in the form of economies of scale or scope and better technologies. However, it may also raise competitive concerns if either one or both parties have significant market power. It may be used as a form of coordination to increase prices, reduce output and foreclose the market for a third party if it relates to the production of essential inputs.[353]

C. Standardization

396. Standardization agreement is an agreement between two or more enterprises as to the technical or quality requirement that the existing or future products, production process or services need to comply with. Standardization agreement may bring about pro-competitive benefits, such as increasing product quality, reducing transaction costs and facilitating new technology and innovation. However, standardization may also have a foreclosure effect if it is used in an anticompetitive manner. For example, if the technology becomes a standard, other competing technology may be prevented from participating in the standard-setting process or competitors may be denied effective access to the standards when the standard has been set by either full denial of access to a standard or grant of access to a standard in a discriminatory manner.[354]

D. Joint Production

397. Joint production agreement involves a collaboration between two or more enterprises to produce certain products jointly. Joint production may bring about economic efficiency by reducing the cost of operation. It may also raise competitive concerns if either one or both parties have significant market power. It may be used as a form of coordination to increase prices, reduce output and foreclose the market for a third party if it relates to the production of essential inputs.[355]

---

353. Guidelines on the applicability of Article 101 of the Treaty on the Functioning of the European Union to horizontal cooperation agreements, https://eur-lex.europa.eu/legal-content/EN/TXT/PDF/?uri=CELEX:52011XC0114(04)&from=EN *see also* Slaughter & May, The EU competition rules on horizontal agreements: A guide to the assessment of horizontal agreements (including the European Commission's guidelines on horizontal cooperation and the block exemption regulations on R&D and specialization agreement) June 2016.

354. Guidelines on the applicability of Article 101 of the Treaty on the Functioning of the European Union to horizontal cooperation agreements, https://eur-lex.europa.eu/legalcontent/EN/TXT/PDF/?uri=CELEX:52011XC0114(04)&from=EN *see also* Slaughter & May, The EU competition rules on horizontal agreements: A guide to the assessment of horizontal agreements (including the European Commission's guidelines on horizontal cooperation and the block exemption regulations on R&D and specialization agreement) June 2016.

355. Guidelines on the applicability of Article 101 of the Treaty on the Functioning of the European Union to horizontal cooperation agreements, https://eur-lex.europa.eu/legalcontent/EN/TXT/PDF/?uri=CELEX:52011XC0114(04)&from=EN *see also* Slaughter & May, The EU competition rules

E. *Joint Purchasing*

398. Joint purchasing agreement is an agreement between two or more enterprises to buy products from sellers jointly. Joint purchasing agreement has significant procompetitive effects and generates economic efficiency in the form of cost-savings (e.g., lower purchase price and transportation costs) and economies of scale. Joint purchasing is a common practice for SME to obtain volume discounts, vis-à-vis their large competitors.[356]

399. Joint purchasing agreement is likely to raise competitive concerns if parties to the agreement have market power in either purchasing or selling market. When joint purchasers have market powers in the purchasing market, they may force the seller to lower the purchase price but do not pass the low price to end consumer. The joint purchasers may restrict the ability of competing purchasers to get access to efficient suppliers or force the sellers to reduce production to increase prices. However, if the joint purchasers are also competitors selling products at the downstream market, joint purchasing may become a platform to collude between them.[357]

F. *Joint-Selling*

400. Enterprises may enter into a joint-selling agreement (e.g., through an association) to jointly sell or distribute their substitute products. Joint-selling may have pro-competitive benefits for SME by increasing their bargaining powers, vis-à-vis their large purchaser. Joint-selling can lead to cost-savings through join-procurement and reduce the cost of transportation and distribution, etc. However, joint-selling can be a disguise of a cartel, such as price-fixing, market sharing or even exchange of sensitive commercial information.[358]

---

on horizontal agreements: A guide to the assessment of horizontal agreements (including the European Commission's guidelines on horizontal cooperation and the block exemption regulations on R&D and specialization agreement) June 2016.

356. Guidelines on the applicability of Article 101 of the Treaty on the Functioning of the European Union to horizontal cooperation agreements, https://eur-lex.europa.eu/legalcontent/EN/TXT/PDF/?uri=CELEX:52011XC0114(04)&from=EN *see also* Slaughter & May, The EU competition rules on horizontal agreements: A guide to the assessment of horizontal agreements (including the European Commission's guidelines on horizontal cooperation and the block exemption regulations on R&D and specialization agreement) June 2016.

357. Guidelines on the applicability of Article 101 of the Treaty on the Functioning of the European Union to horizontal cooperation agreements, https://eur-lex.europa.eu/legalcontent/EN/TXT/PDF/?uri=CELEX:52011XC0114(04)&from=EN *see also* Slaughter & May, The EU competition rules on horizontal agreements: A guide to the assessment of horizontal agreements (including the European Commission's guidelines on horizontal cooperation and the block exemption regulations on R&D and specialization agreement) June 2016.

358. Guidelines on the applicability of Article 101 of the Treaty on the Functioning of the European Union to horizontal cooperation agreements, https://eur-lex.europa.eu/legalcontent/EN/TXT/PDF/?uri=CELEX:52011XC0114(04)&from=EN *see also* Slaughter & May, The EU competition rules

§2. VERTICAL AGREEMENTS

401. Vertical agreement is defined as 'an agreement between enterprises each of which operates at a different level in the production and distribution chain'.[359] Normally, the Commission regards vertical less harmful than horizontal agreement.

402. In determining whether a vertical agreement is anticompetitive, the Commission will take into consideration the following.

403. First, a vertical agreement is normally anticompetitive when one of the parties (either seller or buyer) has enough market power to enable it to influence the conduct of the other party in the market. Only when one of the parties has market power, a vertical agreement may reduce competition either at the market in which seller competes (upstream) or the market in which buyer competes (downstream). However, it is important to note that if the market power of a party to a vertical agreement is very significant (e.g., the market share of the party is 60% and above), the Commission will consider the case under an abuse of dominant position provision.[360]

404. Second, price vertical restraint is more problematic than non-price vertical restraints. Restraints on price will limit or restrict price competition among resellers in the downstream market. It reduces the ability of the resellers to independently determine the prices that they impose on end users. An RPM is a form of price vertical restraint which is prohibited under section 4 of the CA 2010. RPM occurs 'when an upstream seller imposes a fixed or a minimum price that a downstream buyer must resell'.[361] The Commission will take a strong stance against minimum RPM[362] as it reduces the ability of consumers to purchase at a lower price. Another form of RPM, such as maximum or recommended retail pricing, may be deemed to be anticompetitive if it 'serves as a focal point for downstream collusion'.[363] RPM may be used by retailers in a downstream market to enforce a cartel among themselves by asking a manufacturer in an upstream market to set the retail price at which the retailers should sell. In this situation, the Commission may treat this arrangement as a horizontal price fixing.[364]

405. In *MyCC v. Coca-Cola,*[365] Coca-Cola Refreshments issued several notices to targeted supermarkets and hypermarkets in Peninsular Malaysia in 2018 with an

---

on horizontal agreements: A guide to the assessment of horizontal agreements (including the European Commission's guidelines on horizontal cooperation and the block exemption regulations on R&D and specialization agreement) June 2016.

359. Section 2 of Competition Act 2010.
360. Paragraph 3.12, *MyCC Guidelines on Chapter 1 Prohibition.*
361. Paragraph 3.15, *MyCC Guidelines on Chapter 1 Prohibition.*
362. Paragraph 3.14, *MyCC Guidelines on Chapter 1 Prohibition.*
363. Paragraph 3.15, *MyCC Guidelines on Chapter 1 Prohibition.*
364. Paragraph 3.16, *MyCC Guidelines on Chapter 1 Prohibition.*
365. *MyCC v. Coca-Cola Bottlers (Malaysia) Sdn Bhd & Coca-Cola Refreshments Malaysia Sdn Bhd* (No. 700-1/3/2/2018).

attachment containing a product list with recommended retail price (RRP) and recommended consumer price (RCP). The RRP is 'the price at which the customers are required to purchase products from Coca-Cola Refreshments'[366] while RCP 'acts as a guide for the sale of a particular product to the end consumers'.[367] The notices were part of distributor agreements entered into between Coca-Cola Refreshments and its distributors. The distributor agreements clearly state that the RRP is not binding and only acts as a reference.[368]

406. In the *Coca-Cola* case, MyCC concluded that in analysing RPM, 'the Commission is required to carry out an analysis on the effect of the conduct in question on the relevant market'.[369] This means that MyCC needs to determine the relevant market and market power of the parties involved in the agreements. MyCC defined the relevant market as carbonated soft drinks,[370] which are different from other beverages in terms of the characteristic of the product (carbonate) and their intended use.[371] MyCC also found that the market shares of Coca-Cola are above the indicative threshold of 25% (*de minimis*/safe harbour) as stipulated under the *MyCC Guidelines on Chapter 1 Prohibition*: *Anticompetitive Agreement*.[372] However, after a thorough investigation, the Commission found that the RCP issued by Coca-Cola was not strictly complied with by the targeted supermarkets and hypermarkets and did not restrict the ability of the supermarkets and hypermarkets to set their price independently. Neither had Coca-Cola induced the supermarkets and hypermarkets by way of incentives or promotion to ensure adherence to the RRP.

407. Non-price restraints may, on the other hand, foreclose the market or part of the market to competitors in the upstream or downstream market. Anticompetitive non-price vertical agreement may not be considered having a significant effect if the individual market shares (seller or buyer) does not exceed 25% of the relevant market.[373]

408. Third, normally, the Commission adopts an effect-based approach to assess whether a vertical agreement restricts competition ('restriction by effect'). In determining whether a vertical agreement has the effect of significantly preventing, restricting or distorting competition, the Commission will consider few factors, such

366. *MyCC v. Coca-Cola Bottlers (Malaysia) Sdn Bhd & Coca-Cola Refreshments Malaysia Sdn Bhd* (No. 700-1/3/2/2018) para. 82.
367. *MyCC v. Coca-Cola Bottlers (Malaysia) Sdn Bhd & Coca-Cola Refreshments Malaysia Sdn Bhd* (No. 700-1/3/2/2018) para. 84.
368. *MyCC v. Coca-Cola Bottlers (Malaysia) Sdn Bhd & Coca-Cola Refreshments Malaysia Sdn Bhd* (No. 700-1/3/2/2018) para. 85.
369. *MyCC v. Coca-Cola Bottlers (Malaysia) Sdn Bhd & Coca-Cola Refreshments Malaysia Sdn Bhd* (No. 700-1/3/2/2018) para. 58.
370. *MyCC v. Coca-Cola Bottlers (Malaysia) Sdn Bhd & Coca-Cola Refreshments Malaysia Sdn Bhd* (No. 700-1/3/2/2018) para. 64.
371. *MyCC v. Coca-Cola Bottlers (Malaysia) Sdn Bhd & Coca-Cola Refreshments Malaysia Sdn Bhd* (No. 700-1/3/2/2018) para. 67.
372. *MyCC v. Coca-Cola Bottlers (Malaysia) Sdn Bhd & Coca-Cola Refreshments Malaysia Sdn Bhd* (No. 700-1/3/2/2018) para. 75.
373. Paragraph 3.17, *MyCC Guidelines on Chapter 1 Prohibition*.

as the market power of the party imposing such restraints, how and to what extent the vertical agreement contributes to the foreclosure of a market in a vertical relationship, any procompetitive effect or justification arises from the vertical agreement, the extent of entry barriers to the market under investigation and the existence of buyer power which can countervail the power of the sellers.[374]

409. In *MyCC v. Containerchain and Four Container Depot Operators,*[375] the Commission found that Containerchain, a company providing information technology services to shipping and logistic companies had entered into vertical agreements by way of concerted practice with the CDOs which had the effect of the CDOs increasing the DGCs imposing on their customers from MYR 5 to MYR 25 and the CDOs fixing a rebate of MYR 5 offered to hauliers in respect to DGC. Containerchain had approached four CDOs to use its IT system to manage the inflow and outflow of empty containers and informed the CDOs that Containerchain System could be 'one of the catalysts to inform the industry to increase DGC' and 'the implementation of the Containerchain system was a great opportunity for the CDOs to increase their DGC'.[376] The Commission argued that the Containerchain had influenced, facilitated and coordinated the CDOs to increase their DGC and to fix the rebates to be offered to the hauliers in respect of the DGC in the market for the provision of empty container storage, maintenance and handling services within a 5–15 km radius of the Penang Port.

410. In the above case, the Commission also found that the Containerchain system controls about 53.33% of the CDOs operating in the Penang Port which exceeded the 25% indicative 'safe harbour' as stated in the *MyCC Guidelines on Chapter 1 Prohibition.*[377] The target CDOs also have total combine market shares of 64.64%.[378] In elaborating the effect of the anticompetitive arrangement, the Commission stated that 'Containerchain's conduct of influencing the behaviour of the Target CDOs via bringing the CDOs together in meetings; disseminating and sharing information about their revised DGCs; and coordinating the implementation of the agreed revised DGC as well as the rebate are non-trivial'[379] 'have the effect of significantly preventing, restricting or distorting competition in the market'.[380]

374. Paragraph 3.13, *MyCC Guidelines on Chapter 1 Prohibition.*
375. *MyCC v. Containerchain & Four Container Depot Operators* (No. MyCC. 700.2.005.2013).
376. *MyCC v. Containerchain & Four Container Depot Operators* (No. MyCC. 700.2.005.2013) para. 148.
377. *MyCC v. Containerchain & Four Container Depot Operators* (No. MyCC. 700.2.005.2013) para. 152.
378. *MyCC v. Containerchain & Four Container Depot Operators* (No. MyCC. 700.2.005.2013) para. 153.
379. *MyCC v. Containerchain & Four Container Depot Operators* (No. MyCC. 700.2.005.2013) para. 154.
380. *MyCC v. Containerchain & Four Container Depot Operators* (No. MyCC. 700.2.005.2013) para. 155.

I. Distribution

411. An efficient distribution channel is very important for a manufacturer or producer to supply its products to the market. A producer or manufacturer may choose to set up its own retail outlets or establish a subsidiary company to undertake the distribution tasks (vertical integration). A producer who has its own distribution arm is referred to as vertical integration. It is important to note that an agreement between enterprises within a single economic unit, such as the agreement between the parent and subsidiary company falls outside the ambit of section 4 of the CA 2010. A producer may instead appoint an independent distributor who acts as a reseller to distribute the products to as many consumers as possible, which include both the intermediaries and end consumers.

412. A producer may enter into various vertical arrangements with independent distributors, such as exclusive distributorship agreement, selective distribution agreement, exclusive agreement, etc. In order to determine whether a vertical or distribution agreement is anticompetitive, the Commission will assess whether the agreement has the effect of significantly restricting, preventing or distorting competition and whether the agreement produces procompetitive benefits.

A. *Exclusive Distributorship*

413. A supplier may give an exclusive geographical market to a buyer or distributor which restricts competition at the downstream level (intra-brand competition), or a seller may agree to only supply its products to a distributor if the later agrees that to resell the products to a particular group of customers. An exclusive distribution agreement may be examined on a case-to-case basis by assessing whether the agreement has a significant effect on any level of competition. An exclusive agreement may raise competition concerns if there is no effective or significant inter-brand competition (competition among suppliers).[381]

B. *Exclusive Dealing*

414. A supplier of a product may impose a condition that the buyer must buy all of its requirements or a substantial proportion of its supplies from the seller. The Commission may assess whether an exclusive dealing restricts the ability of competitors to compete. If the seller manages to capture a substantial part of the downstream market, an exclusive dealing arrangement may foreclose a substantial part of the downstream market to other suppliers.[382]

---

381. Paragraphs 3.21 & 3.22, *MyCC Guidelines on Chapter 1 Prohibition.*
382. Paragraph 3.19, *MyCC Guidelines on Chapter 1 Prohibition.*

C. Selective Distribution

415. Under a selective distribution system, a producer 'establishes a system in which the products can be bought and resold only by authorized distributors and retailers'.[383] A selective distribution system may reduce intra-brand competition 'foreclosure of certain type(s) of distributors and softening of competition and facilitation of collusion between suppliers or buyers'.[384]

416. However, the selective distribution agreement may fall outside section 4 of the CA 2010 if, for example, distributors or retailers are chosen by a producer on the basis of objective criteria (purely qualitative in nature). Selective distribution system normally involves high-quality and technically advanced consumer goods, such as luxury car and watch.[385] Due to the nature of the goods, a producer will only supply its products to distributors that can guarantee the distribution of the products through a high-quality location and 'specialist sales staff and a suitable after-sales service' to protect the brand image of the producer's product.[386]

417. A producer under selective distribution agreement may require the distributor to comply with pre-sale services to ensure the product's qualities and capabilities for consumers. Therefore, though selective distribution agreement may prevent intra-brand competition by restricting unauthorized distributors and retailers from supplying the products, it may encourage inter-brand competition (encouraging more producers to enter into the market) and prevent free-rider on the pre-sale services provided by the authorized distributors.[387]

D. Franchising

418. Franchising system allows a franchisor to set up a uniform business network with assistance from franchisee without incurring a substantial investment. Franchisee can, on the other hand, enter into a market relying on the franchisor's goodwill and reputable network against a minimal franchise fee. In other words, the franchising system may generate procompetitive benefits encouraging new competitors to enter into a market and increase inter-brand competition. Some restrictions imposed on the licensees do not normally give rise to competitive concerns as it forms an essential part of the franchising system to 'maintain the common identity and reputation of the franchised network' and to protect the know-how and technical assistance provided by the franchisor.[388] This includes as an obligation to

383. *See* Richard Whish & David Bailey, *Competition Law*, 2nd edn 680 (Oxford University Press, 2015).
384. *See,* for example, EU Guidelines on Vertical Restraints (2010/C 130/01) p. 175.
385. *See* Richard Whish & David Bailey, *Competition Law*, 2nd edn 680 (Oxford University Press, 2015).
386. *See* Richard Whish & David Bailey, *Competition Law*, 2nd edn 680 (Oxford University Press, 2015).
387. *See,* for example, EU Guidelines on Vertical Restraints (2010/C 130/01) p. 185.
388. *See,* for example, EU Guidelines on Vertical Restraints (2010/C 130/01) p. 190.

maintain a certain standard of services or uniform business model, not to operate a similar business during the period of the contract, and to sell only product supplies by the franchisor and not to sell the business without the consent of the franchisor.[389]

II. Technology Licensing

419. According to the MyCC Guidelines on IPRs and Competition Law, 'the promotion of intellectual property rights (IPRs) incentivises enterprises to be more innovative and to improve the quality of their products and services, which would then provide wider choices at more competitive prices to consumers. In a similar manner, competition law aims to prohibit or restrain anti-competitive activities which may result in distortion in the market. The conduct of IP owners may, in some circumstances, make it difficult for rival companies to sell substitute products and technology in the market. Intellectual property owners may also reach a dominant position in the market such that they are able to dictate unfair terms and conditions on other market players'.[390]

420. Any conduct related to the IPRs may fall under the purview of the CA 2010 if it involves an anticompetitive agreement (under section 4 of the CA 2010) or abuse of dominant position by the IPRs holders proven to be dominant in the market (under section 10 of the CA 2010).

421. It is important to note that there are few mechanisms under the IP regime which can be used to curb or control abuse of the dominant position of the IPR holders. For example, Part X of the Patents Act 1983 allows for the issuance of compulsory licence if there is no local production, no product produced for sale in Malaysia, or the product is sold at an unreasonably high price or not enough to meet public demand. Compulsory licence may also be issued under section 27(1)(c) of the Industrial Designs of Integrated Circuit Act 2000 and section 36(1) of the Protection of New Plant Varieties Act 2004.

422. Under section 84 of the Patent Act, a Government agency or a third person appointed by the Minister may, subject to complying with certain conditions, exploit a patented invention at any time on several grounds including anticompetitive practices. Section 45 of this Act provides that 'any clause or condition in a license contract shall be invalid in so far as it imposes upon the licensee, in the industrial or commercial field, restrictions not derived from the rights conferred by this Part on the owner of the patent, or unnecessary for the safeguarding of such rights. Examples of such invalid clauses would include tying, mandatory package, post-expiration royalties, non-competition clause, exclusive dealings, grant-back, and price restrictions.

---

389. *See,* for example, *Pronuptia v. Schillgalis*, Case 161/84 (1986).

390. Paragraph 3.2, *Guidelines on Intellectual Property Rights and Competition Law.*

423. Generally, the market definition for conduct involving IP may be divided into three categories.

Good/Product Markets

424. According to the Guidelines on IPRs and Competition Law, it refers to 'markets incorporating IPRs, including final or intermediate goods made using the IP'.[391] In determining the relevant product market, all close substitutes for the goods or services under investigation will be included.

Technology Markets

425. According to the Guidelines on IPRs and Competition Law, it refers to 'the processes or technology incorporating the IP (technology market)'.[392] In determining the relevant market, the Commission will consider 'technologies that are close enough to constitute substitutes to the licensed technology that they significantly prevent the exercise of market power with respect to intellectual property that is licensed'.[393]

Innovation Market or R&D Market

426. According to the Guidelines on IPRs and Competition Law, it refers to 'the intangible knowledge or know-how that constitutes the IP (innovation or R&D)'.[394] An innovation and R&D market include 'the assets (technologies, laboratory, equipment, etc.) comprising R&D related to the identification of commercialisable products or directed to particular new or improved goods or processes, and the close substitutes for that research and development'.[395]

A. Patent Licensing

427. Licensing agreement may involve both horizontal and vertical licensing agreement. The relationship between the IP owner and the licensees is normally vertical in nature. IPR confers certain exclusivity rights to the IPR owners to exploit their innovation and prevent others from exploiting the fruit of their innovation. However, the IPR owners may allow other parties to exploit their IPRs through a licensing agreement. However, it is stated that 'while distinguishing between horizontal and vertical agreements is usually straight forward when considering agreements in production and distribution, it is sometimes more difficult to make the

391. Paragraph 4.3, *Guidelines on Intellectual Property Rights and Competition Law.*
392. Paragraph 4.2, *Guidelines on Intellectual Property Rights and Competition Law.*
393. Paragraph 4.4, *Guidelines on Intellectual Property Rights and Competition Law.*
394. Paragraph 4.2, *Guidelines on Intellectual Property Rights and Competition Law.*
395. Paragraph 4.7, *Guidelines on Intellectual Property Rights and Competition Law.*

distinction when IPRs are involved. Licensing agreements that appear on the surface, to be vertical (between enterprises at different levels in the production/distribution chain) may also have an adverse effect on horizontal competition in either licensing or product markets'.[396]

1. Vertical Restrictions Which May Fall under Section 4(1) of the CA 2010 Including

Territorial and Field-of-Use Restrictions

428. A territorial restriction limits a licensee to produce, use or sell the licensed products or processes to a particular geographical area specified in the license while a field-of-use restriction limits 'the scope of use of the patent or copyright to a particular purpose or use as specified in the license'.[397] Generally, territorial and field-of-use restrictions are not considered to be anticompetitive as both 'enable the licensee to exploit the licensor's technology to the fullest within the use and territory specified'.[398] For example, it is common that a patented product, such as drug can be used in different application, i.e., to cure human and livestock. The field-of-use restriction 'would lead to a more effective exploitation of the patent since the patent owner, or a particular licensee, may not have sufficient resources to practise the invention in all fields'.[399]

429. Nevertheless, territorial and field-of-use restrictions may raise competition concerns if they: '(i) foreclose access to competing technology; (ii) prevent licensees from developing their own technology; (iii) facilitate market allocation; (iv) fix price for any products or service supplied by the licensee; or (v) restrict resale subsequent to the first authorised sale of the patented product (the exhaustion doctrine)'.[400]

Tying

430. Tying can be divided into two, namely, tie-in clause and tie-out clause. Tie-in clause refers to a situation when 'the licensor or vendor makes the purchase, hire or use of a patented article or invention conditional on the purchaser, hirer or licensee also acquiring other goods from the patent owner or his nominee'. Tied-out refers to a situation where 'the purchaser, hirer or licensee is prevented from using certain goods, materials or processes not supplied or owned by the patent owner'.[401] Tying arrangement may be used to the extent a patent's owner rights to

396. Paragraph 6.3, *Guidelines on Intellectual Property Rights and Competition Law.*
397. Paragraph 6.10, *Guidelines on Intellectual Property Rights and Competition Law.*
398. Paragraph 6.10, *Guidelines on Intellectual Property Rights and Competition Law.*
399. Paragraph 6.10, *Guidelines on Intellectual Property Rights and Competition Law.*
400. Paragraph 6.11, *Guidelines on Intellectual Property Rights and Competition Law.*
401. Paragraph 6.14, *Guidelines on Intellectual Property Rights and Competition Law.*

non-patented products. Tying may raise competition concerns when: '(i) the licensor has market power in the tying product; (ii) the arrangement has an adverse effect on competition in the relevant market for the tying product or the tied product; and (iii) efficiency justifications for the arrangement do not outweigh the anti-competitive effects'.[402]

Grant – Backs

431. Technology licensing includes both patented and non-patented IPR, such as know-how and trade secret. Grant-backs refers to 'a clause in a technology license which provides for license or assignment to the licensor of any improvement, patented or non-patented (including trade secret), by a licensee in the products or processes of the licensed patent'.[403] Grant-back arrangement can have procompetitive effect as 'the licensor is able to benefit from any improvements to his licensed technology and he will be more willing to grant the licence in the first place'.[404] However, the grant-back clause is likely to be anticompetitive if the clause requires that full and complete patent rights to the improved technology to be granted to the licensor without adequate compensation given to the licensee. In this situation, the grant-back arrangement discourages the licensee from improving the licensed products.

2. Horizontal Agreement

432. Certain horizontal agreements that relate to the IP may fall under section 4(1) or section 4(2) of the CA 2010. Price fixing agreement is considered to be a hardcore restriction and is likely to fall under section 4(2) of the CA 2010. An agreement to fix trading conditions may fall under section 4(1) or section 4(2) of the CA 2010. For example, two trademark owners who licensed their trademarks and trade secrets of producing certain products may enter into a JV agreement to supply raw material to produce licensed products. If they agreed to impose on their respective licensees the obligation to obtain the raw material supply from this JV as a condition to using the license this may have the effect of restricting the licensees to source the raw material from other suppliers who could supply them at a cheaper price. This conduct could fall under section 4(1) or section 4(2) of the CA 2010.[405]

433. Other examples of horizontal agreements relating to the IP include the following.

Limit of Production Through Pay- for-Delay

434. Pay-for-delay agreement refers to an agreement between patent owners and generic producers whereby the patent owners agree to pay the producers of generic

402. Paragraph 6.15, *Guidelines on Intellectual Property Rights and Competition Law.*
403. Paragraph 6.16, *Guidelines on Intellectual Property Rights and Competition Law.*
404. Paragraph 6.18, *Guidelines on Intellectual Property Rights and Competition Law.*
405. Illustration 4, para. 6.23, *Guidelines on Intellectual Property Rights and Competition Law.*

drug a certain amount of money to delay the production and release of generic drugs to the market before the expiration of the patent. Pay-for-delay may have the effect of delaying competition in the market as the original drug producers may expand their monopolistic power even after the expiration of the after. Thus, the pay-for-delay agreement may infringe section 4(2) or abuse of dominant position under section 10 of the CA 2010.[406]

Cross-Licensing and Patent Pool

435. Cross-licensing arrangement allows two or more patent owners to use each other's patents. Generally, cross-licensing agreements are procompetitive and 'could be beneficial to both the competitors and consumers'.[407] Since the boundaries of patents are often unclear and can only be resolved through expensive litigation, cross-licensing arrangement 'allows new products to be brought more quickly into the market without the need for expansive litigation'.[408] Nevertheless, cross-licensing could impede market access if the licence is restricted to certain members only.[409]

436. Patent pool, on the other hand, refers to 'an agreement among parties to contribute and share access to patented technologies under defined terms and conditions'.[410] The competitive effect of a patent pool depends on whether they involve a complementary/essential patent or substitute technologies. If a patent pool involves substitute technologies, 'competition between substitute technologies may be reduced in the licensing market and so foreclose some of the substitute technologies to licensees thereby reducing competition in the downstream product market'.[411]

3. Abuse of Dominant Position

437. According to the Guidelines on IPRs and Competition Law, market power should not be inferred from the ownership of IPRs only as 'there will often be sufficient actual or potential close substitutes for such product, process or work to prevent the existence of market power'.[412] However, IPR may, in certain circumstances, confer some market power by creating barriers to entry and 'this in itself would be a legal barrier to other competitors from having access to the relevant market'.[413]

---

406. Paragraph 6.26, *Guidelines on Intellectual Property Rights and Competition Law.*
407. Paragraph 6.28, *Guidelines on Intellectual Property Rights and Competition Law.*
408. Paragraph 6.28, *Guidelines on Intellectual Property Rights and Competition Law.*
409. Paragraph 6.30, *Guidelines on Intellectual Property Rights and Competition Law.*
410. Paragraph 6.29, *Guidelines on Intellectual Property Rights and Competition Law.*
411. Paragraph 6.29, *Guidelines on Intellectual Property Rights and Competition Law.*
412. Paragraph 8.3, *Guidelines on Intellectual Property Rights and Competition Law.*
413. Paragraph 8.4, *Guidelines on Intellectual Property Rights and Competition Law.*

438. Based on section 10(1) of the CA 2010, a dominant position can be occupied either singly or collectively and 'in relation to IPRs, collective dominance may occur through various ways, including patent pooling, cross licensing, etc.'.[414] For instance, 'when two or more enterprises were to pool their patents, they appear to be a collective entity in the market'.[415]

439. Abusive conduct can be exploitative, i.e., conduct that directly harms consumers and exclusionary, i.e., conduct that prevent an efficient enterprise from competing in the market. The Commission is only concerned with the impact of particular conduct on the competitive process and not on competitors. For example, a patent and innovation allow an enterprise to enjoy a dominant position in the market due to lower production costs – the reward of innovation. Therefore, pricing just above cost would not be regarded as anti-competitive even though it may drive competitors, 'who do not have access to the patented technology out of the market'.[416]

440. The exercise of legitimate of IPR may affect competition in the short run. However, in determining the effect of exclusionary conduct, the Commission will not only focus on the short term impact (e.g., on price and output) of any conduct complained of but also the impact of the conduct on competition in the long term.[417]

441. The abusive conduct which relates to the IPRs includes but are not limited to the following.

Imposing unfair selling and purchasing price or trading conditions

442. Unfair conduct includes excessive price and post-expiration royalty. In determining whether the price is excessive, the Commission will take into consideration several factors including cost of development, return of investment and reasonable profit.[418] The Commission will treat the issue of excessive price with great caution so as not to reduce the incentive to innovate as the nature of the IPR requires the owner of the IP to impose higher price to recover R&D costs.

443. The imposition of post-expiration royalty is another form of unfair conduct by the IPR owner. It refers to the 'imposition of royalty fee after the expiration of patent rights'.[419] However, in some situations, post-expiration royalty may be allowed. For example, if a licensing agreement relates to both the use of patent rights and trade secrets, any royalty payment beyond the date of the expiration of the last of the patent involved may be valid in relation to a post-expiration payment intended for the use of trade secrets.[420]

---

414. Paragraph 8.6, *Guidelines on Intellectual Property Rights and Competition Law.*
415. Paragraph 8.5, *Guidelines on Intellectual Property Rights and Competition Law.*
416. Paragraph 8.11, *Guidelines on Intellectual Property Rights and Competition Law.*
417. Paragraph 8.12, *Guidelines on Intellectual Property Rights and Competition Law.*
418. Paragraph 8.15, *Guidelines on Intellectual Property Rights and Competition Law.*
419. Paragraph 8.17, *Guidelines on Intellectual Property Rights and Competition Law.*
420. *See* illustration 13, para. 8.17, *Guidelines on Intellectual Property Rights and Competition Law.*

Non-competition Clause

444. A licensing agreement may incorporate a clause restricting a licensee from obtaining patents, know-how or trademarks from other companies in relation to the manufacture or sale of competing products[421] or restricting a licensee to manufacture any other products other than those covered by the patent licensed. In the area of patent licensing, for example, the non-compete clause may have the effect of prohibiting the use of other competing technologies or the production of competing goods not covered by the patent licensed.

Product Hopping

445. Product hopping refers to 'a tactic by which brand name such as pharmaceutical companies can try to obstruct generic competition and preserve monopoly rights on a patented drug by making modest reformulations or incremental changes that offer little or no therapeutic advantages'.[422] This strategy is normally used by an original drug manufacturer to delay the entry of generic competition into the market by withdrawing its original drug before the expiration of the patent and forcing the consumers to switch to the reformulated brand drug. In determining the exclusionary effect of product hoping behaviour, it is 'necessary to distinguish between a conduct that defeats a competitor because of efficiency and consumer satisfaction; and a conduct that impedes competition through means other than competition on the merits'.[423] The Commission will also consider whether the patent owner seeks to force (hard switch) or merely persuade the consumers (soft switch) to switch to the reformulated drug. If the patent owner still continues to sell the first drug brand even though he/she had already stopped promoting it, it is unlikely the conduct will raise anticompetitive concerns.

Refusal to License IPRs

446. Generally, an IP owner is under no obligation to grant a license for the use of his IPRs. In determining whether the refusal to supply is abusive, the Commission needs to distinguish between primary and secondary market involving the IPRs. Refusal to license IPRs in the primary market (i.e., technology and product market) would not normally be anticompetitive. However, when the technology or product is a critical and indispensable input to a derivative product, a refusal to license by the dominant enterprise may constitute an abusive conduct if it harms competition in the secondary market, prevent the emergence of the new product and the refusal is without any commercial justification.[424]

Mandatory Patent Package

447. Mandatory package refers to a situation where 'the patent owner refuses to grant a license under one or more of his/her patents unless the licensee accepts and

---

421. Paragraph 8.19, *Guidelines on Intellectual Property Rights and Competition Law.*
422. Paragraph 8.20, *Guidelines on Intellectual Property Rights and Competition Law.*
423. Illustration 5, para. 8.20, *Guidelines on Intellectual Property Rights and Competition Law.*
424. Illustration 16, para. 8.24, *Guidelines on Intellectual Property Rights and Competition Law.*

pays for additional patents which are not required by him/her'.[425] In considering whether a mandatory patent package is anticompetitive, the Commission will take into consideration whether there is an element of coercion or whether the package license is purely voluntary. Therefore, 'it is only where the patent owner refuses to grant a licence under less than all of his patents, or requires a licensee to accept a licence for unwanted or inapplicable patents in order to obtain the use of the desired patents, that the practice is condemned as mandatory or coercive patent package licensing'.[426]

448. However, a mandatory package may be allowed when it involves blocking or complementary patents, i.e., when two or more patents covered a single product, and the product could not be manufactured under one patent without infringing the other.[427]

Standard-Essential Patent

449. Standard-essential patent (SEP) is 'a patent that protects technology essential to a standard'.[428] When the production of certain goods needs to comply with an agreed and accepted standard, it would be possible to manufacture the products by obtaining a licence to use the technology covered by one or more SEPs and the manufacturers in the relevant industry need to use the SEPs to ensure that their products comply with the agreed standard. Companies owning the SEPs may hold a dominant position in the market and has the ability to foreclose or impair competition by engaging in patent hold-up by '(i) extracting excessive royalties; (ii) compelling the acceptance of unfair cross licensing terms; or (iii) abandoning the invalidity proceedings'.[429]

450. In the case where a patent is set as by the government authority, refusal to license the essential patent could be considered abusive. When a patented technology becomes a standard, 'the patent owners should not be allowed to prevent the use of the patented technologies if their competitors are willing to accept a licence and pay a reasonable royalty'.[430] In this case, the SEP holders are prohibited from increasing the royalty rate simply because the value of the patent has been increased as a result of its SEP status (the evaluation from patent to SEP).

B. Trademark Licensing

451. Sections 4 and 10 of the CA 2010 prohibit anticompetitive IP arrangements/agreements or conduct, which includes trademark licensing. Please see discussion at paragraphs 413 and 425 above.

425. Paragraph 8.29, *Guidelines on Intellectual Property Rights and Competition Law.*
426. Paragraph 8.30, *Guidelines on Intellectual Property Rights and Competition Law.*
427. Illustration 17, para. 8.31, *Guidelines on Intellectual Property Rights and Competition Law.*
428. Paragraph 8.39, *Guidelines on Intellectual Property Rights and Competition Law.*
429. Paragraph 8.40, *Guidelines on Intellectual Property Rights and Competition Law.*
430. Paragraph 8.42, *Guidelines on Intellectual Property Rights and Competition Law.*

C. Know-How and Trade Secret Licensing

452. Sections 4 and 10 of the CA 2010 prohibit anticompetitive IP arrangements/agreements or conduct, which includes trademark licensing. Please see discussion at paragraphs 412, 413 and 424 above.

Chapter 2. Dominant Undertakings' Prohibited Practices

453. Section 10(1) of the CA 2010 prohibits an enterprise holding a dominant position in the relevant market from abusing its dominant position. The Act does not prevent an enterprise from being a dominant or monopoly but rather regulates the behaviour of such an enterprise from engaging in certain conduct that its non-dominant company can do. A dominant enterprise, especially if it is the only producer or supplier in the relevant market, has a special obligation not to disrupt or distort the normal process of competition. Nevertheless, the Act does not prohibit a dominant enterprise from engaging in certain conduct if it has reasonable commercial justifications or if the conduct is a reasonable commercial response to market entry or conduct of its competitor.[431]

454. For the sake of clarity and certainty, section 10(2) of the CA 2010, laid down certain types of abusive conduct. The legal scheme under section 10(2) assists the Commission to focus its enforcement on certain common anticompetitive behaviour by a dominant enterprise. However, it is important to note that the list is not exhaustive and abuse of dominant position provision covers a wide range of abusive conduct. Abusive conducts that are not listed under section 10(2) of the CA 2010 may be dealt with under section 10(1) of the CA 2010.

455. The list of abusive conduct under section 10(2) of the CA 2010 contains both exploitative and exclusionary behaviour. However, it is important to note that the boundary between exploitative and exclusionary conduct is sometimes unclear. Some conduct may be both exploitative and exclusionary, such as predatory pricing and limit of production.

§1. Exploitative Practices

456. Exploitative abuse refers to 'the ability of an enterprise to maintain price above the competitive level for some time without worrying about whether consumers will switch to other products or worrying that new competitors will enter the market'.[432] In assessing the exploitative conduct, the Commission is more concerned about the effect of the conduct on consumers rather than competitors.

I. Excessive/Unfair Pricing

457. Section 10(2)(a) of the CA 2010 prohibits a dominant enterprise from imposing unfair purchase or selling price or other trading condition onto a supplier or customer.

431. Paragraph 1.4, *MyCC Guidelines on Chapter 2 Prohibition* (abuse of dominant position).
432. Paragraph 2.4, *MyCC Guidelines on Chapter 2 Prohibition* (abuse of dominant position).

458. The Act does not define what constitutes 'unfair purchasing or selling price'. Based on *MyCC Guidelines on Chapter 2 Prohibition*, unfair selling price is interpreted in the light of the ability of a dominant enterprise to impose excessive pricing (price above the competitive level) on its customers. Excessive pricing may be the outcome of market structure. For instance, an enterprise holding a monopolistic position may have the incentive to set a higher price to exploit consumers and reap excessive profits. Excessive pricing is only a matter of concern for the Commission if 'there is no likelihood that market forces will reduce dominance in a market'.[433]

459. There is no standard mechanism to determine whether prices are excessive. However, the Commission may, depending on the nature of the goods, take into account 'the actual price set in relation to the costs of supply and other factors such as the dominant enterprises profitability'.[434] The key point in determining excessive pricing is the level of profit margin or the enterprise's profitability. However, the CA 2010 and its subsequent guidelines do not suggest the level at which the profits would be considered as excessive.

460. Under MyCC Guidelines on IPRs and Competition law, in so far as it relates to the IP matters, the determination of excessive pricing, 'several factors, including cost of development, return of investment and reasonable profit will be taken into account'.[435] The Commission may follow several cost benchmarks including:

(i) the historical cost benchmark – a comparison between the prices of the dominant enterprise and the prices it has charged in the past;
(ii) the geographic benchmark – a comparison between the price of a given product over the different neighbouring market, and
(iii) the competitor's benchmark – a comparison between the royalty charged by the dominant enterprise with the royalty charged by its competitors.[436]

461. The word 'unfair purchase price' means that section 10(2)(a) also covers the conduct of a dominant or single buyer in the market. An enterprise may demand excessively lower price (below competitive level) from sellers if the enterprise concerned is the only buyer of the goods (known as monopsony) or faces little competition from other buyers. For example, a single buyer of agricultural products may force small farmers to sell their products at extremely low prices and may cease demand if the farmers refuse to lower their selling prices. The single buyer may then sell the goods to end users at a higher price to gain excessive profits.

462. Section 10(2)(a) condemns both unfair prices and trading conditions. Even though the imposition of trading conditions is a matter of contractual agreement

433. Paragraph 3.3, *MyCC Guidelines on Chapter 2 Prohibition* (abuse of dominant position).
434. Paragraph 3.4, *MyCC Guidelines on Chapter 2 Prohibition* (abuse of dominant position).
435. Paragraph 8.15, *MyCC Guidelines on Intellectual Property Rights and Competition Law.*
436. Paragraph 8.15, *MyCC Guidelines on Intellectual Property Rights and Competition Law.*

between parties, a dominant enterprise may dictate the terms and conditions of supply that it can be imposed on its customers. Since there is no or little competition in the market, the customers have no choice but to accept or agree with the unfair contract terms and conditions.

II. Discrimination

463. Section 10(2)(d) prohibits a dominant enterprise from 'applying different conditions to equivalent transactions with other trading parties to an extent that may:

(i) discourage new market entry or expansion or investment by an existing competitor;
(ii) force from the market or otherwise seriously damage an existing competitor which is no less efficient than the enterprise in a dominant position; or
(iii) harm competition in any market in which the dominant enterprise is participating or in any upstream or downstream market'.

464. Section 10(2)(d) condemns discriminatory behaviour of the dominant enterprise that harms competition in any market in which the dominant enterprise is participating or in any upstream or downstream market. In *MyCC v. MyEG*, the Commission found that:

> MyEG had been abusing its dominant position as the sole concession holder in the provision and management of online PLKS renewal services in Peninsular Malaysia (upstream market) in the market for the sale of the Mandatory Insurances for online PLKS renewal application (downstream market), by imposing different conditions to equivalent transactions with its competitors to an extent that it has harmed competition in the downstream market in which MyEG Commerce is participating.[437]

465. In *MyEG*, MyEG had been given a concession by the Government to provide and manage the online renewal of foreign workers permit. Employers who want to renew their foreign workers permit via MyEG online platform need to purchase mandatory insurance policies for their foreign workers. MyEG was also competing with other insurance companies and agents through its wholly owned subsidiary, MyEG Commerce in the sale of mandatory insurance coverage (MyEG Commerce is an agent of RHB Insurance). The Commission has come to a conclusion that MyEG had induced employers to purchase the mandatory insurance policies from MyEG Commerce for faster and easier renewal. MyEG competitors were 'facing unfavourable conditions as it would invariably take a longer time to obtain PLKS approval as their policies would have to be verified'.[438] If the employers purchase the mandatory insurance through other insurance companies or agents, they

437. *MyCC v. My E.G. Services Berhad* (MyCC (ED) 700-1/1/2/2015) para. 59.
438. *MyCC v. My E.G. Services Berhad* (MyCC (ED) 700-1/1/2/2015) para. 140.

'are required to scan and upload the policies for each foreign worker according to the scanning specification including the size of the file. Furthermore, the MyEG's server file size capacity was small and could not facilitate the uploading of the required documents'.[439] On the other hand, the mandatory insurances purchased directly from MyEG will be automatically verified. This according to the Commission amounts to applying different conditions to equivalent transaction.

466. The Commission has in its Final Decision stated that:

> 'it is apparent that the commission earned by MyEG from the sale of the Mandatory Insurances has increased tremendously over the period of January to June 2015. This is in line with the period when MyEG started to gain its dominant position in the upstream market since 5 January 2015. This further indicated that MyEG has been leveraging its market at the downstream market which is the sale of the Mandatory Insurances'.[440] Similarly, 'RHB Insurance via MyEG has captured increased sales within a short period whereas none of its competing insurance providers experienced any increase in sales despite the increase in number of foreign workers in Peninsular Malaysia.[441]

467. The Commission's decision was upheld by the CAT on 28 December 2017. In affirming the Commission's decision, the CAT stated that:

> In our view, the purchase of the Mandatory Insurances by the employers whether directly with MyEG such as RHB Insurance or with other insurance companies or agents would amount to as 'equivalent transaction' i.e. the same type of transaction. The issue of different methodology does not arise here.[442]

468. The CAT continued stating that:

> The facts of the case before us stated that there is a need for Mandatory Insurance verification imposed by JIM for the renewal of PLKS. The Mandatory Insurances purchased directly through MyEG are automatically verified. However, if the purchase of the Mandatory Insurances is through other than MyEG, it would appear there is additional step imposed by MyEG in the verification exercise. The end users (other insurance and agents) are required to take additional step to scan and upload the insurance policies for each foreign worker according to specification including the size of the file. The additional step constitutes a different condition to equivalent transaction … .The process invariably delays the renewal of PLKS and causes harm to companies in the

439. *MyCC v. My E.G. Services Berhad* (MyCC (ED) 700-1/1/2/2015) para. 141.
440. *MyCC v. My E.G. Services Berhad* (MyCC (ED) 700-1/1/2/2015) para. 150.
441. *MyCC v. My E.G. Services Berhad* (MyCC (ED) 700-1/1/2/2015) para. 153.
442. Paragraph 39, Decision of Competition Appeal Tribunal (Appeal No. TRP 3-2016, 28 Dec. 2017).

downstream market. In our view, it amounts to MyEG putting pressure on end users to purchase Mandatory Insurances from MyEG by virtue of its dominant position in the downstream market.[443]

469. The decision of the CAT was upheld by the High Court on 19 April 2019. In this case, the applicants, *MyEG Services Bhd* and *MyEG Commerce Sdn Bhd* applied for a judicial review to the High Court to quash the decision of the CAT. In relation to the issue of 'equivalent transaction', the High Court agreed with the CAT's finding that since the subject matter of the case is the purchase of mandatory insurance 'the purchase of the Mandatory Insurances by the employers whether directly with My EG such as RHB Insurance or with other insurance companies or agents would amount to the same or equivalent transactions'.[444]

470. With regards to the issue of 'applying different conditions' the High Court also agreed with the CAT's conclusion that 'if the purchase of Mandatory Insurances is directly from My EG, there is automatic verification. But if the purchase of Mandatory Insurances is from other parties, there is a requirement of a verification exercise, and this amounts to "applying different conditions" to equivalent transactions'.[445]

471. The word 'different conditions' obviously includes different prices (or price discrimination). For example, a dominant enterprise may sell the same products to different customers at a different price, and 'the difference in price is not related to any differences in cost of supplying the products'.[446] The Commission will only be concerned with discriminatory behaviour if an enterprise has 'control over price to be able to price- discriminate'.[447] The Commission will consider whether an enterprise has the ability 'to segregate customers into different groups' and has the ability 'to stop arbitrage between the groups'.[448]

472. Price discrimination can cause primary line injury, i.e., an injury suffered by a dominant's competitors or potential competitors by preventing the new entry into the market, impairing the ability of an existing competitor to expand, and forcing the existing equally efficient competitors out of the market. For example, 'a dominant enterprise could charge lower prices in geographic areas where there is more competition and cover losses by charging more in other areas that lack competition. This could force local competitors out of the market in the more competitive areas'.[449] However, the Commission is under no obligation to prove that a dominant enterprise's competitor has left the market before coming to a conclusion that discriminatory behaviour is abusive.

443. Paragraph 40, Decision of Competition Appeal Tribunal (Appeal No. TRP 3-2016, 28 Dec. 2017).
444. Judgment, Application for Judicial Review (No. WA-25-81-03/2018) para. 64.
445. Judgment, Application for Judicial Review (No. WA-25-81-03/2018) para. 66.
446. Paragraph 3.17, *MyCC Guidelines on Chapter 2 Prohibition* (abuse of dominant position).
447. Paragraph 3.18, *MyCC Guidelines on Chapter 2 Prohibition* (abuse of dominant position).
448. Paragraph 3.18, *MyCC Guidelines on Chapter 2 Prohibition* (abuse of dominant position).
449. Paragraph 3.20, *MyCC Guidelines on Chapter 2 Prohibition* (abuse of dominant position).

473. Price discrimination may also hamper competition in the downstream market if it is done by a vertically integrated enterprise. For example, if a dominant enterprise has a subsidiary, offering a lower price to its subsidiary for an important input may reduce the ability of other competitors to compete in the downstream market. In this case price discrimination harms competition in a market in which a dominant enterprise is participating.

474. Price discrimination may also cause secondary line injury, i.e., an injury suffered by a dominant's customers. For example, a dominant enterprise may sell its product which is considered as an important input to customer 'X' cheaper than customer 'Y'. Then X's cost will be lower than 'Y'. As a result, discrimination has put customer 'Y' in a competitive disadvantage and cannot effectively compete with customer 'X'.[450] In this situation, price discrimination distorts competition among the dominant enterprise's customers.

475. Price discrimination may be procompetitive and beneficial for consumers. For example, if patented drugs were to be sold at the same price around the world, many consumers from least developed countries could not afford to buy it. Therefore, 'by charging more to groups who can better afford it, price discrimination can lead to higher output by charging less to lower income groups, which can be welfare enhancing'.[451]

§2. Exclusionary Practices

476. Exclusionary conduct refers to the ability of an enterprise to prevent equally efficient competitors from competing in the same market.[452]

477. In assessing whether exclusionary conduct is abusive, the Commission will adopt an *effect-based* approach. The Commission will use two tests for assessing the anticompetitive effect of exclusionary conduct:

(a) First, does the conduct adversely affect consumers?
(b) Second, does the conduct exclude a competitor that is just as efficient as the dominant enterprise?[453]

478. The requirement to prove consumer harm and harm to an efficient competitor is to ensure that the enforcement against exclusionary conduct is to protect the

---

450. Alison Jones & Brenda Sufrin, *EU Competition Law: Text, Cases and Materials,* 5th edn 398 (Oxford University Press, 2014).
451. Paragraph 3.19, *MyCC Guidelines on Chapter 2 Prohibition* (abuse of dominant position).
452. Paragraph 3.5, *MyCC Guidelines on Chapter 2 Prohibition* (abuse of dominant position).
453. Paragraph 3.9, *MyCC Guidelines on Chapter 2 Prohibition* (abuse of dominant position).

process of competition and not the competitors. Any conduct that benefits consumers should not be prohibited even if it harms inefficient enterprises. This will encourage enterprises in the market to compete on merits.[454]

479. However, the requirement to prove the effect of abusive conduct on consumers is not mandatory. The High Court *My E.G. Services Bhd v. Competition Commission*[455] stated that:

> I am of the considered opinion that the said articles and para 3.6 of MyCC Guidelines on Chapter 2 are general observation in respect of abuse of dominant position in section 10 of Act 712. We must take note that the nature of abuses of dominant position are found in para (a) to (g). It is only in para (b) that there is a reference to 'to the prejudice of consumers', whereas in para (d) (iii), the reference is to 'harm competition' and not to 'harm consumers'. Therefore, if different words have been used by the Legislature, then they must mean different things.[456]

480. The High Court further stated that paragraph 86 that:

> Premised on the aforesaid reasons, I am of the considered opinion that the automatic verification for MyEG related to insurance companies, and the requirement of additional steps for verification for non-My EG insurance companies, is the fact that harms the competition … The conduct of MyEG of using its dominance in upstream market to induce the End Users to use its services in the downstream market has put all the other agents and insurance companies at a competitive disadvantage.

I. Predation

481. Section 10(2)(f) condemns any predatory behaviour towards competitors. The word 'predatory behaviour' includes various conduct, such as predatory pricing.

482. Predatory pricing occurs when an enterprise sells its products or service at a price below cost. Offering price below cost may be procompetitive. For example, a new entrant into a market may offer price below cost to gain initial market share or existing enterprise may offer price below cost to attract consumers.[457]

483. However, a dominant enterprise may set price below cost to drive efficient competitors out of the market. The dominant enterprise will then raise the price

---

454. Paragraphs 3.6 & 3.7, *MyCC Guidelines on Chapter 2 Prohibition* (abuse of dominant position).
455. Judgment, Application for Judicial Review (No. WA-25-81-03/2018).
456. Judgment, Application for Judicial Review (No. WA-25-81-03/2018) para. 85.
457. Paragraph 3.12, *MyCC Guidelines on Chapter 2 Prohibition* (abuse of dominant position).

above the competitive level when there is no competition. In this situation, consumers may only gain benefit in the short run, but they may lose out in the longer run.

484. In determining whether the price is below cost, several concepts will be used depending on the circumstances and particular conditions in the industry under investigation, including:

- Average Variable Cost – this is a short-term concept, which is defined as the sum of all the costs that change as output changes, divided by the total quantity. All fixed costs are excluded.
- Average Avoidable Cost (AAC) – this covers all the costs (i.e., both variable costs and the fixed costs directly related to the product under investigation) that could have been avoided if the dominant enterprise had not engaged in the predatory strategy. If an enterprise does not cover AAC, then it is giving up profits (i.e., scarifying profits).
- Long-run Incremental Cost (LRIC) – this is the change in total costs from the production of an increase in output (which can be either the total output or simply the increase in output due to the predatory conduct). So LRIC includes all the costs associated with the product under investigation even if those costs were sunk (i.e., non-recoverable) before the alleged predatory pricing conduct was engaged in.
- Average Total Cost – this is the sum of fixed and variable costs divided by total output.[458]

485. In assessing whether predatory pricing is abusive, it is crucial for the Commission to determine whether the price offered is below cost using the above-mentioned cost concepts and whether the pricing strategy is able to derive out an efficient competitor from the market. Under the CA 2010, the Commission is not required to prove an intention to drive a competitor out of business in the case of predatory pricing. However, the intention could be relevant to prove the effect of the predatory pricing, i.e., that the predatory strategy is likely to succeed.[459] The Guidelines on Chapter 2 Prohibition is silent on whether it is necessary for the Commission to prove the ability to recoup any losses incurred as a result of predatory price cutting.

II. Tying and Bundling

486. Section 10(2)(e) prohibits a dominant enterprise from making the conclusion of a contract subject to acceptance by other parties of supplementary conditions which by their nature or according to commercial usage have no connection with the subject matter of the contract.

---

458. Paragraph 3.14, *MyCC Guidelines on Chapter 2 Prohibition* (abuse of dominant position).
459. Paragraph 3.16, *MyCC Guidelines on Chapter 2 Prohibition* (abuse of dominant position).

487. Bundling occurs when two or more products are sold together as a package. 'A bundling would normally involve products from the same market which consumer generally would buy together',[460] and the bundled products are normally sold at a cheaper price than separately. Products included in a package are normally related for instance selling car together with its car parts. Bundling can be further divided into the followings:

- Pure bundling – occurs when products are only sold together as a package and are not supplied separately.
- Mixed bundling – occurs when products are sold both individually and in a bundle. However, the customers can get a cheaper price if they purchase the bundled products than buying individual product separately.

488. Tying, on the other hand, occurs when a seller refuses to sell one product unless the buyer also buys another product,[461] for example, a car manufacturer requires a buyer to also purchase a mobile phone that the buyer would not want.

489. Tying and bundling may contribute to cost-efficiency and benefit consumers in the form of a lower price when the product was purchased together as a package. However, tying and bundling may be used as a strategy for an enterprise holding a dominant position in a market to leverage its market power in another market. For example, if a car manufacturer holding a dominant position in the car market requires buyers to also take a mobile phone, other mobile phone operators will lose a significant number the customers who buy the car. Tying arrangement will foreclose the market for other products (tied product market) which is part of the tie.

490. Bundling can also be part of a predatory strategy. For example, the price of one product in a bundle may be set below cost to encourage the customer to buy the bundle package and make it difficult for producers of that individual product to compete.[462]

III. Rebates and Discount

491. Generally, rebates and discount are procompetitive in the sense that it encourages inter-brand competition and benefit consumers in the form of lower price as a reward of their loyalty to a particular enterprise.

492. However, rebates and discount may be used as a strategy to foreclose a market to competitors. For example, a dominant enterprise may use selective

460. Paragraph 3.18, *MyCC Guidelines on Chapter 1 Prohibition.*
461. Paragraph 3.29, *MyCC Guidelines on Chapter 2 Prohibition* (abuse of dominant position).
462. Paragraph 3.31, *MyCC Guidelines on Chapter 2 Prohibition* (abuse of dominant position).

rebates to certain customers who are likely to switch to other competitors.[463] Another form of rebates would be a loyalty rebate (fidelity rebates) when a dominant supplier gives a rebate to a customer who obtains all (or near all) of its requirements from the supplier.[464] This form of the rebate has an exclusivity effect preventing the customer from switching to other competitors.

493. Even though a rebate system does not result in total exclusivity, it may be designed in such a way that strongly encourages the customer to stay with a particular supplier. Loyalty rebates are often set according to a buyer's past purchase and often increase as more are bought. For example, a supplier might give a 20% discount if a buyer buys at least 50% of the requirements from the supplier or 30% discount if a buyer buys at least 70% of the buyer's requirements. The Commission will consider whether the discounts offered are justifiable, such as if they are related to costs.[465] A dominant supplier may award rebates to a customer on all purchases if the customer has hit a certain target. Once the customer hits the target, rebates will be given not only to subsequent but also previous purchases (retroactive rebates). This will definitely discourage the customer to switch to other competitors as the customer will lose its retroactive rebates.[466]

IV. Refusal to Deal

494. Section 10(2)(c) prohibits a dominant enterprise from refusing to supply to a particular enterprise or group or category of enterprises.

495. Generally, an enterprise does not have an absolute obligation to meet each and every demand requested by the customers. However, refusal to supply may be abusive and has an exclusionary effect if a dominant enterprise denies an important input for other enterprises to compete in the market. This is, even so, when the dominant enterprise is actually the only supplier or service provider given a mandate by the government to ensure that all demands on important inputs are met. Refusal to supply may also include 'constructive refusal to supply' where, for example, an enterprise agrees to supply based on unreasonable and unacceptable conditions.

496. Refusal to supply covers a number of different conduct including:

463. *See* Alison Jones & Brenda Sufrin, *EU Competition Law: Text, Cases and Materials*, 5th edn 455 (Oxford University Press, 2014).
464. *See* Alison Jones & Brenda Sufrin, *EU Competition Law: Text, Cases and Materials*, 5th edn 455 (Oxford University Press, 2014).
465. Paragraph 3.24, *MyCC Guidelines on Chapter 2 Prohibition* (abuse of dominant position).
466. *See* Alison Jones & Brenda Sufrin, *EU Competition Law: Text, Cases and Materials*, 5th edn 455 (Oxford University Press, 2014).

- A refusal to supply products to buyers at the downstream market – for example, a refusal to supply is often a business strategy for a vertically integrated enterprise holding a dominant position in an upstream market to eliminate competition in the downstream market. This is, even so, when the dominant enterprise also competes with other enterprises in the downstream market through a subsidiary company. In this situation, the refusal to supply important inputs to the downstream market will impair the ability of the enterprises relying on the inputs supplied to compete effectively with the incumbent at the downstream market. In some situations, a dominant enterprise did not refuse to supply but rather supplies the inputs to its subsidiary company at a cheaper price which make it difficult for other enterprises to compete at the downstream market.
- A refusal to license IPRs – the issue of refusal to license IPRs should be handled with great caution as it has an interface with the IPR law. The IPR law protects the exclusive rights of the IPR owners and forcing the IPR owner to license his/her rights may discourage innovation. According to MyCC Guidelines on IPRs and Competition Law, refusal to license IPRs is only abusive in exceptional circumstances, such as the refusal to license harms the consumer by preventing the emergence of new products, the refusal impairs competition in the secondary market where the enterprise's technology is an indispensable input to the market, and the refusal is without commercial justification.[467]

  A refusal to license IPRs may also cover the case of SEP. For example, if a certain patented technology becomes an essential standard in producing and manufacturing products, a manufacturer in the relevant industry needs to obtain a licence to use that technology to ensure compliance with the standard. Therefore, refusal to license or granting a license based on unreasonable, unfair and discriminatory terms and condition may amount to abusive conduct.[468]
- A refusal to grant access to an essential facility- – Essential facility, also known as 'bottleneck facility', is an important facility or infrastructure that competitors need to get access to in order to provide services to their customers. This bottleneck facility is often considered as a natural monopoly as it involves a very large investment and is not economically duplicated. Refusal to get access to essential facility or allowing access to it in an unfair and discriminatory manner may amount to abusive conduct, especially when access to the facility is indispensable with no actual or potential substitute and denial to access is without reasonable commercial justification.

497. The obligation of a designated monopoly (sanctioned by the government) to allow the competitor to get access to the essential facility was discussed in *MyCC v. My E.G. Services Bhd.* In this case, MyEG had been awarded a concession by the government to provide online service for the renewal of foreign workers permit. The Commission stated that:

> Being dominant by itself is not a breach of the Act. However, as a sole concession holder there is a higher burden on MyEG to comply with the Act. There

467. *See* Illustration 16, para. 8.24, *MyCC Guidelines on Intellectual Rights and Competition Law.*
468. *See* paras 8.39–8.42, *MyCC Guidelines on Intellectual Rights and Competition Law.*

is an obligation on MyEG to grant equal access to its facilities and therefore promotes competition in the downstream market.[469]

498. However, the Commission will treat this issue with great caution as forcing the essential facility owner to supply may reduce the incentive to invest and may harm incentives for innovation and investment in the long term.[470]

V. Price Squeeze

499. Margin squeeze is another form of abusive conduct under the CA 2010 even though it is not listed under section 10(2) of the Act.

500. Margin squeeze occurs when an enterprise holding a dominant position in the upstream market for an input 'set prices at such a level that its competitors on the downstream market cannot compete with it for the supply of goods or services to customers. The dominant enterprise can apply a margin squeeze by setting a high price for the input, charging lower prices on the downstream market, or by a combination of the two'.[471]

501. If the dominant enterprise is a vertically integrated business where it also competes in the downstream market, margin squeeze may be used to leverage its market power in the upstream market so as to drive out the rivals in the downstream market. In this regard, margin squeeze is likely to hinder the competitive process in the downstream market.

502. In *MyCC v. Megasteel Bhd*, the Commission in its Proposed Decision found that Megasteel deliberately had maintained a low margin between the contract prices that the company offered for the upstream supply of HRC to a competitor on the downstream market (CRC market) and the actual prices for which Megasteel sold its CRC on the downstream market. HRC is an important input to produce other kinds of steel, i.e., CRC. Megasteel is also competing with other downstream players to produce and sell CRC using HRC. The Commission viewed that the margin squeeze was done by the sales of CRC at prices that were insufficient to recover the transformation costs that were actually incurred by Megasteel in converting HRC into CRC. The Commission is of the view that Megasteel holds a special responsibility as a dominant HRC supplier to not engage in any pricing policy for its supply of HRC that will distort, or has the effect of distorting competition in the downstream market for CRC.

503. However, after careful reassessment of the case, based on more detailed information obtained through the written and oral submission submitted by

469. *MyCC v. My E.G. Services Berhad* (MyCC (ED) 700-1/1/2/2015) para. 36.

470. Paragraph 3.27, *MyCC Guidelines on Chapter 2 Prohibition* (abuse of dominant position).

471. *See* Alison Jones & Brenda Sufrin, *EU Competition Law: Text, Cases and Materials*, 5th edn 426 (Oxford University Press, 2014).

Megasteel, 'the Commission has come to the conclusion that Megasteel did not abuse its dominant position nor practice margin squeeze in the relevant domestic markets'.[472] Further data obtained by the Commission did not support the allegation that 'Megasteel often undercut its CRC prices. In addition, inconclusive data indicate that there is no practice of margin squeeze by Megasteel.'[473] The Commission had also wrongly defined the relevant market in the proposed decision as HRC market whereas Megasteel only produces the scrap metal-based HRC.[474]

472. Decision of the Competition Commission, 15 Apr. 2016 (No. MyCC/002/2012) para. 51.
473. Decision of the Competition Commission, 15 Apr. 2016 (No. MyCC/002/2012) para. 50.
474. Decision of the Competition Commission, 15 Apr. 2016 (No. MyCC/002/2012) para. 43.

Chapter 3. Concentrations

§1. Horizontal Mergers

I. Aviation Service Market

504. Horizontal merger refers to 'mergers between enterprise that operate at the same level of the supply chain in the same economic market'.[475] Horizontal merger may lead to both unilateral and coordinated anticompetitive effects.

505. Unilateral effect refers to the ability of a merged entity to exercise its market power by imposing a price increase or behave anticompetitively in a sustainable and profitable manner.[476] A horizontal merger may also incentivize non-merger parties to increase their prices due to the overall reduction of competitive pressure in the relevant aviation market.[477]

506. Coordinated effect refers to the ability of the merger parties to tacitly or explicitly collude or coordinate their behaviour to reduce competition. Coordinated effects are more likely to occur if:[478]

- Enterprises are able to align their behaviour in a relevant aviation service market.
- Enterprises have the incentive to maintain coordinated behaviour.
- The coordinated behaviour could be sustained in light of other competitive constraints in a relevant aviation service market.

II. Communications Market

507. Coordinated effects of a horizontal merger may arise when a merger 'reduces the competitive constraints in a market, creating or strengthening conditions that facilitate the ability of competitors to coordinate their competitive behaviour and engage in conduct which would be anti-competitive'.[479]

508. Unilateral effects of a horizontal merger 'flow from the non-coordinated action of M&A parties and arise when the elimination of competition between M&A parties enables the exercise of market power'.[480] For example:

> if these two (2) firms were to merge, any decrease in sales in response to an increase in price in one product are internalised as customers switch to the

475. Paragraph 3.7, *Guidelines on Substantive Assessment of Mergers.*
476. Paragraph 7.4, *Guidelines on Substantive Assessment of Mergers.*
477. Paragraph 7.5, *Guidelines on Substantive Assessment of Mergers.*
478. Paragraph 7.12, *Guidelines on Substantive Assessment of Mergers.*
479. Paragraph 12.34, *Guidelines on Mergers and Acquisitions.*
480. Paragraph 12.37, *Guidelines on Mergers and Acquisitions.*

other product which is now also sold by the merged or acquired entity. This has the result of removing a constraint on a firm's ability to engage in anticompetitive conduct.[481]

509. Non- merger parties may also benefit from a horizontal merger if it finds that it is 'profitable to raise prices in response to the now merged or acquired firm raising its prices due to limited competition remaining post-M&A'.[482]

§2. VERTICAL MERGERS

I. Aviation Service Market

510. A vertical merger refers to 'a merger between enterprises that operate at different levels of the supply chain in the same economic market', such as a merger between an airline and a ground handling company.[483] A vertical merger may be procompetitive resulting from an increase in efficiencies and reduction of costs in providing better aviation services.[484] A vertical merger may also be anticompetitive, giving rise to both unilateral and coordinated effects.

511. Unilateral effects – a vertical merger may increase the ability of a merger party to foreclose competing enterprises from any aviation service market. For example:

> 'If a merger party refuses to supply an aviation service to its competitors in another aviation service market or sells the aviation service to its competitors at a price that makes them uncompetitive, it may affect competition or foreclose that market to the competitors.'[485]
> 'if a merger party controls an essential facility to an aviation service market, it might be able to reduce competition from its competitors by refusing to provide them with access to that essential facility. The merger party may also place competitors at a cost disadvantage by granting access only at discriminatory prices that favour the merger party's own business'.[486]

512. In considering the foreclosure effect of a vertical merger the Commission may take into consideration the market power of a merger party in at least one of the relevant aviation service markets involved in that merger,[487] and whether a merger party has any incentive to foreclose competition, i.e., whether the foreclosure would be profitable to the merger party.[488]

481. Paragraph 12.38, *Guidelines on Mergers and Acquisitions.*
482. Paragraph 12.40, *Guidelines on Mergers and Acquisitions.*
483. Paragraph 8.1, *Guidelines on Substantive Assessment of Mergers.*
484. Paragraph 8.2, *Guidelines on Substantive Assessment of Mergers.*
485. Paragraph 8.6(c), *Guidelines on Substantive Assessment of Mergers.*
486. Paragraph 8.6(d), *Guidelines on Substantive Assessment of Mergers.*
487. Paragraph 8.7, *Guidelines on Substantive Assessment of Mergers.*
488. Paragraph 8.8, *Guidelines on Substantive Assessment of Mergers.*

513. Coordinated effects – A vertical merger may also give rise to coordinated effects. For example, a vertical merger may facilitate coordinated behaviour by allowing a merger party to gain access to confidential information relating to the activities of other enterprises in a relevant aviation service market,[489] or allow a merger party to 'acquire better knowledge of the selling prices in upstream or downstream aviation service markets resulting from a vertical merger which may facilitate coordination in either the upstream or downstream aviation service markets'.[490]

II. Communications Market

514. Unilateral effects – a vertical merger refers to the ability of an integrated firm to exercise unilateral market power by foreclosing competitors from any communications market. A new integrated firm may engage in the following anticompetitive behaviour:[491]

(a) charging a higher price for an important input into the production process of downstream (non-integrated) rivals to eliminate a competitor or potential competitor from entering the market; or
(b) refusing to supply products or services or limiting supply by downstream or upstream rivals to important inputs.

515. Coordinated effects – a vertical merger in communications market may also 'increase the potential for coordination between firms' as a result of 'an increase in transparency, greater scope for alignment, and the ability to monitor adherence to a coordinated strategy which create conditions for coordination between firms'.[492]

§3. Market/Product Extension Mergers

516. Product extension mergers are mergers between two firms that produce different but related products in the same market. The MAVCOM and MCMC do not specifically address market extension mergers within their guidelines, but they may be considered as conglomerate mergers (*see* below).

§4. Pure Conglomerate Mergers

I. Aviation Service Market

517. A conglomerate merger refers to a merger between enterprises that operate in different markets.

489. Paragraph 8.10(a), *Guidelines on Substantive Assessment of Mergers.*
490. Paragraph 8.10(c), *Guidelines on Substantive Assessment of Mergers.*
491. Paragraph 12.47, *Guidelines on Mergers and Acquisitions.*
492. Paragraph 12.53, *Guidelines on Mergers and Acquisitions.*

518. Unilateral effects – A conglomerate merger may be problematic if it involves a merger between 'enterprises that provide complementary services or services that are generally provided to the same set of buyers'[493] as it allows 'a merger party to strengthen its market positions or market power through tying or bundling practices' resulting 'in the foreclosure of a relevant market to competing enterprises'.[494]

519. Coordinated effects – In addition to unilateral behaviour, 'a conglomerate merger may also increase the potential for coordination especially where the merger party's competitors in one aviation service market are also its competitors in another market'.[495]

II. Communications Market

520. As in the case of the aviation service market, an integrated firm as a result of a conglomerate merger may devise foreclosure strategies in the form of bundling or tying of complementary products. It creates an incentive to the buyers 'to source products from the merged or acquired entity so as to reduce any transactions costs that would be involved in sourcing products from multiple suppliers'.[496]

521. A conglomerate merger increases the need for a merger party to offer a full range of complementary products or services to compete. This will create entry barriers as future entrant needs to offer 'the full range of products, potentially increasing the sunk costs associated with entry or exit which may have the purpose or effect of substantially lessening competition'.[497]

§5. Joint Ventures

522. In assessing the competitive effects of JVs, the MAVCOM Guidelines on Substantive Assessment of Mergers and MCMC Guidelines on Mergers and Acquisitions do not specifically distinguish between mergers and JVs. Accordingly, JVs are assessed in substantively the same way as other mergers are assessed.

493. Paragraph 9.2, *Guidelines on Substantive Assessment of Mergers.*
494. Paragraph 9.3, *Guidelines on Substantive Assessment of Mergers.*
495. Paragraph 9.5, *Guidelines on Substantive Assessment of Mergers.*
496. Paragraph 12.48, *Guidelines on Mergers and Acquisitions.*
497. Paragraph 12.51, *Guidelines on Mergers and Acquisitions.*

Part III. Administrative Procedure

Chapter 1. Administrative Investigations Before the Antitrust Authority

§1. INITIATIVE

I. General Sectors Inquiries

523. MyCC has the power based on its own initiative or upon the request of the Minister to conduct a market review into any market in order to determine whether any feature or combination of features of the market prevents, restricts or distorts competition in the market.[498] The market includes a study into:

(a) the structure of the market concerned;
(b) the conduct of enterprises in the market;
(c) the conduct of suppliers and consumers to the enterprises in the market; or
(d) any other relevant matters.[499]

524. The Commission is required to publish a report of its findings and recommendations after conducting the market review and make it available to the public as a source of reference.[500] So far, MyCC had conducted four market reviews, namely.

A. Review on Fixing Prices/Fees by Professional Bodies (2013)

525. The study focused on the 131 bodies/associations that are grouped into thirty-four sectors. The grouping of these sectors is guided by the relevant laws pertaining to the sectors (where available) and the WTO services Sectoral Classification. The study had come into four conclusions:

498. Section 11 of Competition Act 2010.
499. Section 11(2) of Competition Act 2010.
500. Section 12 of Competition Act 2010.

- Ten sectors are found to be governed by respective bodies/associations that are empowered by legislation to regulate such sector, and scales of fees are established for their members, namely, architects, engineers, quantity surveyors, land surveyors, valuers, appraisers and estate agents, town planners, accountants, legal, medical and dental practitioners.
- There are three sectors in which the governing authorities are empowered by a specific provision to fix scales of fees but have yet to do so, namely, midwives and nurses, counsellors and food analysts.
- There are five sectors in which the governing bodies are given the general power to regulate the sector, but no scales of fees have been fixed, namely optometrists, pharmacists, chemists, veterinary, surgeons and medical assistants.
- There are five sectors prescribe fees/prices for their members even though they are not empowered by any law, namely, company secretaries, arbitrators, mediators, landscape architects and dental practitioners.

B. Review on the Domestic Broiler Market (2014)

526. The market review 'focused on the current structure of the domestic broiler market; and the interactions of farmers, wholesalers and retailers across the broiler supply chain'.[501]

527. The research revealed that changes in upstream market prices are transmitted asymmetrically and positively to standard broiler retail in downstream market. Asymmetric price transmission may be the result of market power of an integrated firm (or a group of integrated firms) and/or the exercise of oligopolistic behaviour in the intermediate (wholesale) stages of the supply chain. Thus, 'when there is a change in price at the farm level, firms along the supply chain may be colluding tacitly when they all immediately pass-on an upstream price change to minimise or completely avoid any reductions of their margins. Likewise, they would be keen to maintain prices above the competitive level and earn a higher margin by not passing-on any reduction in price at the farm level'.[502]

528. The research also found that broiler market is highly integrated and argued that 'when players in a sector become increasingly vertically integrated, there will be a lower number of competing businesses in each stage of the supply chain. This is the main reason for MyCC's concern with price transmission effects. The lower the level of competition, the more likely it will be for upstream price increases (but not price reductions) to be passed-on downstream':[503]

> While acknowledging the need to impose a 'permitted maximum' retail price for no more than 2 weeks before and after a festival will prevent consumers

501. Review of Domestic Broiler Market (Final Report, 21 Mar. 2014) p. 1.
502. Review of Domestic Broiler Market (Final Report, 21 Mar. 2014) p. 38.
503. Review of Domestic Broiler Market (Final Report, 21 Mar. 2014) p. 44.

from being charged exorbitantly by retailers, the research argued that maximum retail prices 'may also inadvertently weaken retailers' competition with one another, as well as create market distortions and a lack of transparency in the commercial relationships between wholesalers and retailers'.[504]

C. Review on Pharmaceutical Sector (2017)

529. The market review focused on three levels of supply chain: (1) manufacturer and importer, (2) wholesaler and distributor, and (3) general practitioner, but the main focus is on the first two levels. In relation to market concentration, the market review report concluded that:

- There is a stiff competition of generic drugs manufacturing between local and imported producers.
- However, there is a high degree of market power from global multinational companies for originator drugs.
- There is a high concentration of foreign distributors.

530. The market review had conducted studies of anticompetitive conduct in the pharmaceutical industry by other competition authorities and found some similar patterns or trends in Malaysia, especially patent strategies to delay the entry of generic drug. It is stated that 'some of the requirements and standards pose significant challenges to the domestic generic industry. The main concern is delay in generics entering the market and high costs to the local manufacturers and importers. Thus there should be attention on such regulatory requirements becoming regulatory barriers without adding value to quality, safety and efficacy considerations'.[505] The market review also highlights other issues, such as price discrimination between pharmacists and physicians in terms of the prices charged by originators for patented drugs supplied. It is stated that 'a common complaint among community pharmacists interviewed for this Review was that they were being charged more for a particular drug than the pricing given to clinics and/or private hospitals. There were cases where pharmacists were at risk of losing customers because of the higher prices they charged for medicines due to higher procurement prices. There were also some cases of refusal by the originator company to supply medicines to the community pharmacist'.[506]

504. Review of Domestic Broiler Market (Final Report, 21 Mar. 2014) p. 35.
505. Market Review of Pharmaceutical Sector, 27 Dec. 2017, p. 147.
506. Market Review of Pharmaceutical Sector, 27 Dec. 2017, p. 172.

D. Review on Building Materials in Construction Industry (2017)

531. Market review of building materials focused on long steel, cement, ready-mixed concrete and sand-mining and distribution of building materials. These are the most utilized building materials in the construction industry. In relation to market concentration, the review found that:

- the 'long' steel production is dominated by four major players, which capture about 79% of total market shares;
- cement manufacturers are vertically integrated with four major players, which control about 82% of total market shares;
- ready-mixed concrete market is dominated by four major players, which control about 50% of total market shares;
- market concentration for distributors of building materials is low.

532. According to the market review report, there is no major or obvious anti-competitive conduct. However, there are several areas that may raise competitive concerns in the future, for example, high barriers entry and vertical integration strategy (compliant of lower price to drive out competitors at the downstream market) in the long steel market, market dominant (in East Malaysia) and exclusive dealing in the cement market, and possible sharing of information in the distribution of building materials market, etc.

533. In relation to the vertical integration in the long steel market, the market review report stated that 'If a manufacturer is able to leverage its vertically integrated structure, it should translate to more competitive pricing to the end consumers. However, it may be considered a breach of the CA if the prices offered are much lower than market price with the intention of driving competitors out of the market, i.e. predatory pricing. A vertically integrated company may also violate the CA if they prioritize supply to their own downstream operations and refuse to sell to others with the purpose of increasing market share.'[507]

II. Ex Officio Investigations

534. The CA 2010 empowers the Commission to launch an investigation at any time if the Commission has reason to suspect that any enterprise has infringed or is infringing any prohibition of the CA 2010 or is committing any offence under the Act.[508]

535. The Commission shall conduct an investigation on any suspected infringement of any prohibition or any commission of an offence under the Act based on the direction of the Minister in charge of overseeing the CA 2010.[509]

---

507. Market Review on Pharmaceutical Sector, 27 Dec. 2017, p. 146.
508. Section 14(1) of Competition Act 2010.
509. Section 14(2) of Competition Act 2010.

III. Complaints

536. MyCC has the power to conduct an investigation based on a complaint made by the public. The Commission has the discretion to conduct an investigation on enterprise, conduct or agreement that has infringed or is infringing any prohibition under the CA 2010 or is committing any offence under the CA 2010.[510] The CA 2010 requires the complainant to provide details of the alleged infringement or offence, including the person against whom the complaint is made.[511] Information submitted to the Commission will be treated as confidential, and the Commission may protect the identity of the complainant if necessary.

537. Upon receiving a complaint, the Commission will assess whether the complaint falls within the scope of its powers and will forward the complaint to any relevant agency if the complaint is not within its jurisdiction. In deciding whether to start a formal investigation, the Commission may make inquiries on the complainant[512] and will take into account its strategic priorities.[513]

538. The Commission may not proceed with the formal investigation based on several grounds, such as the complaint is related to non-competition matters, there are no competition issues arising from the complaint, the subject matter of complaint falls under other regulators' jurisdiction, the complainant fails to provide further information to assist the Commission in its formal investigation, etc.

539. If the Commission decides not to proceed with an investigation, the Commission must as soon as practicable inform the complainant of the decision and reasons for the decision.[514] The Commission had previously issued a brief assessment paper (Executive Summary) after closing a complaint against an electronic payment system. For an example, the Commission had received a complaint on the surcharge that is being imposed at parking lots over and above the parking fees that are being paid by Touch 'n Go (TNG) card users. After a careful assessment, the Commission found there was no competition issue arising from the complaint based on the following reasons:

- the surcharge is justified as it is due to the investment and maintenance costs of the TNG system, incurred by the operators;
- the TNG facility offers cashless convenience to the customer;
- a cash alternative is also made available to the customer apart from the TNG option at the parking entry points.[515]

510. Section 15(1) of Competition Act 2010.
511. Section 15(2) of Competition Act 2010.
512. Section 16(1) of Competition Act 2010.
513. Page 7, *MyCC Guidelines on Complaint Procedures.*
514. Section 16(2) of Competition Act 2010.
515. Assessment by the Malaysia Competition Commission on Parking Surcharge by Touch n' Go Sdn Bhd at http://www.mycc.gov.my/sites/default/files/Executive%20Summary%20TNG%200711201 6.pdf.

540. The Commission after deciding to investigate a complaint under section 15 of the CA 2010, may at any time close the investigation if:

(a) it has accepted an undertaking from an enterprise under section 43 of the CA 2010;
(b) the investigation would not constitute the making of the best use of the Commission's resources.[516]

541. When the Commission decides to close an investigation, it shall publish a statement that the investigation has been closed and set out a brief summary of the Commission's reasons for closing that investigation.[517] The statement to close an investigation may take the form of an undertaking or a finding of non-infringement.

542. The Commission had issued non-infringement decisions to the following enterprises:

No	*Enterprise*	*Date*
1.	Finding of Non-Infringement under section 39 of the CA 2010 – Pangsapuri Perdana	12 February 2015
2.	Finding of Non-Infringement under section 39 of the CA 2010 – Members of the Sarawak Restaurants Association April 2015	16 April 2015
3.	Finding of Non-Infringement under section 39 of the CA 2010 – My Egg Consortium Sdn. Bhd	4 June 2015
4.	Finding of Non-Infringement under section 39 of the CA 2010 – Federation of Stationers and Booksellers Association of Malaysia	26 October 2015
5.	Finding of Non-Infringement under section 39 of the CA 2010 – Wood sellers	7 February 2017
7.	Finding of Non-Infringement under section 39 of the CA 2010 – Label stock Makers	7 February 2017

§2. Powers

I. Requests for Information

543. The Commission has the power to require any person whom the Commission believes are familiar with the facts and circumstances of the case to provide or produce to the Commission any information or document which is relevant to the performance of the Commission's powers and functions or to make statements to

516. Section 16(3) of Competition Act 2010.
517. Section 16(4) of Competition Act 2010.

the Commission explaining on any information or document so provided.[518] The notice for the request of information will be sent by the Commission to the relevant person setting out the period within which and the manner in which the document or information shall be provided.

544. If the documents or information are not in possession of the person directed by the Commission, the person is required to at least:

(a) state, to the best knowledge and belief, where the document may be found; and
(b) identify, to the best of his knowledge and belief, the last person who had custody of the document and to state, to the best of his knowledge and belief, where the last-mentioned person is to be found.[519]

545. Any person required or directed by the Commission to provide information shall ensure that the information is true, accurate and completed. Providing untrue or misleading information is an offence under the CA 2010 unless the person is not aware of any other information which would make the information provided untrue or misleading.[520]

546. The Commission in the course of an investigation may retain or take possession of any document for such duration that it deems necessary and must return the document as soon as practicable when the document is no longer needed.[521] The Commission also has the power to get access to records, books or accounts or any other things which are relevant in the performance of its functions or powers under the CA 2010.[522]

547. In providing information, any person should abide by two important rules, namely, rule of confidentiality and privileged communication.

548. The CA 2010 prohibits the disclosure and use of confidential information relating to a particular enterprise or the affairs of an individual obtained by virtue of any provision of the CA 2010.[523] The Act, however, laid down certain circumstances in which disclosure of confidential information can be made, such as when the disclosure is made with the consent of the person from whom the information is obtained or when the disclosure is necessary for the performance of the functions of the Commission.[524]

549. The CA 2010 protects the communication between a professional legal adviser and his client.[525] The advocate and solicitor are not bound to comply with

518. Section 18(1)(a), (b) of Competition Act 2010.
519. Section 18(2) of Competition Act 2010.
520. Section 18(3) of Competition Act 2010. *See also* s. 23 of Competition Act 2010.
521. Section 19(1) & (3) of Competition Act 2010.
522. Section 20(1) of Competition Act 2010.
523. Section 21(1) of Competition Act 2010.
524. *See* s. 21(2)(a)–(e) of Competition Act 2010.
525. Section 22(1) of Competition Act 2010.

the request of the Commission made under section 18 of the CA 2010 in respect of any document or information that contains a privileged communication made by or on behalf of or to the advocate and solicitor except the person to whom or by or on behalf of whom the communication was made agrees to the advocate and solicitor complying with the request.[526]

550. A person is prohibited under the CA 2010 to destroy, conceal mutilate or alter, or remove from its premise any record, book, account, document, computerized data with the intent to defraud the Commission or interfere or obstruct the Commission from carrying out its powers and functions under the CA 2010.[527]

II. Investigating and Search Powers

551. The Commission may conduct search and seizure with and without a warrant. The Commission may obtain a warrant from a Magistrate to enter into a premise if it is believed that the premise has been used for or there is evidence in the premise that is necessary to the conduct of the investigation into the infringement of any prohibition or the commitment of an offence under the CA 2010.

552. The warrant issued may authorize the Commission officer to enter into a premise at any reasonable time with or without assistance and if necessary, be by force.[528] The warrant may also authorize the officer of the Commission to search and seize any documents including record, book, account or computerized data or any other things which are relevant to the investigation.[529] The officer may if necessary conduct search on any person who is in or on the premises.[530] The warrant may also allow the office of the Commission to take possession of all things which are suspected to be instrument or evidence of infringements.[531] If it is not practicable to remove any documents or records, the Commission can seal such documents, records, etc.[532]

553. The Commission may enter into a premise without a warrant from the Magistrate if the Commission has reasonable ground that the delay of obtaining the warrant may affect the Commission's investigation or the evidence of the commission of infringement is likely to be tampered with or removed or destroyed. In conducting a search, the Commission officer has the right to get access to computerized data whether stored in a computer or otherwise.[533]

526. Section 22(2) of Competition Act 2010.
527. Section 24 of Competition Act 2010.
528. Section 25 of Competition Act 2010.
529. Section 25(2) of Competition Act 2010.
530. Section 25(3) of Competition Act 2010.
531. Section 25(4) of Competition Act 2010.
532. Section 25(6) of Competition Act 2010.
533. Section 27 of Competition Act 2010.

554. When the Commission officer seized any documents, records or data, the said officer is required to prepare a list of items that have been seized and a written notice containing the grounds for the seizure.[534] The list of the items and the written notice should be served to the occupier of the premises which have been searched by his agent or servant at those premises[535] unless the seizure is made in the presence of the person against whom proceedings under the CA 2010 are intended to be taken or in the presence of the owner of such property or his agent.[536] The seized items should be released to the lawful owner if it is no longer required in any proceedings under the Act or for any prosecution under any other written law.[537]

555. In order to ensure smooth investigation process, the CA 2010 prohibits any conduct that would obstruct, hinder or delay the Commission officer in the execution of any power or duty conferred by the Act[538] and prohibits the disclosure to any person of information which may prejudice the investigation or proposed investigation (tipping-off).[539] The CA 2010 also provides protection for the whistleblower who makes a complaint to the Commission or cooperates with the Commission in an investigation from being subject to threat or reprisal which may put the complainant in commercial or other disadvantages.[540] The act of threat and reprisal includes a threat of late payment of amount properly due to the complainant, the unreasonably bringing or conduct of litigation against the complainant, the cancellation of orders with the complainant, or the diversion of business from or refusal to trade with the complainant.[541]

III. Cooperation with Other State Institutions

556. The CA 2010 gives the power to the Minister to direct the Commission regarding the interworking arrangement between the Commission and other authority in Malaysia or in a foreign jurisdiction or any international organization.[542]

557. Since there are various sector regulators who have the mandate to oversee competition matters in specific sectors, such as Malaysian Communication and Multimedia Commission, Malaysian Aviation Commission, Energy Commission, etc., MyCC had established a Special Committee (SC) which consists of various sector regulators to coordinate the enforcement of the competition laws in the country. The SC has become an avenue for all regulators to come together and discuss common issues on competition, complaints by consumers on competition-consumer-related

534. Section 29(1)(a)(i) & (ii) of Competition Act 2010.
535. Section 29(1)(b) of Competition Act 2010.
536. Section 29(2) of Competition Act 2010.
537. Section 30 of Competition Act 2010.
538. Section 32 of Competition Act 2010.
539. Section 33 of Competition Act 2010.
540. Section 34 of Competition Act 2010.
541. Section 34(2) of Competition Act 2010.
542. Section 39 of Competition Commission Act 2010.

matters, recent updates and development from the respective sectors, and any other policy matters related to competition. The SC is also a good platform to coordinate and jointly undertake activities relating to the promotion and enforcement of competition law, such as joint research and advocacy programme. All complaints received by MyCC which fall under the jurisdiction of other regulators will be forwarded to the respective regulators.

558. A special committee meeting will be conducted once or twice a year to discuss how sector regulators address competitive concerns based on the complaints forwarded. Any policy changes proposed new policy and laws or amendment to the law will also be presented and discussed in the meeting. It allows MyCC to provide input and recommendation on competition-related matters to ensure that any future implementation of law or policy is in line with the CA 2010. The main objectives of the establishment of the SC among others to ensure where possible harmonization and uniformity of competition principles, interpretation and application of the competition laws and to allow peer review of related competition policy framework in the respective sectors.

559. MyCC had entered into a MoUs with the Central Bank of Malaysia which provides a platform for both regulators to collaborate and cooperate in areas of common regulatory objective in carrying out their respective mandates given or permitted by the laws which govern both parties. The MoU allows both parties to consult each other, to share information and coordinate competition law enforcement in fostering the stability of the financial sector and minimizing the duplicative efforts as well as addressing regulatory gaps. The cooperation between MyCC and the Central Bank covers the investigation and enforcement actions, exchange of confidential information and effective and efficient coordination and collaboration.

§3. Right of Defence

I. Content and Notification of Opening Decisions

560. After the completion of an investigation, MyCC may decide to issue a proposed decision to the effect that one of the prohibitions under Part II has been or is being infringed. For this purpose, the Commission must give written notice of its proposed decision to each enterprise that may be directly affected by the decision, including the infringing enterprise.[543] The notice will state the following:

(a) The reasons for the Commission's proposed decision in sufficient detail to enable the enterprise to whom the notice is given to sufficiently comment on or respond to the issued proposed decision on an informed basis.
(b) Penalties or remedial action that the Commission proposes to impose.

543. Section 36 of Competition Act 2010.

561. The notice shall also inform each enterprise to whom the notice is given the opportunity to submit within a reasonable period written representation to the Commission and to indicate whether the enterprise intends to make an oral representation before the commission.[544]

II. Proceedings: Hearings, Access to File, Briefs

562. If an enterprise wishes to make an oral representation before the Commission, the Commission will convene a session for oral representation to be held at a date, time and place determined by the Commission.[545] The written notice of the date, time and place will be sent to:

(i) The enterprise concerned.
(ii) Any person who had lodged a complaint with the Commission concerning the practice that was the subject of the Commission's investigation.
(iii) Any other person whose presence at the session of the oral representation is considered necessary by the Commission.[546]

563. It is important to note that oral representation is not a full hearing and does not involve weighing evidence through examination and cross-examination of witnesses. It can only be conducted after the infringing enterprise submitted its written submission in response to the Commission's proposed decision. Only the infringing enterprise is allowed to make an oral representation before the Commission under the CA 2010.

564. However, the Commission may at any time conduct a full hearing to determine whether an enterprise had infringed or is infringing any prohibition under Part II of the CA 2010.[547] If the Commission decides to conduct a hearing, it must give at least fourteen days' notice to the infringing enterprise and to other interested parties stating its decision to convene the hearing, the date, time and place for conducting the hearing and matters to be considered at the hearing.[548] The Commission may also decide:

(a) whether to hold separate/individual hearings with each of the enterprise and any other interested third parties or to hold a single hearing attended by all enterprises involved and the interested third parties; and
(b) whether to hold a hearing in public or in a closed session for the purpose of protecting confidential information.[549]

544. Section 36(c)(i)(ii) of Competition Act 2010.
545. Section 37(a) of Competition Act 2010.
546. Section 37(b)(i), (ii) & (iii) of Competition Act 2010.
547. Section 38(1) of Competition Act 2010.
548. Section 38(2) of Competition Act 2010.
549. Section 38(3)(a) & (b) of Competition Act 2010.

565. An enterprise is given the right to be represented at a hearing conducted by an advocate and solicitor or any of its officers or employees or any other person with the consent of the Chairman of the Commission.[550] All matters raised by the enterprises concerned or any other person participating in the hearing will be recorded and kept by the Commission.[551]

566. Even though the CA 2010 does not contain provisions on access to file by the infringing enterprise, as a matter of procedure, any enterprise which has been issued with a proposed decision will be given the right to access to the Commission's file and documents within a reasonable period of times. The infringing party needs to submit a notice via a form provided and to pay a minimal amount of fees. However, certain documents are considered as non-accessible documents, such as the Commission's internal document, classified documents under Official Secrets Act 1972, documents related to leniency, privilege communication under section 22 of the CA 2010, etc.

III. Statement of Objections

567. MyCC does not issue a statement of objections but instead issues a proposed infringement decision.

IV. Final Hearing and Decision

568. If the Commission decides that there is no infringement of a prohibition under Part II of the CA 2010, the Commission must without delay give notice of the decision (non-infringement decision) to any person who is affected by the decision stating the basis of the decision and the Commission's reason for making the decision.[552]

569. If the Commission decides that there is an infringement, the Commission must, within fourteen days of its making a decision, notify any person affected by the decision. The Commission must prepare and publish reasons for each decision it makes under the CA 2010. The Commission may specify any appropriate steps which are required to be taken by the infringing enterprise to bring the infringement to an end, to impose a financial penalty or any other direction as it deems appropriate.[553]

550. Section 38(6) of Competition Act 2010.
551. Section 38(5) of Competition Act 2010.
552. Section 39 of Competition Act 2010.
553. Section 40(1)(b), (c) & (d) of Competition Act 2010.

Chapter 2. Voluntary Notifications and Clearance Decisions

§1. Aviation Service Market

I. Notification

570. The Malaysian Aviation Commission (MAVCOM) adopts a voluntary merger regime for an anticipated merger or a merger. This means that the parties to the anticipated merger or a merger need not notify the Commission.

571. The party may choose to either notify the merger or apply for a decision as to whether the merger infringes or will infringe the prohibition of section 54.[554] However, the parties should notify if they are of the view that the merger may result in SLC.[555]

572. If the party decide to execute while a merger application is being assessed, the Commission may treat the application as if it were an application for a merger made in accordance with section 56 or require the merger party to submit a new application for the merger assessment.[556]

573. The voluntary merger regime does not open for any consultation or guidance from the Commission.[557] Enterprises providing aviation services are expected to carry out their self-assessment whether merger occurs within section 54 and whether it will infringe the section.[558]

574. Even though it is voluntary in nature, the Commission still has the power to carry out an investigation if the Commission has reason to suspect that the anticipated merger or a merger would infringe section 54 and consequently impose remedial action, including to cease, modify or dissolve the merger.[559]

575. For anticipated merger, the applicant must notify the Commission when the merger has been made public by any party or by the Commission when the commission published a summary of merger application.[560]

---

554. Paragraph 2.1, *Guidelines on Notification and Application Procedure for an Anticipated Merger or a Merger.*
555. Paragraph 2.3, *Guidelines on Notification and Application Procedure for an Anticipated Merger or a Merger.*
556. Paragraph 3.27, *Guidelines on Notification and Application Procedure for an Anticipated Merger or a Merger.*
557. Paragraph 2.5, *Guidelines on Notification and Application Procedure for an Anticipated Merger or a Merger.*
558. Paragraph 2.3, *Guidelines on Notification and Application Procedure for an Anticipated Merger or a Merger.*
559. Paragraph 2.6, *Guidelines on Notification and Application Procedure for an Anticipated Merger or a Merger.*
560. Paragraph 3.2(c), *Guidelines on Notification and Application Procedure for an Anticipated Merger or a Merger.*

576. For a completed merger, the notification and application may be made at any time, but the party is encouraged to notify as soon as possible.[561] The application must be made in the prescribed form and accompanied by the relevant important documents.

577. In making a final decision, the Commission will consider any feedback received through public consultation as well written representation made by the applicants in the case of proposed infringement decision.[562] The Commission will give notice of the final decision to the applicant and give the applicant, a merger party or any relevant person an opportunity to request for any confidential information to be redacted.[563]

II. Clearance Decision

578. The final decision can be divided into non-infringement decision and infringement decision:

(i) The Commission will issue a non-infringement decision based on the following factors:[564]
  - The anticipated merger will not infringe, and the merger has not infringed section 54 of the Act.
  - The prohibited merger falls under an exclusion.
  - The Commission accepts an undertaking pursuant to section 62 of the Act.

(ii) Infringement decision.

579. If the Commission finds that an anticipated merger or a merger infringes the prohibition of section 54, the Commission shall give directions including:[565]

- prohibiting an anticipated merger from being carried into effect;
- requiring a merger to be dissolved or modified;
- requiring a merger party to enter into agreements designed to prevent or lessen the anticompetitive effects arising from an anticipated merger or a merger;
- requiring a merger party to dispose of such businesses, assets, shares or rights in a manner that may be specified by the Commission; or
- providing a performance bond, guarantee or other forms of security on such terms and conditions as may be determined by the Commission.

---

561. Paragraph 3.3, *Guidelines on Notification and Application Procedure for an Anticipated Merger or a Merger.*
562. Paragraph 3.28, *Guidelines on Notification and Application Procedure for an Anticipated Merger or a Merger.*
563. Paragraph 3.29, *Guidelines on Notification and Application Procedure for an Anticipated Merger or a Merger.*
564. Paragraph 3.31, *Guidelines on Notification and Application Procedure for an Anticipated Merger or a Merger.*
565. Paragraph 3.39, *Guidelines on Notification and Application Procedure for an Anticipated Merger or a Merger.*

580. The Commission may also impose a financial penalty which must not exceed 10% of the worldwide turnover or give any other direction as it deems appropriate.

§2. COMMUNICATIONS MARKET

I. Notification

581. The Malaysian Communications and Multimedia Commission (MCMC) also adopts a voluntary notification regime which allows the merging parties to proceed with the merger, but they bear the risk of an investigation by the Commission. The voluntary regime allows the merger parties to:

(a) seek the commission's view on the effect of the merger on competition; and
(b) decide whether to apply to the Commission for authorization of a merger subject to various undertakings.[566]

582. The MCMC does not encourage the notification of merger unless it has been publicly announced and the parties to the merger have a bona fide intention to proceed with the merger.[567] The Commission may conduct an investigation into a merger that has not been voluntarily submitted if it has reasonable ground to believe that the merger has, or will lead to a criminal or civil offence being committed.[568]

II. Clearance Decision

583. Upon completion of the merger assessment, the Commission may either issue:

(1) a favourable decision by not objecting to the merger (both after Phase 1 and Phase 2 assessment; or
(2) make an unfavourable decision by objecting to the merger (after Phase 2 assessment only).

A. No Objection

584. The Commission may make a favourable decision if it finds that a merger does not have the purpose, or does not have or is not likely to have the effect of

566. Paragraph 1.27, *Guidelines on Mergers and Acquisitions.*
567. Paragraph 3.22, *Guidelines on Mergers and Acquisitions.*
568. Paragraph 10.1; *see* the Commission's investigation process para. 10.3.

substantially lessening competition in a communications market or result in a dominant position.[569] A Notice of No Objection will be issued to the applicant confirming that the party may proceed with the merger in the structures submitted to the Commission for assessment.[570]

B. Objection

585. The Commission may object to an M&A by issuing a Notice of Objection if it finds that an M&A has contravened, or a proposed M&A (upon completion) will contravene, the prohibition in section 133 of the CMA or may involve the MCMC exercising its power to direct a licensee in a dominant position under subsection 139(1) of the CMA.[571]

569. Paragraph 6.4, *Guidelines on Mergers and Acquisitions.*
570. Paragraph 6.5, *Guidelines on Mergers and Acquisitions.*
571. Paragraph 6.16, *Guidelines on Mergers and Acquisitions.*

Chapter 3. Merger Control

§1. Preliminary Filing Obligations

I. Criteria and Thresholds

586. The MCMC considers that a merger may only raise SLC concern and suitable for notification if:

(1) In the case of a proposed horizontal and non-horizontal merger – at least one of the parties to the merger is a licensee who is already in a dominant position in a communications market.[572]
(2) In the case of a proposed horizontal merger – if the threshold above is not met, the Commission will consider whether the merger results or may result in a licensee obtaining a dominant position in a communications market.[573] The Commission considers if the merged or acquired entity is likely to have a post-merger market share of 40% or more to be indicative of dominant.[574]
(3) In the case of a completed horizontal and non-horizontal merger – the merged entity or acquired entity is a licensee in a dominant position.
(4) If all of the above thresholds are not met, the Commission may also take into account other factors, such as at the least one party to the merger is subject to ongoing investigation under the CMA or if there is significant cross-shareholding between the parties, to a merger of 40% or more.[575]

587. If the merger does not meet the stipulated threshold, the parties to the merger may not need to notify the Commission. However, the Commission reserves the right to investigate the merger at any time. The threshold only serves as a screening tool to suggest whether a merger warrants investigation or suitable for notification. The decision to object or not to object a merger depends on the outcome of the substantive assessment of the merger.[576]

II. Turnover Calculation

588. The MAVCOM is more likely to investigate into an anticipated merger or a merger if:

(i) the combined turnover of the merger parties in Malaysia in the financial year preceding the anticipated merger or the merger is at least MYR 50 million, or

572. Paragraphs 3.17 & 3.33, *Guidelines on Mergers and Acquisitions.*
573. Paragraphs 3.17 & 3.33, *Guidelines on Mergers and Acquisitions.*
574. Paragraphs 3.20 & 3.33, *Guidelines on Mergers and Acquisitions.*
575. Paragraphs 3.21(b) & 3.33, *Guidelines on Mergers and Acquisitions.*
576. Paragraph 3.29, *Guidelines on Mergers and Acquisitions.*

(ii) the combined worldwide turnover of the merger parties in the financial year preceding the anticipated merger or the merger is at least MYR 500,000.[577]

589. Even if the above threshold is not met, the Commission reserves the power to investigate the anticipated merger or a merger if it has a reason to suspect that the merger has resulted or may be expected to result in an SLC in any aviation service market.

III. Market Share Calculation

590. According to MCMC Guideline on Dominant Position, a firm is likely to be dominant if it holds more than 40% market share in a communications market.[578] The Commission considers if the merged or acquired entity is likely to have a post-merger market share of 40% or more to be indicative of dominant.[579]

IV. Other Relevant Notions

A. *The Relevant Market*

591. Aviation service market refers to a market for aviation services in Malaysia or in any part of Malaysia, which would include a group of services which are substitutable or competitive with one another.[580] Aviation service is defined by section 2 of the MACA to mean:

(a) the carriage of passengers, mail or cargo for hire or reward by air or by the use of any aircraft between two or more places, of which at least one place is in Malaysia;
(b) the provision in Malaysia of any of the ground handling services;
(c) the operation of an aerodrome in Malaysia for the take-off and landing of any aircraft engaged in the carriage of passengers, mail or cargo for hire or reward; or
(d) any other service determined by the Commission to be necessary or expedient for the carriage of passengers, mail or cargo.

592. Section 6 of the CMA defines 'communications market' as:

577. Paragraph 2.7, *Guidelines on Notification and Application Procedure for an Anticipated Merger or a Merger.*
578. Paragraph 4.17(a), *Guideline on Dominant Position.*
579. Paragraph 3.20, *Guidelines on Mergers and Acquisitions.*
580. Paragraph 2.1, *Guidelines on Aviation Service Market Definition.*

an economic market for a network service, or an applications service, or for goods or services used in conjunction with a network service or applications service, or for access to facilities used in conjunction with a network service or an applications service.

B. Substantial Lessening of Competition

593. According to MAVCOM Guidelines on Substantive Assessment of Mergers, 'an SLC may occur where a merger has a significant effect on rivalry between enterprises over time, reducing the competitive pressure on enterprises in any aviation service market to improve their services offered to buyers in terms of quality, efficiency or innovation'.[581] An SLC may be determined through the following steps:

(1) Define the relevant aviation service market.
(2) Develop a theory of harm, i.e., the identification of possible harm and effects of a merger on competition in a relevant aviation service market.
(3) Develop a counterfactual scenario, i.e., the conditions and the degree of competition in a relevant aviation service market in the absence of a merger based on prevailing conditions in the market if the merger does not occur.

594. According to MCMC Guidelines on Mergers and Acquisitions, 'a lessening of competition may be equated with an increase in market power for one (1) or more participants in a market, or can also occur if a firm engages in conduct which maintains its market power'.[582] In determining the SLC, the Commission sets out the following steps:

(1) Define the boundaries of the relevant communications market.
(2) Consider whether the licensee is in a dominant position in the relevant communications market.
(3) Assess whether a merger has the purpose (if the licensee is not dominant) or effect (if the licensee is dominant) of substantially lessening competition.

595. In assessing whether a merger has the purpose or effect to substantially lessen competition in a communications market, the MCMC adopts 'the with or without test' which considers what competition in the market would look like with and without the merger taking place;[583] and 'if the level of competition in the market with the M&A is substantially lower than the level of competition in the market without the M&A, the M&A will be considered by the Commission to substantially lessen competition'.[584]

581. Paragraph 4.2, *Guidelines on Substantive Assessment of Mergers.*
582. Paragraph 12.5, *Guidelines on Mergers and Acquisitions.*
583. Paragraph 12.25, *Guidelines on Mergers and Acquisitions.*
584. Paragraph 12.26, *Guidelines on Mergers and Acquisitions.*

§2. STRUCTURE OF PROCEEDINGS

I. Preliminary Assessment and Full Investigation

A. *MAVCOM*

596. For anticipated merger, the applicant must notify the Commission when the merger has been made public by any party or by the Commission when the commission published a summary of merger application.[585]

597. For a completed merger, the notification and application may be made at any time, but the party are encouraged to notify as soon as possible. The application must be made in the prescribed form and accompanied by the relevant important documents:[586]

(1) Upon receiving a complete application, the Commission will first determine whether the merger will occur or has occurred within the meaning of section 54.[587] If the Commission finds that the anticipated or completed merger is within the meaning of section 54, the Commission will publish a summary of the application for the purpose of getting feedback from the public. Any person may submit feedback to the Commission within thirty days from the date of publication. At the end of thirty days, the Commission will start Phase 1 Assessment.[588]
(2) The Phase 1 Assessment – the purpose of Phase 1 assessment is to gather information on the anticompetitive effect of an anticipated merger or a merger from various sources.[589] If after the assessment, the Commission found the anticipated merger or a merger will not raise competitive concern, the Commission will issue a proposed decision to the applicant containing the facts relied upon by the Commission and reasons for a decision.[590] The applicant has the opportunity to peruse the proposed decision and may request any confidential information to be redacted.[591] The Commission will publish its proposed decision for the purpose of public consultation. Any person may submit

585. Paragraph 3.2, *Guidelines on Mergers and Acquisitions.*
586. Paragraph 3.3, *Guidelines on Mergers and Acquisitions.*
587. Paragraph 3.8, *Guidelines on Notification and Application Procedure for an Anticipated Merger or a Merger.*
588. Paragraph 3.10, *Guidelines on Notification and Application Procedure for an Anticipated Merger or a Merger.*
589. Paragraph, 3.11, *Guidelines on Notification and Application Procedure for an Anticipated Merger or a Merger.*
590. Paragraph 3.12(a), *Guidelines on Notification and Application Procedure for an Anticipated Merger or a Merger.*
591. Paragraph 3.12(b), *Guidelines on Notification and Application Procedure for an Anticipated Merger or a Merger.*

feedback within thirty days from the date of publication of the proposed decision.[592] Based on the feedback obtained from the public consultation, the Commission may issue a non-infringement decision[593] or proceed with Phase 2 Assessment.[594]

(3) Phase 2 Assessment – The Phase 2 Assessment involves more detailed information and extensive examination of the effects of an anticipated merger or a merger.[595] The Commission may require the applicant to furnish detailed information relating to the business of the merger parties. The Commission will then issue a proposed decision providing details, such as whether there will be or has been an infringement, the fact relied upon by the commission and reasons for a decision.[596] The merger party may request any confidential information to be redacted.[597] The Commission will publish its proposed decision for the purpose of obtaining feedback from the public. Any party may give feedback within thirty days for the date of the publication.[598] The applicant will be given an opportunity to submit written representation to the Commission pertaining to the proposed decision within a period determined by the Commission.[599]

B. MCMC

598. The application for merger assessment can be made by the acquiring party in the case of a proposed merger and the merged entity or the entity that has acquired control in the case of a completed merger.[600] The Commission will not accept multiple parallel application for merger assessment.[601]

599. Before commencing Phase 1 and Phase 2 assessment, the Commission will review the validity of an application. The Commission will consider any application without sufficient information as invalid and will reject the application by issuing a Notice of Rejection to the applicant within ten days from the date of the

592. Paragraph 3.12(c), *Guidelines on Notification and Application Procedure for an Anticipated Merger or a Merger.*
593. Paragraph 3.13(a), *Guidelines on Notification and Application Procedure for an Anticipated Merger or a Merger.*
594. Paragraph 3.13(b), *Guidelines on Notification and Application Procedure for an Anticipated Merger or a Merger.*
595. Paragraph 3.15, *Guidelines on Notification and Application Procedure for an Anticipated Merger or a Merger.*
596. Paragraph 3.16, *Guidelines on Notification and Application Procedure for an Anticipated Merger or a Merger.*
597. Paragraph 3.16(b), *Guidelines on Notification and Application Procedure for an Anticipated Merger or a Merger.*
598. Paragraph 3.17, *Guidelines on Notification and Application Procedure for an Anticipated Merger or a Merger.*
599. Paragraph 3.16(d), *Guidelines on Notification and Application Procedure for an Anticipated Merger or a Merger.*
600. Paragraph 4.3, *Guidelines on Mergers and Acquisitions.*
601. Paragraph 4.2, *Guidelines on Mergers and Acquisitions.*

application was received.[602] If the application is considered as valid, the Commission will notify the applicant in writing within five days from the date the application was received.[603]

600. Merger assessment involves three stages, namely, preliminary review, Phase 1 assessment and Phase 2 assessment:

(1) Preliminary review – before commencing Phase 1 assessment, the Commission will determine whether a transaction falls within the definition of merger and whether the transaction meets the relevant threshold or other justifications.[604]
(2) Phase 1 assessment – the Commission will assess whether the merger has the purpose or effect of substantially lessening competition in the communications market based on information obtained from the applicant or third parties. The Commission is required to complete Phase 1 assessment within thirty days from the date of the Commission notifies the applicants of receipt of a valid application.[605] However, the timeframe is indicative only and can be extended at the Commission's absolute discretion[606] Upon the completion of Phase 1 assessment, the Commission will issue either a Notice of No Objection[607] or a notice informing an applicant that a Phase 2 of assessment is necessary.[608]
(3) Phase 2 assessment – the Commission will conduct Phase 2 assessment if it cannot determine whether a merger has the purpose or effect of substantially lessening competition in the communications market during the Phase 1 assessment due to the complexity of the merger.[609] The Phase 2 assessment process requires more detailed information and extensive analysis of the effects of the merger. The Commission is required to commence the Phase 2 assessment within ten business days from the date of the receipt of a valid application.[610] The Phase 2 assessment should be completed within 120 days from the date of the commencement[611] and can be expanded at the Commission's absolute discretion.[612]

II. Time Framework

601. The MAVCOM merger regime does not provide a specific timeframe for the assessment of a merger application. This gives the Commission more flexibility

602. Paragraph 4.14, *Guidelines on Mergers and Acquisitions.*
603. Paragraph 4.10, *Guidelines on Mergers and Acquisitions.*
604. Paragraph 5.8, *Guidelines on Mergers and Acquisitions.*
605. Paragraph 5.12, *Guidelines on Mergers and Acquisitions.*
606. Paragraph 5.13, *Guidelines on Mergers and Acquisitions.*
607. Paragraph 5.15(a), *Guidelines on Mergers and Acquisitions.*
608. Paragraph 5.15(b), *Guidelines on Mergers and Acquisitions.*
609. Paragraph 5.17, *Guidelines on Mergers and Acquisitions.*
610. Paragraph 5.18, *Guidelines on Mergers and Acquisitions.*
611. Paragraph 5.19, *Guidelines on Mergers and Acquisitions.*
612. Paragraph 5.29, *Guidelines on Mergers and Acquisitions.*

in determining the duration for assessment, taking into consideration factors, such as the complexity of a merger and the completeness of the information provided by the parties.[613]

602. For MCMC, The Commission is required to complete Phase 1 Assessment within thirty days from the date of the Commission notifies the applicants of receipt of a valid application. However, the timeframe is indicative only and can be extended at the Commission's absolute discretion.[614] The Phase 2 Assessment should be completed within 120 days from the date of the commencement and can be expanded at the Commission's absolute discretion.[615]

III. Right of Defence

A. Submission

603. MAVCOM gives the right to any person to submit feedback on its proposed decision at the stage of Phase 1 and Phase 2 Assessment. The applicant will be given an opportunity to submit written representation to the Commission in relation to its proposed decision at the Phase 2 Assessment stage.

604. At the end of the Phase 2 Assessment stage, if the MCMC forms a view, it is likely to issue an unfavourable decision the Commission will issue a Statement of Issue (SOI) to an applicant before making a final decision. The SOI must state the grounds on which the Commission believes that the merger may contravene or has contravened the prohibition in section 133 of the CMA or requires or may require the Commission to exercise its power to direct a licensee in a dominant position under subsection 139(1) of the CMA[616] The applicant is given thirty days to submit a response to the Commission.

B. Failing Firm Defence

605. In the case of a failing firm, a merger party may invoke a defence that without a merger, the failing firm would exit the relevant market anyway. In invoking the failing firm defence, the merger party should establish the following:[617]

(i) the failing firm must be in such a deteriorated financial situation that it and its assets would exit the market in the near future without the M&A;

613. Paragraph 3.7, *Guidelines on Notification and Application Procedure for an Anticipated Merger or a Merger.*
614. Paragraph 5.13, *Guidelines on Mergers and Acquisitions.*
615. Paragraph 5.29, *Guidelines on Mergers and Acquisitions.*
616. Paragraph 5.23, *Guidelines on Mergers and Acquisitions.*
617. Paragraph 12.58, *MCMC Guidelines on Mergers and Acquisition*; Paragraph 4.4(c), *MAVCOM Guidelines on Substantive Assessment of Mergers.*

(ii) there must be no serious prospect of restructuring the business without the M&A; and
(iii) there should be no available alternatives to the M&A which would be less anticompetitive.

606. The claim of failing firm should be substantiated with evidence that 'a merger party is genuinely failing and that it would fail should the merger not occur'.[618]

C. *Efficiencies and Social Benefits*

607. Merger that has resulted or may be expected to result in an SLC in any aviation service market may be excluded if the merger parties can prove economic efficiencies and social benefits.

608. Economic efficiencies include:[619]

- Cost reduction resulting from economies of scale and scope, more efficient processes or working methods across a portfolio of services.
- Removal of double marginalization of profits in different levels of a supply chain.
- Increase the level of differentiation of aviation services.
- Increase in capacity and network of aviation services, including expanding scheduled air transport services and opening up new routes to passengers.
- Reduce prices for complementary aviation services as compared to the prices previously charged by different enterprises.
- Create one-stop shopping where buyers can buy a range of services from the merger party due to the reduction of transaction costs or increased quality assurance.

609. Social benefits include improvement of connectivity, environmental protection, health, safety and employment.[620]

618. Paragraph 4.4(c), *Guidelines on Substantive Assessment of Mergers.*
619. Paragraphs 12.5–12.7, *Guidelines on Substantive Assessment of Mergers.*
620. Paragraph 12.9, *Guidelines on Substantive Assessment of Mergers.*

§3. Clearance and Conditional Clearance

I. Conditions and Undertakings

A. Contents

1. MAVCOM

610. The merger party may propose an undertaking to address the anticompetitive effect of the merger or anticipated merger at any time during Phase 1 or Phase 2 Assessment or in responding to a proposed decision by the Commission at the conclusion of the Phase 2 Assessment.[621] In some circumstances, the Commission may invite the merger party to offer an undertaking if the Commission finds that the effect or likely effect of the merger on competition (SLC effect) may be remedied by the undertaking.[622]

611. The undertakings proposed must be clear, sufficient to address the merger SLC's effects, proportionate, capable of being implemented and should not give rise to new competition concerns or require substantial monitoring by the Commission.[623] The Commission may publish the proposed undertaking to gain feedback from the public before accepting it. If the Commission decides to accept the undertaking, the Commission must close the investigation without making any finding of infringement and must not impose any penalty on the party.[624]

2. MCMC

612. The Commission may require the parties to the merger to submit an undertaking pursuant to section 140(3) before making an authorization of any conduct.[625] The undertaking may include, but not limited to, the following:[626]

- An undertaking to proceed with the merger in a substantially restructured form.
- An undertaking that a specific division will be sold off.
- An undertaking that the negative competitive effects of the merger will be addressed in some other form.
- An undertaking to expand or allow fair and reasonable access to vital infrastructure or services to customers or competitors.

621. Paragraph 3.20, *Guidelines on Notification and Application Procedure for an Anticipated Merger or a Merger.*
622. Paragraph 3.21, *Guidelines on Notification and Application Procedure for an Anticipated Merger or a Merger.*
623. Paragraph 3.22, *Guidelines on Notification and Application Procedure for an Anticipated Merger or a Merger.*
624. Paragraph 3.25, *Guidelines on Notification and Application Procedure for an Anticipated Merger or a Merger.*
625. Paragraph 8.9, *Guidelines on Mergers and Acquisitions.*
626. Paragraph 8.9, *Guidelines on Mergers and Acquisitions.*

- An undertaking to not acquire assets within a specific time period, if doing so would have the effect of strengthening the merged or acquired entity's market power.
- In the case of a merger involving a firm acquiring direct or indirect control of another firm, an undertaking that all dealings between the parties will be done on an arm's length basis and the measures will be put in place to ensure this remains the case.

B. Timing

1. MAVCOM

613. The Commission may specify a period within which the non-infringement will be valid and allow the merger party to proceed with the anticipated merger within the specified limit.[627] If the merger party is unable to execute the merger within the stipulated period, it may apply to the Commission for an extension of the period. Before granting extension, the Commission will consider the reason for the extension put forward by the merger party, whether there is a change in the competitive environment since the decision was issued and how it may be expected to change further within the proposed period of extension.[628]

614. The Commission will grant such extension if there is no material change in the competitive environment since the decision was issued and the competitive impact of the anticipated merger within the proposed period of extension will not be materially different from the competitive impact of the said merger if carried within the original stipulated period.[629] The Commission will not grant the extension if the application requires an extensive analysis of the competitive impact of the anticipated merger due to material change in the competitive environment.[630]

2. MCMC

615. Any favourable decision issued by the Commission is only valid for a period specified in the notice (normally for one year), and the Commission may object to the merger effected outside the stipulated period. Parties to the merger may apply to the Commission in writing to extend the validity of the Notice of No

627. Paragraph 3.32, *Guidelines on Notification and Application Procedure for an Anticipated Merger or a Merger.*
628. Paragraph 3.34, *Guidelines on Notification and Application Procedure for an Anticipated Merger or a Merger.*
629. Paragraph 3.35, *Guidelines on Notification and Application Procedure for an Anticipated Merger or a Merger.*
630. Paragraph 3.36, *Guidelines on Notification and Application Procedure for an Anticipated Merger or a Merger.*

Objection[631] no later than ninety days prior to the expiry of the validity of period.[632] The application must set out, for example, the reason for the extension, how the competitive environment in the relevant market has changed since the issuance of the Notice of No Objection and how the merger's effect on competition will differ if effected outside the original period.[633] If the request for an extension was rejected, the parties to a merger might reapply for assessment.[634]

616. The Commission may revoke the Notice of No Objection before the expiry of the period of validity if the information given to the Commission is false and misleading, or if the merger which has been completed is materially different to the transaction submitted to the Commission for assessment, or if there has been a material change of circumstance since the Commission issued the Notice of No Objection.[635] If the Notice of No Objection was revoked after the merger has been completed, the Commission might proceed with an investigation.[636] However, if the merger has not been completed yet, the Commission may allow the parties to a merger to re-apply for assessment of the merger.[637]

C. Remedies

1. MAVCOM

617. In determining the appropriate remedy, the Commission may take into consideration various factors including the ability of the remedy to restore the competitive structure, to bring the anticompetitive effect to an end or prevent or mitigate an SLC as well as the cost of monitoring the remedy.[638] In general, the remedy that may be imposed by the Commission can be divided into two categories.

Structural Remedy

618. The structural remedy may be the most appropriate remedy to maintain and restore the competitive structure since the merger itself may alter the existing competitive landscape in the aviation sector.[639] Besides, structural remedy may be simple and certain and can be implemented with a short period of time with little supervision and minimum costs. Structural remedy may involve the sale of one or more businesses, physical assets or other rights of any merger party. In proposing the sale of a business, the Commission needs to ensure that the business must be

631. Paragraph 6.9, *Guidelines on Mergers and Acquisitions.*
632. Paragraph 6.12, *Guidelines on Mergers and Acquisitions.*
633. Paragraph 6.9, *Guidelines on Mergers and Acquisitions.*
634. Paragraph 6.11, *Guidelines on Mergers and Acquisitions.*
635. Paragraph 6.13, *Guidelines on Mergers and Acquisitions.*
636. Paragraph 6.14, *Guidelines on Mergers and Acquisitions.*
637. Paragraph 6.15, *Guidelines on Mergers and Acquisitions.*
638. Paragraph 3.42, *Guidelines on Notification and Application Procedure for an Anticipated Merger or a Merger.*
639. Paragraph 3.40, *Guidelines on Notification and Application Procedure for an Anticipated Merger or a Merger.*

capable of being separated from the merger party and the potential purchaser has the necessary expertise, resource and incentives to act as an effective competitor in the aviation service market.[640]

619. The Commission may also stipulate time within which the sale of the business must be completed. If the sale fails to be completed within the specified period, an independent trustee may be appointed to monitor the operation of the business pending disposal or to handle the sale at the expense of such merger party.[641]

Behavioural Remedy

620. Behavioural remedy is aimed to regulate the future conduct of the merger parties. The Commission may impose condition or prohibition on the merger party to ensure that their behaviour will not further weaken competition in the aviation service market. Behavioural remedy is preferable when the divestment is not practical or disproportionate to the effect of the merger on competition or to support structural divestment.[642]

Financial Penalty

621. Generally, the Commission will not impose a penalty in relation to an anticipated merger or a merger that has been notified to the Commission. However, the Commission may impose a financial penalty on the merger party if the anticipated merger had been executed after the Commission had issued a proposed infringement decision.[643]

2. MCMC

622. The Commission may take remedial action or enforcement measures depending on the circumstances of the merger including whether the merger has been completed or merely proposed, whether the merger has the purpose or effect of substantially lessening competition or whether the merger involves a licensee in a dominant position.[644]

---

640. Paragraph 3.40, *Guidelines on Notification and Application Procedure for an Anticipated Merger or a Merger.*
641. Paragraph 3.40, *Guidelines on Notification and Application Procedure for an Anticipated Merger or a Merger.*
642. Paragraph 3.40, *Guidelines on Notification and Application Procedure for an Anticipated Merger or a Merger.*
643. Paragraph 3.44, *Guidelines on Notification and Application Procedure for an Anticipated Merger or a Merger.*
644. Paragraph 7.3, *Guidelines on Mergers and Acquisitions.*

Proposed Merger

623. A proposed merger involves a licensee holding a dominant position, and the merger would have the effect of substantially lessening competition in a communications market or results in a dominant position:

- the Commission may in pursuant to subsection 139(1) direct the licensee to stop the merger and prohibit transfer any licenses or spectrum assignments granted to another entity;[645]
- the Commission may seek an interim or interlocutory injunction under section 142 of the CMA against parties to the merger for failures to comply with section 133 of the CMA or take action under section 53 of the CMA for failures to comply with a direction issued by the Commission in a notice of objection.[646]

624. If a proposed merger which does not involve a licensee in a dominant position or likely to result in a dominant position but has the purpose of substantially lessening competition in a communications market, the Commission may seek an interim or interlocutory injunction against the parties to the merger if the merger is continued or completed.[647]

Completed Merger

625. If the merger does not involve a licensee in a dominant position or will result in a dominant position but has the purpose of substantially lessening competition in a communications market, the Commission may obtain an interim or interlocutory injunction pursuant to section 142 of the CMA, to prevent further integration between the parties to the merger, or to prevent the merged or acquired entity from trading.[648]

626. If the merger involves a licensee in a dominant position and has the effect of substantially lessening competition in a communications market:

- The Commission may issue a direction under section 51 of the CMA to prevent further integration between merger parties, or to prevent the merged or acquired entity from trading.
- The Commission might impose penalties under section 53 of the CMA if the parties to merger failed to comply with the direction in the Notice of Objection.[649]

645. Paragraph 7.5, *Guidelines on Mergers and Acquisitions.*
646. Paragraph 7.6, *Guidelines on Mergers and Acquisitions.*
647. Paragraph 7.7, *Guidelines on Mergers and Acquisitions.*
648. Paragraph 7.8, *Guidelines on Mergers and Acquisitions.*
649. Paragraph 7.9, *Guidelines on Mergers and Acquisitions.*

D. Appeal and Authorization

627. MAVCOM is required to notify the infringement decision to any person affected by the decision. However, any person affected by the decision may appeal to the Minister for the anticipated merger or the merger to be exempted from the prohibition on the ground of public interest. The term 'public interest' is confined to matters of public or national security and defence only.[650] Any person affected by the decision of the Commission (under part VII) may appeal to the High Court within three months from the date on which the decision was communicated (section 88).[651]

628. Under section 140 of the CMA, the MCMC shall authorize conduct that construed to have the purpose or effect of substantially lessening competition in a communications market if it satisfied that the authorization is in the national interest and subject to certain restrictions or limitations imposed on the parties to a merger.[652] The rights to apply for authorization is only limited to a merger where at least one of the merger parties is a licensee, and the proposed merger has not yet taken place.

629. The MCMC shall authorize conduct that construed to have the purpose or effect of substantially lessening competition in a communications market if it satisfies that the authorization is in the national interest and subject to certain restrictions or limitations imposed on the parties to a merger.[653]

630. Pursuant to section 120 of the CMA, parties to a merger may apply to the Appeal Tribunal for review of:

- a decision of the Commission in respect of the purpose, effect or likely effect of a merger submitted to it for assessment; or
- any direction of the Commission under subsection 139(1) of the CMA to a licensee in a dominant position.

§4. Relations with Other Merger Control Authorities

I. Other Authorities Within the Local Jurisdiction

631. The CA 2010 does not contain merger control provisions. The Malaysian merger regime is sector-specific focusing on aviation services and communications market.

650. Paragraph 5.2, *Guidelines on Notification and Application Procedure for an Anticipated Merger or a Merger.*
651. *See* s. 88 of the MACA 2015; *see also* para. 5.5, *Guidelines on Notification and Application Procedure for an Anticipated Merger or a Merger.*
652. Paragraph 8.8, *Guidelines on Mergers and Acquisitions.*
653. Paragraph 8.8, *Guidelines on Mergers and Acquisitions.*

II. International Coordination

632. Pursuant to section 269 of the CMA, the Minister may direct the MCMC to enter into interworking arrangements with any other authority in Malaysia or in a foreign jurisdiction, or any international organizations. The Minister may also produce rules and determine arrangements for interworking arrangements between the licensee and international organizations.

Chapter 4. Challenging of the Administrative Decision

§1. COMPETENT COURTS

633. Any person who is aggrieved or whose interest is affected by the decision of the Commission may appeal to the CAT under sections 35 (interim measures), 39 (finding of non-infringement) or 40 (finding of an infringement)[654] by submitting a notice of appeal in writing to the CAT within thirty days from the date of the decision of the Commission.[655]

634. Under the CA 2010, the CAT has the powers of a subordinate court under the Subordinate Courts Act 1948 [Act 92] in relation to the enforcement of attendance of witnesses, hearing evidence on oath or affirmation and punishment for contempt.[656] Specifically, the CAT has the power to summon any person including parties to the proceeding before it to give evidence, to receive evidence on oath or affirmation and to examine all such persons as witnesses, to require the production of any information, document or other things necessary for the purposes of the appeal.[657]

635. A decision of the CAT is final and binding on the parties to the appeal.[658] The decision of the CAT may confirm or set aside the decision of the Commission. In addition, the CAT may:

(a) remit the matter to the Commission;
(b) impose or revoke, or vary the amount of, a financial penalty;
(c) give such direction, or take such other step as the Commission could itself have given or taken; or
(d) make any other decision which the Commission could itself have made.

636. In *MAS-AirAsia*, the CAT set aside the Commission's decision and directed the financial penalty, if paid, to be refunded the Appellant.[659]

637. In *My E.G. Services Bhd*, the CAT affirmed the Commission's decision with consequential amendments including: (a) the imposition of financial penalty of MYR 2,272,200.00 inclusive of daily penalty; (b) cease and desist order to MyEG from imposing different conditions to the equivalent transaction in the processing

654. Section 51(1) of Competition Act 2010.
655. Section 51(2) of Competition Act 2010.
656. Section 57(2) of Competition Act 2010.
657. Section 57(1) of Competition Act 2010.
658. Section 58(2) of Competition Act 2010.
659. Decision of Competition Appeal Tribunal (Appeal No. TRP 1-2014, TRP 2-2014, 18 Feb. 2016) para. 162.

of Mandatory Insurances for Online PLKS renewal application; (c) provide an efficient gateway for all its competitors and potential new entrants in the relevant market for the sale of Mandatory Insurances; and (d) allow the other competitors to compete at the same level within sixty days from the date of the CAT's decision.[660]

638. The decision of the CAT may by the leave of the High Court be enforced in the same manner of judgment or order to the same effect.[661]

639. The decision of the CAT may be appealed to the higher courts for a judicial review. Order 53, Rule 3(1) of Rules of Court 2012 states that an application of a judicial review shall not be made unless leave has been granted. The applicant may seek any of the reliefs, including a prayer of a declaration.[662] The application for leave must be made ex parte to a Judge in Chamber and must be supported by a statement setting out the name and description of the applicant, the relief sought and the grounds on which it is sought and by an affidavit verifying the facts relied on.[663]

§2. Time Limits

640. A written notice of appeal should be submitted to CAT within thirty days from the date of the decision of the Commission.[664] An applicant may apply for a stay of the decision of the Commission to the CAT on or after the day on which the notice of appeal has been filed with the CAT.[665]

641. An application for judicial review must be made promptly and in any event within three months from the date when the grounds of the application first arose or when the decision is first communicated to the applicant.[666] However, the Court may extend the specified time if it considers that there is a good reason for doing so.[667] Where the leave has been granted, the applicant needs to file a notice in the provided form within fourteen days after the grant of such leave.[668]

§3. Scope of Judicial Review

642. In *Competition Commission v. Competition Appeal Tribunal, Malaysia Airlines Bhd and AirAsia Bhd*, the Commission applied for a judicial review against the CAT's decision and seeking a certiorari order to quash the decision of the CAT a declaration that the CAT's decision is illegal, irrational, suffers from procedural

660. Decision of Competition Appeal Tribunal (Appeal No. TRP 3-2016, 28 Dec. 2017) para. 58.
661. Section 59 of Competition Act 2010.
662. Order 53, Rule 2(2) of Rules of Court 2012.
663. Order 53, Rule 3(2) of Rules of Court 2012.
664. Section 51(2) of Competition Act 2010.
665. Section 53(2) of Competition Act 2010.
666. Order 53 Rule 3(6) of Rules of Court 2012.
667. Order 53 Rule 3(7) of Rules of Court 2012.
668. Order 53 Rule 4(1) of Rules of Court 2012.

impropriety, an abuse of process and/ or an error of law, an arbitrary.[669] The High Court stated that 'the position of the law on judicial review now is well settled that the court not only can review the decision making process but is also allowed to delve into the merits of the decision'.[670]

643. In determining the application of judicial review the High Court in *Competition Commission v. Competition Appeal Tribunal, Malaysia Airlines Bhd and AirAsia Bhd*, had referred to the case of *Akira Sales & Service (M) Sdn Bhd v. Nadiah Zee bt Abdullah and another appeal* (2018) 2 MLJ 537 which re-emphasized the liberal approach on judicial review taken in *R. Rama Chandran v. The Industrial Court Malaysia & Anor* (1997) 1 MLJ 145.

644. There are three important grounds for impugning a decision susceptible to judicial review, namely (i) illegality, (ii) irrationality and (iii) procedural impropriety:

- Illegality means that 'the decision maker must understand directly the law that regulates his decision making power and must give effect to it. Whether he has or not is par excellence a justiciable question to be decided, in the event of a dispute, by those persons, the judges, by whom the judicial power of the state is exercisable'.[671]
- Irrationality 'applies to a decision which is so outrageous in its defiance of logic or of accepted moral standards that no sensible person who had applied his mind to the question to be decided could have arrived at it. Whether a decision falls within this category is a question that judges by their training and experience should be well equipped to answer, or else there would be something badly wrong with our judicial system'.[672]
- Procedural impropriety covers 'failure by an administrative tribunal to observe procedural rules that are expressly laid down in the legislative instrument by which its jurisdiction is conferred, even where such failure does not involve any denial of natural justice'.[673]

645. A decision which involves an error of law is also subject to a judicial review.[674] In case of *Competition Commission v. Competition Appeal Tribunal, Malaysia Airlines Bhd and AirAsia Bhd*, the High Court had referred to the case of *Syarikat Kenderaan Melayu Kelantan v. Transport Workers Union* (1995) 2 MLJ 317:

---

669. Decision of Competition Appeal Tribunal (Appeal No. TRP 3-2016, 28 Dec. 2017) para. 1.
670. Judgment, Application for Judicial Review (No. WA-25-82-05/2016) para. 25; *Akira Sales & Service (M) Sdn Bhd v. Nadiah Zee bt Abdullah and another appeal* (2018) 2 MLJ 537 para. 45.
671. Judgment, Application for Judicial Review (No. WA-25-82-05/2016) para. 26; *Akira Sales & Service (M) Sdn Bhd v. Nadiah Zee bt Abdullah and another appeal* (2018) 2 MLJ 537 para. 45.
672. Judgement, Application for Judicial Review (No. WA-25-82-05/2016) para. 26; *Akira Sales & Service (M) Sdn Bhd v. Nadiah Zee bt Abdullah and another appeal* (2018) 2 MLJ 537 para. 45.
673. Judgment, Application for Judicial Review (No. WA-25-82-05/2016) para. 26; *Akira Sales & Service (M) Sdn Bhd v. Nadiah Zee bt Abdullah and another appeal* (2018) 2 MLJ 537 para. 45.
674. Judgment, Application for Judicial Review (No. WA-25-82-05/2016) para. 29.

> It is neither feasible nor desirable to attempt an exhaustive definition of what amounts to error of law, for the categories of such an error are not closed. But it may be said that an error of law would be disclosed if the decision-maker asks himself the wrong question or takes into account irrelevant consideration or omits to take into account relevant considerations (what may be conveniently termed an Anisminic error) or if he misconstrues the terms of any relevant statute, or misapplies or misstates a principle of the general law.

646. In *My E.G. Services Bhd v. Competition Commission,* the applicants, My E.G Services Bhd and My E.G Commerce Sdn Bhd applied for a judicial review to quash the decision made by the CAT on 28 December 2017 on the ground among others the CAT has failed to take into consideration the relevant factors and materials put forward by the applicants showing that they had not infringed section 10(2)(d) (iii) of the CA 2010 and the CAT had erred in its finding that the applicants had abused its dominant position under section 10(2)(d)(iii) of the CA 2010 in relation to the provision of the Online Renewal System to the End Users.[675] The High Court dismissed the application as it could not find any irrationality and unreasonableness in the CAT's decision. The High Court concluded that as a dominant enterprise in the upstream market, MyEG 'has a special responsibility to ensure that its conduct did not have exclusionary effect in the downstream market'[676] and MyEG as the dominant concession holder in the upstream market 'has failed to ensure that there is a platform equally available to all, so that there is no abuse in the downstream market'.[677]

647. In *Federation of Sabah Industries & Ors v. Competition Commission & Ors,*[678] the applicants, the Federation of Sabah Industries and two others had applied for a judicial review for an order of mandamus and certiorari to quash the Competition (Block Exemption for Vessel Sharing Agreements (VSA) and Voluntary Discussion Agreements (VDA) in Respect of Liner Shipping Services) Order 2014 (BEO 2014).

648. The grounds for the judicial review submitted by the applicants, among others, are:

- The conditional BEO in relation to 'restriction on price fixing of liner shipping services is self-contradictory and impossible to enforce since the pricing information is shared'.[679]

675. Judgment, Application for Judicial Review (No. WA-25-81-03/2018) para. 2.
676. Judgment, Application for Judicial Review (No. WA-25-81-03/2018) para. 94.
677. Judgment, Application for Judicial Review (No. WA-25-81-03/2018) para. 95.
678. [2015] MLJU 2024 para. 1; Application of Judicial Review (No. BKI-25-2/10-2014 2) April 2015.
679. [2015] MLJU 2024 para. 19; Application of Judicial Review (No. BKI-25-2/10-2014 2) April 2015.

- The conditional BEO 2014 in relation to 'confidential contracts by the liner operators allows them to maintain their dominant position and contradicts s. 10 which prohibits abuse of dominant position'.[680]
- 'There is no benchmark to ensure that the objectives of the conditional BEO is achieved and hence is ultra vires the Act' and 'there is no established mechanism to ensure that the condition of the conditional BEO are complied with and is null and void'.[681]

649. The High Court in dismissing the judicial review application stated that there are no merits in the applicant's application.[682] The Court stated at paragraph 52 that:

> *Reading the Act, the Ordinance, the Cabotage Policy and the BEO 2014, there is no conflict between them. The Applicants complained that the BEO allow the liners to maintain their dominant position and would reduce competition, affect the high shipping costs for Sabah and increase the prices of consumer goods in Sabah. It is not in dispute that there are not many vessels registered in Sabah or owned by businesses in Sabah providing shipping services between Sabah and West Malaysia and there are not many or enough products being exported or transported to West Malaysia from Sabah on the return leg of ships serving between Sabah and West Malaysia.* This is a key factor which contributes to higher shipping costs between the two.

650. The Court also stated in paragraph 63 that:

> The Applicants have also not produced any evidence, data on statistics which showed that the BEO 2014 has resulted in anticompetitive practices which increase the prices of consumer goods in Sabah or that the conditions set out in paragraph 5 of BEO 2014 are irrational or perverse. Any block exemption granted is subject to the conditions authorised by S.8(5)(a) of the Act. Should any of these conditions not be complied with, the 1st Respondent is empowered to cancel the block exemption under S.8(5)(b).

680. [2015] MLJU 2024 para. 19; Application of Judicial Review (No. BKI-25-2/10-2014 2) April 2015.
681. [2015] MLJU 2024 para. 19; Application of Judicial Review (No. BKI-25-2/10-2014 2) April 2015.
682. [2015] MLJU 2024 para. 64; Application of Judicial Review (No. BKI-25-2/10-2014 2) April 2015.

Selected Bibliography

Book

Ahmad Ibrahim & Ahilemah Joned, *The Malaysian Legal System* 57–58 (Dewan Bahasa dan Pustaka, 1987).

Ahmad Ibrahim, *Towards a History of Law in Malaysia and Singapore* (Dewan Bahasa dan Pustaka, Kuala Lumpur, 1992).

Alison Jones & Brenda Sufrin, *EU Competition Law: Text, Cases and Materials*, 5th edn (Oxford University Press, 2014)

Jomo Kwame Sundaram (ed.), *Malaysian Industrial Policy* 6 (NUS Press, 2007).

Jonathan Faull & Ali Nikpay, *The EC Law of Competition*, 2nd edn (Oxford University Press, 2007)

Nasarudin Abdul Rahman & Haniff Ahamat, *Competition Law in Malaysia* (Sweet and Maxwell, 2016).

Richard Whish & David Bailey, *Competition Law* 2nd edn (Oxford University Press, 2015)

Samuel Bassey Okposin, Abdul Halim Abdul Hamid & Hway Boon Ong, *The Changing Phases of Malaysian Economy* (Pelanduk, 1999).

Sharifah Suhanah Syed Ahmad, *Malaysian Legal System*, 2nd edn (Malayan Law Journal, 2007)

Wan Arfah Hamzah, *A First Look at the Malaysian Legal System* 27 (Oxford Fajar, 2009).

Article/Report

E.T. Gomez, 'Targeting Horizontal Inequalities: Ethnicity, Equity, and Entrepreneurship in Malaysia', *Asian Economic Papers*, 11(2) (2012) 31–57.

H. Ahamat & N.A.Rahman, 'Defining "Government Authority"' in the Malaysian Competition Act 2010: A Quest for Objectivity', *International Journal of Public Law and Policy,* 5(2) (2015).

Haniff Ahamat, *The Legal Framework for the Inclusion of Consumer Interests within Anti-dumping Regimes with Special Reference to the EC and Malaysian Anti-dumping Regimes* 235 (unpublished PhD Thesis, University of Essex, 2008).

Jomo Kwame Sundaram, *The New Economic Policy and Interethnic Relations in Malaysia* 1–2 (United Nations Research Institute for Social Development, 7 September 2004).

N. Yasuda, 'Malaysia's New Economic Policy and the Industrial Coordination Act', *The Developing Economies,* XXIX(4) (December 1991) 331.

Selected Bibliography

Wan Saiful Wan Jan, *Malaysia's New Economic Model: Is the Malaysian Government Serious about Economic Liberalization?*, Friedrich Neumann Stiftung Background Paper No. 14/September 13 (2011).

C.Y. Whah, & B.T.C. Guan, 'Malaysia's Protracted Affirmative Action Policy and the Evolution of the Bumiputera Commercial and Industrial Community', *SOJOURN: Journal of Social Issues in Southeast Asia,* 32 (2017) 336–373.

Legislation

Competition Act 2010.
Competition Commission Act 2010.
Energy Commission Act 2001.
Financial Services Act 2013.
Gas Supply Act (Amendment) 2016.
Malaysian Aviation Commission Act 2015.
Multimedia Commission Act 1998.

Guidelines

Guidelines on Chapter 1 Prohibition.
Guidelines on Chapter 2 Prohibition.
Guidelines on Financial Penalties.
Guidelines on Leniency Regime.
Guidelines on Market Definition.
Guidelines on Complaints Procedures.
Guidelines on Competition Law and Intellectual Property Right.

Index

The numbers here refer to paragraph numbers.

Index

www.ingramcontent.com/pod-product-compliance
Lightning Source LLC
Chambersburg PA
CBHW071447230926
51846CB00001B/377
* 9 7 8 9 4 0 3 5 2 6 8 3 6 *